FOURTH EDITION

SEQUEL

A Handbook for the Critical Analysis of Literature

Richard C. Guches, Ed.D.

Department of English
American River College, CA

T. H. Peek, Publisher • P.O. Box 50123 • Palo Alto, California 94303

ISBN: 0-917962-97-4

07 06 05 04 03
19 18 17 16 15

Manufactured in the United States of America

Preface

"And this I believe: that the free, exploring mind of the individual human is the most valuable thing in the world. And this I would fight for: the freedom of the mind to take any direction it wishes, undirected. And this I must fight against: any idea, religion, or government which limits or destroys the individual. This is what I am and what I am about. I can understand why a system built on a pattern must try to destroy the free mind, for this is one thing which can by inspection destroy such a system. Surely I can understand this, and I hate it and I will fight against it to preserve the one thing that separates us from the uncreative beasts. If the glory can be killed, we are lost."

From *East of Eden* by John Steinbeck

Copyrights and Acknowledgments

Contents

To the Student:

To write an effective critical analysis you must first have a basic understanding of sentence structure and paragraphing, as well as the skill to arrange the parts of an analysis logically and coherently. Possessing the skill to organize information and ideas, however, will not result in a successful paper unless you also have an understanding of the subject about which you wish to write. Information about a subject can usually be gained from library research, but sound analytical abilities require training and practice.

SEQUEL is designed to familiarize you with new concepts and analytical skills, and to offer you a new understanding about the nature of literature. To become truly skillful and confident in your abilities to analyze fiction, drama, film, and poetry, you need to develop a background in literature beyond the selection offered here. SEQUEL has been expressly planned to enhance your understanding, expand your background, and promote your appreciation of the literature you read now and in the future.

Read carefully and critically, write clearly and coherently and you will do well—not only in these chapters but also in other courses. In addition, you will feel a personal gain and a sense of accomplishment in being able to understand better what you read and view—and in being able to write effective and critical analyses.

Analyzing Poetry

Many people seem to feel that while they enjoy novels and are fond of movies, poetry is somehow alien to their lives. Often, however, this belief derives from a genuine lack of understanding of what it is poets are trying to do and the techniques they generally employ. Like the other genres discussed in this book, poetry has specific characteristics, and to learn these is to enhance your understanding and your appreciation of its forms.

Indeed, by analyzing poetry you can see a great many literary techniques in action. Technical literary devices that would need long passages of prose to demonstrate may be illustrated with but a few lines in poetry. Moreover, the same techniques used by prose writers and dramatists are readily observed in the creations of poets. Observation and identification of these will lead you to an understanding and the potential for appreciation. In short, you are not being asked to like poetry, or any of the literary selections in this book, but rather to understand it and to demonstrate that understanding. If your understanding leads to appreciation and then to real joy in the literature, so much the better. You must remember, however, that only the understanding is required, not the appreciation and certainly not the joy. What is important in this book, and for the rest of your life, is not what specifically you like or dislike but your ability to understand the "why" of either, and that is discovered only through sound critical analysis. A close study of poetry is a logical beginning for analyzing other literature, for literary techniques are easily illustrated and quickly understood in short poetic selections.

Objectives:

After completing this chapter you will be able to:
1. Define poetry.
2. Describe allusions and identify referents.
3. Illustrate the use of imagery.
4. Explain the difference between denotation and connotation.
5. Assess the contribution of metaphor to poetry.
6. Interpret symbols.
7. Illustrate three uses of irony.
8. Write an analysis of a poem.
9. Identify common figures of speech.
10. Express confidence in your understanding of poetry.

Pre-assessment:

Place the letter of the correct answer in the space at the left of each statement.

_____ 1. Most poetry is intended to be (A) spoken (B) heard (C) printed (D) memorized (E) thrilling.

2. Most poetry involves (A) description of emotional experience (B) the poets' ideas on morality (C) the sense of touch (D) true experience (E) love.

_____ 3. A word's connotation is its meaning (A) as written in a contemporary dictionary (B) to only one character in the poem (C) defined by using only synonyms (D) devoid of emotion (E) beyond its dictionary definition.

_____ 4. When writers employ imagery they are appealing to readers' (A) logic (B) emotion (C) feelings (D) senses (E) reason.

_____ 5. Readers are able to make reference to events, people, or places in history or previous literature by using (A) metonymy (B) allusion (C) hyperbole (D) irony (E) synecdoche.

_____ 6. Metaphor is a form of comparison which (A) attempts to reveal a relationship between two aspects of life (B) reveals both what it is and something more also (C) shows the intended meaning of the words to be the opposite of their expected meaning (D) contrasts what the audience expects with what is expected by the characters (E) represents abstract ideas as people.

_____ 7. Images, metaphors, and symbols (A) never appear in the same poem (B) are rarely used in normal speech (C) often overlap (D) depend upon dictionary definitions of words (E) belong only to the world of poetry and not to fiction or drama.

_____ 8. When writers' meanings are the opposite of what is expected, they are using the technique called (A) tone (B) allegory (C) denotation (D) simile (E) irony.

_____ 9. When readers of a poem or story or the audience at a play knows something that a character does not know, the writer is using a technique known as (A) verbal irony (B) metaphor (C) dramatic irony (D) allegory (E) tone.

10. The use of allusion presupposes (A) familiarity with drama (B) course work (C) an interest on the part of readers (D) literate and knowledgeable readers (E) readers' naivete.

ANALYZING POETRY

Lesson 1

Characteristics

Poetry differs from both prose and drama in its arrangement of words and its expression of experiences, ideas, and emotions. Historically, poetry may be defined as a rhythmical composition, occasionally rhymed, presented in a style that is highly concentrated, very imaginative, and typically more powerful than ordinary prose. Most poetry is intended to be heard—either orally or in the mind's ear—as you read it. The arrangement of the words is usually an aid in understanding a poem since it allows the reader to determine the emphasis visually. Some poets have such strikingly distinctive visual styles that their work is instantly recognizable. For example:

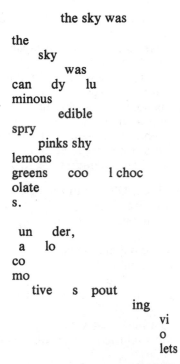

—*e.e. cummings (1894-1962)*

Beyond the obviousness of style, however, there exists the inner meaning of poetry. Poetry, like prose and drama, involves the feelings of emotional experience. Poetry, however, concentrates the experience and compresses the emotion until,

3

with very few words, the compressed feeling is imparted from the poem to the reader.

To understand this concept you must become aware of the experiential idea underlying any poem that you wish to analyze. Each poem has an event or idea from which the poet derives inspiration. Often this inspiration comes from life experiences. These may be as universal as birth, love, or death—but need not be so profound.

Looking at a specific poem should help you begin to see how poetic visions may be derived from life events. Robinson Jeffers is an American poet whose poetry frequently reflects his rugged Pacific coast environment. Once he found a redtail hawk with a broken wing; he tried to save it but failed. From this incident, the death of the wild hawk, he created a poem in which he not only shares the experience and his feelings about it, but also generalizes, based upon the experience, to comment upon some philosophical values that he holds.

HURT HAWKS

The broken pillar of the wing jags from the clotted shoulder,
The wing trails like a banner in defeat,
No more to use the sky forever but live with famine
And pain a few days: cat nor coyote
Will shorten the week of waiting for death, there is game without talons.
He stands under the oak-bush and waits
The lame feet of salvation; at night he remembers freedom
And flies in a dream, the dawns ruin it.
He is strong and pain is worse to the strong, incapacity is worse.
The curs of the day come and torment him
At distance, no one but death the redeemer will humble that head,
The intrepid readiness, the terrible eyes.
The wild God of the world is sometimes merciful to those
That ask mercy, not often to the arrogant.
You do not know him, you communal people, or you have forgotten him;
Intemperate and savage, the hawk remembers him;
Beautiful and wild, the hawks, and men that are dying, remember him.

I'd sooner, except the penalties, kill a man than a hawk; but the great redtail
Had nothing left but unable misery
From the bone too shattered for mending, the wing that trailed under his talons
    when he moved.
We had fed him six weeks, I gave him freedom,
He wandered over the foreland hill and returned in the evening, asking for death,
Not like a beggar, still eyed with the old
Implacable arrogance. I gave him the lead gift in the twilight.
    What fell was relaxed,
Owl-downy, soft feminine feathers; but what
Soared: the fierce rush: the night-herons by the flooded river cried fear at its
    rising
Before it was quite unsheathed from reality.

—Robinson Jeffers (1887-1962)

The poet, obviously, is moved by the events. The depth of his feelings comes through in his words, yet the poem itself is not long. In prose, the author would have written much, much more to convey the same ideas. You can see, then, the compression that has taken place by using the poetic style. This illustrates one of the main characteristics and most important virtues of poetry. Many believe that this compression enhances the emotion readers feel about the experience and ideas expressed in poetry.

EXERCISE 1.1

Write a one-paragraph summary of each of the following poems.

THERE WAS A CHILD WENT FORTH

There was a child went forth every day,
And the first object he looked upon, that object he became,
And that object became part of him for the day or a certain part of the day,
Or for many years or stretching cycles of years.

The early lilacs became part of this child, 5

And grass and white and red morning-glories, and white and red clover,
    and the song of the phoebe-bird,
And the Third-month lambs and the sow's pink-faint litter, and the mare's
    foal and the cow's calf,
And the noisy brood of the barnyard or by the mire of the pond-side,
And the fish suspending themselves so curiously below there, and the beautiful
    curious liquid,
And the water-plants with their graceful flat heads, all became part of him. 10

The field-sprouts of Fourth-month and Fifth-month became part of him,
Winter-grain sprouts and those of the light-yellow corn, and the esculent roots
    of the garden,
And the apple-trees covered with blossoms and the fruit afterward, and wood-
    berries, and the commonest weeds by the road,
And the old drunkard staggering home from outhouse of the tavern
    whence he had lately risen,
And the schoolmistress that passed on her way to the school, 15
And the friendly boys that passed, and the quarrelsome boys,
And the tidy and fresh-cheeked girls, and barefoot negro boy and girl,
And all the changes of city and country wherever he went.

His own parents, he that had fathered him and she that had conceived him
    in her womb and birthed him,
They gave this child more of themselves than that, 20
They gave him afterward every day, they became part of him.

The mother at home quietly placing the dishes on the supper-table,
The mother with mild words, clean her cap and gown, a wholesome odor
    falling off her person and clothes as she walks by,
The father, strong, self-sufficient, manly, mean, angered, unjust,
The blow, the quick loud word, the tight bargain, the crafty lure, 25
The family usages, the language, the company, the furniture, the yearning
    and swelling heart,

Affection that will not be gainsayed, the sense of what is real, the thought if
    after all it should prove unreal,
The doubts of day-time and the doubts of night-time, the curious whether
    and how,
Whether that which appears so is so, or is it all flashes and specks?
Men and women crowding fast in the streets, if they are not flashes and
    specks what are they?   30
The streets themselves and the facades of houses, and goods in the
    windows,
Vehicles, teams, the heavy-planked wharves, the huge crossing at the ferries,
The village on the highland seen from afar at sunset, the river between,
Shadows, aureola and mist, the light falling on roofs and gables of white or
    brown two miles off,
The schooner near by sleepily dropping down the tide, the little boat slack-
    towed astern.   35
The hurrying tumbling waves, quick-broken crests, slapping,
The strata of colored clouds, the long bar of maroon-tint away solitary by
    itself, the spread of purity it lies motionless in,
The horizon's edge, the flying sea-crow, the fragrance of salt marsh and
    shore mud,
These became part of that child who went forth every day, and who now
    goes, and will always go forth every day.

—Walt Whitman (1819-1892)

ON FLUNKING A NICE BOY OUT OF SCHOOL

I wish I could teach you how ugly
decency and humility can be when they are not
the election of a contained mind but only
the defenses of an incompetent. Were you taught
meekness as a weapon? Or did you discover,   5
by chance maybe, that it worked on mother
and was generally a good thing—
at least when all else failed—to get you over
the worst of what was coming. Is that why you bring
these sheepfaces to Tuesday?   10
                        They won't do.
It's three months work I want, and I'd sooner have it
from the brassiest lumpkin in pimpledom, but have it,
than all these martyred repentances from you.

—John Ciardi (1916-1986)

6

THE CHIMNEY SWEEPER

When my mother died I was very young,
And my father sold me while yet my tongue
Could scarcely cry "'weep! 'weep! 'weep! 'weep!"
So your chimneys I sweep, and in soot I sleep.

There's little Tom Dacre, who cried when his head,   5
That curled like a lamb's back, was shaved; so I said,
"Hush, Tom! never mind it, for, when your head's bare,
You know that the soot cannot spoil your white hair."

And so he was quiet, and that very night,
As Tom was asleeping, he had such a sight!   10
That thousands of sweepers, Dick, Joe, Ned, and Jack,
Were all of them locked up in coffins of black.

And by came an Angel who had a bright key,
and he opened the coffins and set them all free;
Then down a green plain leaping, laughing, they run,   15
And wash in a river, and shine in the sun.

Then naked and white, all their bags left behind,
They rise upon clouds and sport in the wind;
And the Angel told Tom, if he'd be a good boy,
He'd have God for his father, and never want joy.   20

And so Tom awoke, and we rose in the dark,
And got with our bags and our brushes to work.
Though the morning was cold, Tom was happy and warm;
So if all do their duty they need not fear harm.

—William Blake (1757-1827)

Lesson 2

Connotation

Denotation is what a word means according to the dictionary. Obviously, a word's definition, what it means according to the "experts," is important to everyone. A word, however, often means more than what the dictionary indicates. The meaning of a word beyond its dictionary definition is called **connotation**. The connotative meanings of words are of primary importance to poets, for they want readers to share images and feelings that may be evoked through the emotional value of certain words.

To understand words' connotative values, consider how some words cause certain emotional responses while other words, meaning nearly the same thing, leave you unaffected. For example, in a romantic ballad, you will never hear of a knight leaping upon his *horse* to race to the rescue of the princess. Neither will he race forth upon his *nag*, *equine quadruped*, or *filly*. Invariably, romantic heroes leap upon waiting steeds. The word *steed* has the most romantic connotation; certainly, a steed is a horse, but it is the kind of high-spirited horse suitable for a ballad hero.

Think, for a moment, about how connotation is used in our daily lives to reflect our intended meaning. When we are stopped for speeding, the person who stopped us is a *cop*; when we want to pursue that occupation ourselves, we wish to become *police officers*. If you are on the faculty in a high school, you are a *teacher*; if you teach in a college or university, you are usually a *professor*.

Likewise, out of the consideration for others, we often use words and terms with neutral connotations, avoiding usages that imply a negative judgment:

Neutral	*Negative*
alcoholic	drunk
substance abuse	addict
disabled	crippled
dentures	false teeth
economically disadvantaged	poor
undocumented worker	illegal alien
soldier of fortune	mercenary

In the world of business and marketing, an understanding of connotation can determine success or failure. The real estate profession offers several good examples:

What they say	*What they mean*
home	house
charming	small
gracious	overly large
homesite	lot
initial investment	down payment
purchase agreement	sales contract
financing	mortgage
additional financing	second mortgage
value	price
marketing fee	commission

EXERCISE 1.2

For each group of words, circle the word or phrase with the most favorable connotation.

1. female parent, dame, mother, the old lady, mom
2. spy, secret agent
3. average, mediocre, ordinary, commonplace, middling
4. lawyer, shyster, mouthpiece, attorney
5. dwelling, house, abode, residence, home
6. doctor, sawbones, physician, quack
7. senator, politician, statesman
8. bureaucrat, administrator

The connotation of a word is its associated meanings, what it implies, and its emotional overtones. The denotation of a word is a more limited definition, based on clear categories that do not depend on emotional subtlety. For instance, think of the word "mother"; the denotation is a female who has given birth. The connotation, however, is associated with the feelings, attitudes, and responses that you have associated with your mom since childhood. In another example, home denotes that building where you live; however, home connotes privacy, intimacy, coziness, perhaps also love, warmth and security—mom, dad, the children and the dog. These connotative elements are what poets wish to emphasize as they attempt to involve their readers in the emotional images they create.

After reading the poem "There Is No Frigate Like a Book" complete the exercises that follow.

THERE IS NO FRIGATE LIKE A BOOK

There is no frigate like a book
   To take us lands away,
Nor any coursers like a page
   Of prancing poetry:
This traverse may the poorest take
   Without oppress of toll;
How frugal is the chariot
   That bears the human soul!

—*Emily Dickinson (1830-1886)*

EXERCISE 1.3

In two or three sentences, write a prose summary of the poem.

_____

_____

_____

_____

EXERCISE 1.4

For each of the following words from the poem write a sentence or two explaining the word's connotation.

1. frigate

_____

_____

_____

2. coursers

_____

_____

_____

3. chariot

_____

_____

_____

EXERCISE 1.5

In line 2, why does the poet use the word "lands" rather than "miles"?

_____

_____

_____

_____

_____

_____

Allusion

As connotation is beyond denotation, so **allusion** encourages readers to consider either history or another work of literature apart from the one being read. Like connotation, allusion adds meanings. Allusion is a reference to an event, a person, a place, or an object in history or previous literature. Through the use of an allusive reference, readers can make connections that greatly enhance their understanding of what they read. Sometimes the allusion is crucial to the understanding of the selection.

IN THE GARDEN

In the garden there strayed
A beautiful maid
As fair as the flowers of the morn;
The first hour of her life
She was made a man's wife,
And was buried before she was born.

—Anonymous

This brief anonymous poem seems, at first reading, to contain a paradox that makes it nonsense. How, after all, can a beautiful maid be married when she is but an hour old and die before she is born? (Have you resolved the paradox?) The allusion is to the Book of Genesis in the King James version of the Bible where in the story of creation, Eve is said to have been created (therefore, never born) and immediately married to Adam. The understanding of this poem presupposes a familiarity with the Bible story, for without that understanding the seeming paradox can never be resolved.

Identify the following allusion.

QUATRAIN

Jack, eating rotten cheese, did say
Like Samson I my thousands slay;
I vow, quoth Roger, so you do.
And with the self-same weapon too.

—Benjamin Franklin (1706-1790)

1. What is alluded to in this poem?

_____

_____

_____

2. Write a prose summary of this poem.

_____

_____

_____

Allusions to previous literature are most frequently to Greek mythology, the Bible (typically the King James Version), and Shakespeare. These are by no means the only references for allusions. Since these are so commonly employed, however, readers need at least a casual familiarity with them or much of literature's richness will pass them unnoticed.

Some literary allusions are quite subtle and demand critical thinking and a broad background on the part of readers. Here is a Robert Frost poem. See if you can find the allusion.

"OUT, OUT—"

The buzz-saw snarled and rattled in the yard
And made dust and dropped stove-length sticks of wood,
Sweet-scented stuff when the breeze drew across it.
And from there those that lifted eyes could count
Five mountain ranges one behind the other   5
Under the sunset far into Vermont.
And the saw snarled and rattled, snarled and rattled,
As it ran light, or had to bear a load.
And nothing happened: day was all but done.
Call it a day, I wish they might have said   10
To please the boy by giving him the half hour

That a boy counts so much when saved from work.
His sister stood beside them in her apron
To tell them "Supper." At the word, the saw,
As if to prove saws knew what supper meant,   15
Leaped out at the boy's hand, or seemed to leap—
He must have given the hand. However it was,
Neither refused the meeting. But the hand!
The boy's first outcry was a rueful laugh,
As he swung toward them holding up the hand   20
Half in appeal, but half as if to keep
The life from spilling. Then the boy saw all—
Since he was old enough to know, big boy
Doing a man's work, though a child at heart—
He saw all spoiled. "Don't let him cut my hand off—   25
The doctor, when he comes, Don't let him, sister!"
So. But the hand was gone already.
The doctor put him in the dark of ether.
He lay and puffed his lips out with his breath.
And then—the watcher at his pulse took fright.   30
No one believed. They listened at his heart.
Little—less—nothing!—and that ended it.
No more to build on there. And they, since they
Were not the one dead, turned to their affairs.

—Robert Frost (1874-1963)

If you spent time looking through the lines of this poem and ignored the title then you missed the allusion altogether. It is all too common to ignore titles and, in this case, it is all important. You should have noticed, first, that the title is in quotation marks. As you know, quotation marks are used with poetry when writing out the titles in compositions but not when the title is at the head of the poem itself. Consequently, these quotation marks should have tipped you to the fact that the poet is quoting some other source. Since it is a quotation, it is not very likely that the poet would select an obscure source. Where in history or literature is the expression, "Out, Out" used? If you were unable to think of any reference with these words then you might consult some secondary source like *Familiar Quotations* by John Bartlett. In the index section, under "out," the phrase "Out brief candle" is listed. On that page, in the middle of a longer quotation is the allusion.

Tomorrow, and tomorrow, and tomorrow,
Creeps in this petty pace from day to day,
To the last syllable of recorded time;
And all our yesterdays have lighted fools
The way to dusty death. **Out, out** brief candle!

Life's but a walking shadow, a poor player
That struts and frets his hour upon the stage
And then is heard no more: it is a tale
Told by an idiot, full of sound and fury,
Signifying nothing.

MACBETH Act V, Scene 5, *William Shakespeare (1564-1616)*

The theme of this passage, spoken by Macbeth just after he learns of his wife's death, is the meaninglessness and brevity of life. The philosophy of this passage coupled with the content of Frost's poem reveals a universal comment about the human condition. The poem's content is a specific incident, but the allusion indicates that the poet has broader concerns than the death of one boy on a Vermont farm. Frost is writing about life and death everywhere.

Although Frost's reference is subtle, it illustrates the power of allusion to suggest so much with so few words. Also, it illustrates that the use of allusion presupposes a literate and knowledgeable reader.

EXERCISE 1.7

Identify and explain the allusions in the following poems.

in Just—

in Just-
spring   when the world is mud-
luscious the little
lame balloonman

whistles   far   and wee   5

and eddieandbill come
running from marbles and
piracies and it's
spring

when the world is puddle-wonderful   10

the queer
old balloonman whistles
far   and   wee
and bettyandisbel come dancing

from hop-scotch and jump-rope and   15

it's spring
and
    the

        goat-footed

balloonMan   whistles   20
far
and
wee

—*e. e. cummings (1894–1962)*

_____

_____

_____

_____

_____

FIRE AND ICE

Some say the world will end in fire,
Some say ice.
From what I've tasted of desire
I hold with those who favor fire.
But if it had to perish twice,
I think I know enough of hate
To say that for destruction ice
Is also great
And would suffice.

—*Robert Frost (1874-1963)*

THE PARABLE OF THE OLD MAN AND THE YOUNG

So Abram rose, and clave the wood, and went,
And took the fire with him, and a knife.
And as they sojourned both of them together,
Isaac the first-born spake and said, My Father,
Behold the preparations, fire and iron,   5
But where the lamb for this burnt offering?
Then Abram bound the youth with belts and straps,
And builded parapets and trenches there,
And stretched forth the knife to slay his son.
When lo! an angel called him out of heaven,   10
Saying, Lay not thy hand upon the lad,
Neither do anything to him. Behold,
A ram, caught in a thicket by its horns;
Offer the Ram of Pride instead of him.
But the old man would not so, but slew his son,   15
And half the seed of Europe, one by one.

—*Wilfred Owen (1893-1918)*

Imagery

When writers wish to share an experience with readers, when they want readers to understand fully what something is like, they appeal to the senses: sight, sound, smell, touch, and taste. The term used for this technique is **imagery**—which seems to suggest that the words form a mental picture. While it is true this is often a visual image, imagery as used in literature means an appeal to any of the senses. Ernest Hemingway's stories, for example, involve the senses. In his short stories, readers can see the sun's rays streak through the treetops down into the river; feel the icy water and cold, crisp air; hear the rippling water and the frying fish; smell the early morning dampness and the aroma of cooking; and taste the breakfast trout. Through this kind of appeal, readers are able to identify with the characters and their feelings. In poetry, imagery allows readers to experience vicariously the sights, sounds, and feelings that poets wish to share.

Look for appeals to your senses in the following poem.

THE FISH

I caught a tremendous fish
and held him beside the boat
half out of water, with my hook
fast in a corner of his mouth.
He didn't fight.   5
He hadn't fought at all.
He hung a grunting weight,
battered and venerable
and homely. Here and there
his brown skin hung in strips   10
like ancient wall-paper,
and its pattern of darker brown
was like wall-paper:
shapes like full-blown roses
stained and lost through age.   15
He was speckled with barnacles,
fine rosettes of lime,
and infested
with tiny white sea-lice,
and underneath two or three   20
rages of green weed hung down.
While his gills were breathing in
the terrible oxygen
—the frightening gills,
fresh and crisp with blood,   25
that can cut so badly—
I thought of the coarse white flesh
packed in like feathers,
the big bones and the little bones,
the dramatic reds and blacks   30
of his shiny entrails,
and the pink swim-bladder
like a big peony.

I looked into his eyes
which were far larger than mine   35
but shallower, and yellowed,
the irises backed and packed
with tarnished tinfoil
seen through the lenses
of old scratched isinglass.   40
They shifted a little, but not
to return my stare.
—It was more like the tipping
of an object toward the light.
I admired his sullen face,   45
the mechanism of his jaw,
and then I saw
that from his lower lip
—if you could call it a lip—
grim, wet, and weapon-like,   50
hung five old pieces of fish-line,
or four and a wire leader
with the swivel still attached,
with all their five big hooks
grown firmly in his mouth.   55
A green line, frayed at the end
where he broke it, two heavier lines,
and a fine black thread
still crimped from the strain and snap
when it broke and he got away.   60
Like medals with their ribbons
frayed and wavering,
a five-haired beard of wisdom
trailing from his aching jaw.
I stared and stared   65
and victory filled up
the little rented boat,
from the pool of bilge
where oil had spread a rainbow
around the rusted engine   70
to the bailer rusted orange,
the sun-cracked thwarts,
the oarlocks on their strings,
the gunnels—until everything
was rainbow, rainbow, rainbow!   75
And I let the fish go.

—*Elizabeth Bishop (1911-1979)*

EXERCISE 1.8

Before each line of the following poem write which sense the poet is appealing to in illustrating the experience.

MEETING AT NIGHT

1. _____ The gray sea and the long black land;

2. _____ And the yellow half-moon large and low;

3. _____ And the startled little waves that leap

4. _____ In fiery ringlets from their sleep,

5. _____ As I gain the cove with pushing prow,

6. _____ And quench its speed i' the slushy sand.

7. _____ Then a mile of warm sea-scented beach;

8. _____ Three fields to cross till a farm appears;

9. _____ A tap at the pane, the quick sharp scratch

10. _____ And blue spurt of a lighted match,

11. _____ And a voice less loud, through its joys and fears,

12. _____ Than the two hearts beating each to each!
                                              —*Robert Browning (1812-1889)*

EXERCISE 1.9

Circle each sense image used in the following poem.

SPRING

1. sight
2. sound
3. touch
4. smell
5. taste

Nothing is so beautiful as spring—
    When weeds, in wheels, shoot long and lovely and lush;
    Thrush's eggs look little low heavens, and thrush
Through the echoing timber does so rinse and wring
The ear, it strikes like lightnings to hear him sing;   5
    The glassy peartree leaves and blooms, they brush
    The descending blue; that blue is all in a rush
With richness; the racing lambs too have fair their fling.

What is all this juice and all this joy?
    A strain of the earth's sweet being in the beginning   10
In Eden garden.—Have, get, before it cloy,

    Before it cloud, Christ, lord, and sour with sinning,
Innocent mind and Mayday in girl and boy,
    Most, O maid's child, thy choice and worthy the winning.

                                              —*Gerard Manley Hopkins (1844-1889)*

18

Figurative Language

Figurative language is a term that includes a number of categories, some of which are very important to writers and to readers. Failure to comprehend fundamental language use in literature can prevent full understanding, thus inhibiting appreciation. Some of the most common figurative language techniques are included in this lesson. Other examples of figurative language may be presented in class or researched in the library.

A. Metaphor and Simile

Similes and metaphors are forms of comparison; they indicate some relationship between essentially different things. Simply defined, a simile *states* a comparison ("My love is like a red, red rose") whereas a metaphor *implies* the comparison ("My love is a red, red rose"). In actual use, however, the difference is much more complex. Metaphors tend to be more extensive than similes, but both metaphor and simile must reveal a significant relationship between two things (for example, roses and love). The foundation of much poetry is this metaphoric relationship, whether it is explicit or implied.

THE EAGLE

Metaphor: He clasps the crag with *crooked hands;*
Close to the sun in lonely lands,
Ringed with the azure world, he stands.

The wrinkled sea beneath him crawls;
He watches from his mountain walls,
Simile: And *like a thunderbolt* he falls.

—*Alfred, Lord Tennyson (1809-1892)*

The simile in "The Eagle" compares, from a bird's-eye view, the dive of an eagle with the speed of a thunderbolt. This *hyperbole* (that is, intentional exaggeration for effect) allows the reader to identify with the bird, to feel its dive toward earth, and to experience the rush of the dive as compared to a thunderbolt. The power of the simile rests with this ability to compare experiences explicitly.

Metaphor:

METAPHORS

I'm a riddle in nine syllables,
An elephant, a ponderous house,
A melon strolling on two tendrils.
O red fruit, ivory, fine timbers!
This loaf's big with its yeasty rising.
Money's newminted in this fat purse.
I'm a means, a stage, a cow in calf.
I've eaten a bag of green apples,
Boarded the train there's no getting off.

—*Sylvia Plath (1932-1963)*

Metaphor employs more subtlety and requires more thoughtful contemplation than most similes. The figures of speech in "Metaphors" make several comparisons, some of which may be humorous. The poet has compared an expectant mother with a riddle, an elephant, a house, a melon, a fruit, a loaf, a purse, a means, a stage, and a cow; yet in her humorous metaphors, the poet recognizes a resigned finality in the condition of pregnancy: "having boarded the train," she writes, "there's no getting off." Through this series of metaphors, we can recognize the poet's observation about the experience of pregnancy; we can both see the physical awkwardness and share the feeling of resignation. In this example the author achieves an intensified statement by representing each of the poem's images by a metaphor.

Simile:

A VALEDICTION: FORBIDDING MOURNING

As virtuous men pass mildly away,
   And whisper to their souls to go,
While some of their sad friends do say,
   The breath goes now, and some say, "No,"

So let us melt, and make no noise,   5
   No tear-floods, nor sigh-tempests move,
'Twere profanation of our joys
   To tell the laity our love,

Moving of th' earth brings harms and fears,
   Men reckon what it did and meant,   10
But trepidation of the spheres,
   Though greater far, is innocent.

Dull sublunary lovers' love
   (Whose soul is sense) cannot admit
Absence, because it doth remove   15
   Those things which elemented it.

But we by a love so much refined,
   That ourselves know not what it is,
Inter-assured of the mind,
   Care less, eyes, lips, and hands to miss.   20

Our two souls therefore, which are one,
   Though I must go, endure not yet
A breach, but an expansion,
   Like gold to airy thinness beat.

If they be two, they are two so   25
   As stiff-twin compasses are two,
Thy soul the fixed foot, makes no show
   To move, but doth, if th' other do.

And though it in the center sit,
   Yet when the other far doth roam,   30
It leans, and hearkens after it,
   And grows erect, as that comes home.

Such wilt thou be to me, who must
   Like other foot, obliquely run;
Thy firmness makes my circle just,   35
   And makes me end, where I begun.
                   —*John Donne (1572-1631)*

The similes of "A Valediction: Forbidding Mourning" begin with a comparison of the impending separation of a pair of lovers with the death of a virtuous man. Since a virtuous man has nothing to fear after death, he anticipates no afterlife punishments; his passing is peaceful. Likewise, the lovers should as easily and peacefully part, thereby not cheapening their love nor fearing the separation.

In his next simile, the poet compares the lovers' separation with the movements of the planets. If movement is detected in the lowest sphere, as with earthquakes, then people are worried and fretful; but if the movement is in the highest spheres, as with the movement of other planets, it goes unnoticed. Since their love is in the highest spheres, the parting should not cause trepidation. The poet also compares the lovers' separation to a stretching of gold as it is beaten into foil, and last, to the movement of a compass; while one leg remains at home the other leg moves away yet around. Even so, the two legs remain attached at the top; their love binds them forever together.

A metaphoric comparison of two things often strives toward a closer definition of some human emotion. The poet accomplishes this by transferring the meaning of a known thing or experience, called a referent, to something else. For example:

l(a

l(a

le
af
fa

ll

s)
one
l

iness

—*e.e. cummings (1894-1962)*

In Cummings's poem, "a leaf falls" is the referent with which everyone is familiar, while the emotion of loneliness is compared to the falling leaf. The poet expresses loneliness as a falling leaf, as well as conveying both the emotion and the image in the poem's shape. This poem is an effective compressed metaphor.

EXERCISE 1.10

List each metaphoric comparison contained in the following poem.

TO SEE A WORLD IN A GRAIN OF SAND

To see a world in a grain of sand
And a heaven in a wild flower,
Hold infinity in the palm of your hand
And eternity in an hour.

—*William Blake (1757-1827)*

_____   _____

_____   _____

_____   _____

_____   _____

EXERCISE 1.11

List five examples of metaphoric use of language from your reading, viewing, or conversations outside of class.

1. _____

_____

_____

2. _____

_____

_____

3. _____

_____

_____

4. _____

_____

_____

5. _____

_____

_____

EXERCISE 1.12

Is the following poem an example of the use of metaphor or simile? Circle one.

Metaphor   Simile

UPON MISTRESS SUSANNA SOUTHWELL, HER FEET
Her pretty feet
Like snails did creep
A little out, and then,
As if they played at bo-peep,
Did soon draw in again.

—*Robert Herrick (1591-1674)*

B. Symbolism

Images, metaphors, and symbols often overlap and are sometimes difficult to distinguish. Generally, however, an image *means nothing more* than what it is. (The small brown bear rubbed its backsides against the rough bark of a large sugar pine tree.) A metaphor *means something other* than what it states.

Hope is the thing with feathers—
That perches in the soul—
And sings the tune without the words—
And never stops—
At all—

—*Emily Dickinson (1830-1886)*

A symbol *means both what it is and other things as well*. In fact, symbols often have multiple meanings.

Tiger! Tiger! burning bright
In the forests of the night,
What immortal hand or eye
Could frame thy fearful symmetry?

—*William Blake (1757-1827)*

In this example we can see the image of a tiger, and we can also visualize its ferocity. An image does not stop being an image simply because it is used in a metaphor or a symbol. This may be seen in some of the many objects that we regard as symbols. The flag is a symbol, so is a backyard swimming pool. Volkswagen buses, Cadillacs, and Harley Davidson motorcycles are all symbols, too. All symbols are subject to various interpretations, but many remain consistent in their meaning (the Cross, for example).

In literary use, symbols depend upon their context for meaning. Some symbols are widely used and give little problem in their interpretation: water = life; sleep = death; winter = old; age = death; dove = peace; sunrise = birth; sunset = death.

But sometimes a poet employs personal symbols, and these depend entirely upon their context for interpretation. Contextual use and emphasis directs readers from an interpretation based on image or metaphor to the symbolic intent of the poet.

Consider the following poem:

THE ROAD NOT TAKEN

Two roads diverged in a yellow wood,
And sorry I could not travel both
And be one traveler, long I stood
And looked down one as far as I could
To where it bent in the undergrowth;   5

Then took the other, as just as fair,
And having perhaps the better claim,
Because it was grassy and wanted wear;
Though as for that the passing there
Had worn them really about the same,   10

And both that morning equally lay
In leaves no step had trodden black.
Oh, I kept the first for another day!
Yet knowing how way leads on to way,
I doubted if I should ever come back.   15

I shall be telling this with a sigh
Somewhere ages and ages hence:
Two roads diverged in a wood, and I—
I took the one less traveled by,
And that has made all the difference.   20

—Robert Frost (1874-1963)

In its first three stanzas, Frost's poem describes a place in the woods where a road forks and the narrator ponders which direction to take. The imagery is vivid; consequently, the road and its appearance is clear. Also the dilemma is clear: the narrator wishes to experience both roads but realizes that for now a choice must be made. The first three stanzas include the following visual images:

a yellow wood

the undergrowth

grassy

leaves

Frost begins to develop the symbolic nature of the poem at the end of the third stanza. Here the narrator suggests that, while wishing to save the road not taken for another day, the realization is inescapable that *"way leads on to way,"* that is, each road leads to other divisions and these lead to yet others, on and on. This is true of roads and also true of other experiences. Here, alert readers begin to realize that the poet has something more in mind than an image of a particular forked road. This preliminary judgment is confirmed in stanza four where the narrator reveals that the result of the choice *"has made all the difference."* You might well ask *"made all the difference"* in what? The answer will not become clear, however, until you realize that the roads diverging in the woods is a symbol. Everything the poem states about

24

roads in the woods is true, but the observations are also true about any great decision in life. We can all look back upon decisions that we have made and feel that the decisions, the road we chose, *"has made all the difference."* You should see clearly that Frost's poem is symbolically both about roads diverging in the woods and about decisions. From neither can we return to explore what it would have been like to travel the other way.

The use of symbols is not unique to poetry, of course. Much of the world's great literature is filled with symbolism. Perhaps that is, in part, what makes it great. Certainly, it is a symbolic quality that makes such novels as Herman Melville's *Moby Dick* live for generations. Symbols possess multiple meanings and this is partly what makes good literature rewarding to experience again and again. It is possible to find new meanings and different interpretations each rereading, even with old and often-read literary favorites.

EXERCISE 1.13

Read the following poems and complete the exercises.

A WHITE ROSE

The red rose whispers of passion
    And the white rose breathes of love;
Oh, the red rose is a falcon,
    And the white rose is a dove.

But I send you a cream-white rosebud,
    With a flush on its petal tips;
For the love that is purest and sweetest
    Has a kiss of desire on the lips.

          —John Boyle O'Reilly (1844-1890)

Write what is symbolized in the above poem by each of the following:

the white rose _____

the red rose _____

the rosebud _____

THE TIGER

Tiger! Tiger! burning bright
In the forests of the night,
What immortal hand or eye
Could frame thy fearful symmetry?

In what distant deeps or skies   5
Burnt the fire of thine eyes?
On what wings dare he aspire?
What the hand dare seize the fire?

And what shoulder, and what art
Could twist the sinews of thy heart?   10
And when thy heart began to beat,
What dread hand? and what dread feet?

What the hammer? what the chain?
In what furnace was thy brain?
What the anvil? what dread grasp   15
Dare its deadly terrors clasp?

When the stars threw down their spears,
And water'd heaven with their tears,
Did he smile his work to see?
Did he who made the Lamb make thee?   20

Tiger! Tiger! burning bright
In the forests of the night,
What immortal hand or eye,
Dare frame thy fearful symmetry?

—*William Blake (1757-1827)*

What are a few of the things that might be symbolized in this poem by each of the following?

the Tiger _____

the Lamb _____

THE NOISELESS PATIENT SPIDER

A noiseless patient spider,
I mark'd where on a little promontory it stood isolated,
Mark'd how to explore the vacant vast surrounding,
It launch'd forth filament, filament, filament, out of itself,
Ever unreeling them, ever tirelessly speeding them.

And you O my soul where you stand,
Surrounded, detached, in measureless oceans of space,
Ceaselessly musing, venturing, throwing, seeking the spheres to connect them,
Till the bridge you will need be form'd, till the ductile anchor hold,
Till the gossamer thread you fling catch somewhere, O my soul.

—*Walt Whitman (1819-1892)*

In two or three sentences, identify the symbol in the above poem and explain its meaning.

_____

_____

_____

_____

_____

_____

_____

_____

C. Irony

Verbal Irony:

Often the freshness of literature comes from a unique observation of an experience or idea. The freshness may be achieved overtly but the most successful employ a subtlety of expression that forces readers to think. One of the most subtle kinds of expression is **irony**, a technique that may be humorous or sarcastic in which the intended meaning of the words or the situation is the opposite of their expected meaning. We use **verbal irony** frequently when we wish to emphasize a point humorously or sarcastically.

(Trying to look out into a valley filled with smog she says, "What a lovely view.")

From the context the real meaning is clear, though the meaning is the opposite of what is said. A famous example of verbal irony, laced with sarcasm, occurs in Shakespeare's play, *Julius Caesar,* when Mark Antony, orating over the body of the murdered Julius Caesar, says of one of the chief assassins, "Brutus is an honorable man." The crowd (and the audience) soon see that Antony means just the opposite.

OF ALPHUS

No egg on Friday Alph will eat,
  But drunken he will be
On Friday still. Oh, what a pure
  Religious man is he!

Anonymous—Sixteenth Century

Situational Irony:

A kind of irony with which you may be less familiar but that is often used in literature is situational irony. In situational irony a discrepancy exists between what is expected and what actually happens.

OZYMANDIAS

I met a traveller from an antique land
Who said: Two vast and trunkless legs of stone
Stand in the desert . . . Near them, on the sand,
Half sunk, a shattered visage lies, whose frown,
And wrinkled lip, and sneer of cold command,   5
Tell that its sculptor well those passions read
Which yet survive, stamped on these lifeless things,
The hand that mocked them, and the heart that fed:
And on the pedestal these words appear:
"My name is Ozymandias, king of kings: 10
Look on my works, ye Mighty, and despair!"
Nothing beside remains. Round the decay
Of that colossal wreck, boundless and bare
The lone and level sands stretch far away.

—Percy Bysshe Shelley (1792-1822)

The situational irony lies in the discrepancy between what Ozymandias expects (that we will despair) and what actually occurs (that nothing is left).

Dramatic Irony:

Another kind of irony, **dramatic irony,** is most often found in drama, where the audience knows something a character does not. A classic example of dramatic irony occurs in Sophocles' play *Oedipus*, when Oedipus curses whoever caused the plague in the city of Thebes; however, the audience knows, as Oedipus does not, that he has cursed himself.

Dramatic irony also may be used in poems and stories.

THE WORKBOX

"See, here's the workbox, little wife,
  That I made of polished oak."
He was a joiner*, of village life;   *carpenter
  She came of borough folk.

He holds the present up to her   5
  As with a smile she nears
And answers to the profferer,
  "Twill last all my sewing years!"

"I warrant it will. And longer too.
  'Tis a scantling that I got   10
Off poor John Wayward's coffin, who
  Died of they knew not what.

"The shingled pattern that seems to cease
  Against your box's rim
Continues right on in the piece   15
  That's underground with him.

"And while I worked it made me think
  Of timber's varied doom:
One inch where people eat and drink,
  The next inch in a tomb.   20

"But why do you look so white, my dear,
  And turn aside your face?
You knew not that good lad, I fear,
  Though he came from your native place?"

"How could I know that good young man,   25
  Though he came from my native town,
When he must have left far earlier than
  I was a woman grown?"

"Ah, no. I should have understood!
  It shocked you that I gave   30
To you one end of a piece of wood
  Whose other is in a grave?"

"Don't, dear, despise my intellect,
  Mere accidental things
Of that sort never have effect   35
  On my imaginings."

Yet still her lips were limp and wan,
  Her face still held aside,
As if she had known not only John,
  But known of what he died.   40

—Thomas Hardy (1840-1928)

The dramatic irony in "The Workbox" occurs with the growing knowledge that the wife in the poem obviously knew John Wayward much better than she admits to her husband, who has only limited knowledge. (Note also the verbal ironies in lines 25 to 28 and in line 34.)

EXERCISE 1.14

Identify and describe the irony in each of the following poems. (Note there may be more than one in each.)

EPIGRAM

As Thomas was cudgeled one day by his wife,
He took to the street, and fled for his life.
Tom's three dearest friends came by in the squabble,
And saved him at once from the shrew and the rabble,
Then ventured to give him some sober advice.   5
But Tom is a person of honor so nice,
Too wise to take counsel, too proud to take warning,
That he sent to all three a challenge next morning.
Three duels he fought, thrice ventured his life,
Went home, and was cudgeled again by his wife.   10

—*Jonathan Swift (1667-1745)*

_____

_____

_____

_____

_____

_____

_____

_____

_____

_____

_____

FORMAL APPLICATION

The poets apparently want to rejoin the human race.   TIME

I shall begin by learning to throw
the knife, first at trees, until it sticks
in the trunk and quivers every time;

next from a chair, using only wrist
and fingers, at a thing on the ground,   5
a fresh ant hill or a fallen leaf,

then at a moving object, perhaps
a pieplate swinging on twine, until
I pot it at least twice in three tries.

Meanwhile, I shall be teaching the birds   10
that the skinny fellow in sneakers
is a source of suet and bread crumbs,

first putting them on a shingle nailed
to a pine tree, next scattering them
on the needles, closer and closer   15

to my seat, until the proper bird,
a towhee, I think, in black and rust
and gray, takes tossed crumbs six feet away.

Finally, I shall coordinate
conditioned reflex and functional   20
form and qualify as Modern Man.

You see the splash of blood and feathers
and the blade pinning it to the tree?
It's called an "Audubon Crucifix."

The phrase has pleasing (even pious)   25
connotations, like *Arbeit Macht Frei,* [1]
"Molotov Cocktail," [2] and *Enola Gay,* [3]
                    —*Donald W. Baker (b. 1923)*

---

[1]"Labor liberates"—Nazi party slogan
[2]Homemade firebomb
[3]The name of the airplane that dropped the atomic bomb

MY LAST DUCHESS

Ferrara

That's my last Duchess painted on the wall,
Looking as if she were alive. I call
That piece a wonder, now; Fra Pandolf's hands
Worked busily a day, and there she stands.
Will 't please you sit and look at her? I said   5
"Fra Pandolf" by design, for never read
Strangers like you that pictured countenance,
The depth of passion of its earnest glance,
But to myself they turned (since none puts by
The curtain I have drawn for you, but I)   10
And seemed as they would ask me, if they durst,
How such a glance came there, so, not the first
Are you to turn and ask thus. Sir, 'twas not
Her husband's presence only, called that spot
Of joy into the Duchess' cheek; perhaps   15
Fra Pandolf chanced to say, "Her mantle laps
Over my lady's wrist too much," or, "Paint
Must never hope to reproduce the faint
Half-flush that dies along her throat." Such stuff
Was courtesy, she thought, and cause enough   20
For calling up that spot of joy. She had
A heart—how shall I say? too soon made glad,
Too easily impressed; she liked whate'er
She looked on, and her looks went everywhere.
Sir, 'twas all one! My favor at her breast,   25
The dropping of the daylight in the West,
The bough of cherries some officious fool
Broke in the orchard for her, the white mule
She rode with round the terrace—all and each
Would draw from her alike the approving speech,   30
Or blush, at least. She thanked men—good! but thanked
Somehow—I know not how—as if she ranked
My gift of a nine-hundred-years-old name
With anybody's gift. Who'd stoop to blame
This sort of trifling? Even had you skill   35
In speech—which I have not—to make your will
Quite clear to such a one, and say, "just this
Or that in you disgusts me; here you miss,
Or there exceed the mark"—and if she let
Herself be lessoned so, nor plainly set   40
Her wits to yours, forsooth, and made excuse—
E'en then would be some stooping; and I choose
Never to stoop. Oh, sir, she smiled, no doubt,
Whene'er I passed her; but who passed without
Much the same smile? This grew; I gave commands;   45
Then all smiles stopped together. There she stands
As if alive. Will 't please you rise? We'll meet
The company below, then. I repeat,
The Count your master's known munificence
Is ample warrant that no just pretense   50
Of mine for dowry will be disallowed;

Though his fair daughter's self, as I avowed
At starting, is my object. Nay, we'll go
Together down, sir. Notice Neptune, though,
Taming a sea-horse, thought a rarity,   55
Which Claus of Innsbruck cast in bronze for me!

—*Robert Browning (1812-1889)*

It is easier to write a mediocre poem than to understand a good one—Montaigne

Other Literary Techniques—
Poetry and Prose

1. **Allegory**—a metaphoric genre (or device briefly appearing within another genre) in which abstract ideas or concepts are represented as people, objects, or situations. Often concepts behind these representations are easily identified; sometimes, however, they are hard to grasp, provoking thought rather than supplying definite answers.

MATTHEW 13:24-30

24   Another parable put he forth unto them, saying, The kingdom of heaven is likened unto a man which sowed good seed in his field:

25   But while men slept, his enemy came and sowed tares* among the wheat, and went his way.

26   But when the blade was sprung up, and brought forth fruit, then appeared the tares also.

---

*weeds

27   So the servants of the householder came and said unto him, Sir, didst not thou sow good seed in thy field? from whence then hath it tares?

28   He said unto them, An enemy hath done this. The servants said unto him, Wilt thou then that we go and gather them up?

29   But he said, Nay; lest while ye gather up the tares, ye root up also the wheat with them.

30   Let both grow together until the harvest: and in the time of harvest I will say to the reapers, Gather ye together first the tares, and bind them in bundles to burn them: but gather the wheat into my barn.

Bible—King James Version

THE PILGRIM'S PROGRESS

Now they began to go down the hill into the Valley of Humiliation. It was a steep hill, and the way was slippery; but they were very careful, so they got down pretty well.

Then said Mr. Great-Heart, "We need not to be so afraid of this valley; for here is nothing to hurt us unless we procure it to ourselves. 'Tis true, Christian did here meet with Apollyon, with whom he also had a sore combat; but that fray was the fruit of those slips that he got in his going down the hill. For they that get slips there must look for combats here; and hence it is that this valley has got so hard a name. For the common people, when they hear that some frightful thing has befallen such an one in such a place, are of an opinion that that place is haunted with some foul fiend or evil spirit; when, alas, it is for the fruit of their doing that such things do befall them there."

—John Milton (1608-1674)

A MAN HIDES IN A WELL

A man who has committed a crime is fleeing; the guards are close behind. He comes upon a dry well into which are growing some vines. Desperate, he tries to hide himself by descending into the well on the vines. As he descends, he sees a deadly snake in the bottom; consequently, he decides to cling to the vines for safety. After a time, as his arms begin to tire, he notices two mice, one white and one black, gnawing at the vines. If the vines break, he will fall on the snake and perish. Suddenly, upon looking upward, he sees a bee-hive just above his head. Occasionally a drop of honey falls from the hive. The man, forgetting all his danger, tastes the honey with delight.

—the teachings of Buddha

2. **Personification**—(a form of metaphor) like allegory that gives substance to abstract ideas, but that represents such ideas specifically with human characteristics.

I WANDERED LONELY AS A CLOUD

I wandered lonely as a cloud
   That floats on high o'er vales and hills,
When all at once I saw a crowd,
   A host, of golden daffodils,
Beside the lake, beneath the trees,   5
Fluttering and dancing in the breeze.

Continuous as the stars that shine
   And twinkle on the milky way,
They stretched in never-ending line
   Along the margin of a bay: 10
Ten thousand saw I at a glance,
Tossing their heads in sprightly dance.

The waves beside them danced; but they
   Out-did the sparkling waves in glee;
A poet could not but be gay,   15
   In such a jocund company;
I gazed—and gazed—but little thought
What wealth the show to me had brought:

For oft, when on my couch I lie
   In vacant or in pensive mood,   20
They flash upon that inward eye
   Which is the bliss of solitude;
And then my heart with pleasure fills,
And dances with the daffodils.

       —*William Wordsworth (1770-1850)*

3. **Apostrophe**—(a from of metaphor) addressing an object as though it were living—or speaking as though an absent person were present.

PAPA ABOVE!

Papa above!
Regard a Mouse
O'erpowered by the Cat!
Reserve within thy kingdom
A "Mansion" for the Rat!

Snug in seraphic Cupboards
To nibble all the day,
While unsuspecting Cycles
Wheel solemnly away!

       —*Emily Dickinson (1830-1886)*

4. **Metonymy**— (a form of metaphor) use of a word in place of another word that is closely associated with it.

> The boy's first outcry was a rueful laugh,
> As he swung toward them holding up the hand
> Half in appeal, but half as if to keep
> The *life* from spilling.

[''Life'' and blood are interchanged. See Frost's poem on page 12.]

> *The White House* reaction was requested.

[The president is considered ''the White House'' when expressing an official opinion.]

5. **Synecdoche**—(a form of metaphor) use of a significant part to represent the whole.

> Unpleasing to *a married ear!*

[In the context of the poem ''Spring,'' ear represents the married man. See page 56.]

> I should have been *a pair of ragged claws*
> Scuttling across the floors of silent seas.

[''Claws'' represent a crab. See ''The Love Song of J. Alfred Prufrock,'' page 209.]

6. **Tone**— a writer's or narrator's attitude toward his or her subject, audience, or self, as indicated by choices of words, tempo, or imagery.

LOVE

> There's the wonderful love of a beautiful maid,
>   And the love of a staunch true man,
> And the love of a baby that's unafraid—
>   All have existed since time began.
>
> But the most wonderful love, the Love of all loves,
>   Even greater than the love for Mother,
> Is the infinite, tenderest, passionate love
>   Of one dead drunk for another.
>
> *—Anonymous*

THE CAREFUL ANGLER

> The careful angler chose his nook
> At morning by the lilied brook,
> And all the noon his rod he plied
> By that romantic riverside.
> Soon as the evening hours decline
> Tranquilly he'll return to dine.
> And, breathing forth a pious wish,
> Will cram his belly full of fish.
>
> *—Robert Louis Stevenson (1850-1894)*

7. **Other Types of Irony**—(not discussed earlier in this chapter)

    A. Socratic Irony:

        Pretense of ignorance in a discussion to expose an opponent's fallacious logic.

    B. Romantic Irony:

        Writers creating a serious mood only to make light of themselves.

    C. Irony of Fate:

        The difference between what a human's hopes and expectations are and what is decreed by the gods, fate, fortune, or sheer chance.

8. **Paradox**—a contradiction that is nevertheless true.

MY LIFE CLOSED TWICE

My life closed twice before its close;
    It yet remains to see
If Immortality unveil
    A third event to me,

So huge, so hopeless to conceive,
    As these that twice befell.
Parting is all we know of heaven,
    And all we need of hell.

        —*Emily Dickinson (1830-1886)*

9. **Hyperbole**—deliberate, often ironic exaggeration.

THE EAGLE

He clasps the crag with crooked hands;
Close to the sun in lonely lands,
Ringed with the azure world, he stands.

The wrinkled sea beneath him crawls;
He watches from his mountain walls,
And like a thunderbolt he falls.

        —*Alfred, Lord Tennyson (1809-1892)*

10. **Understatement**—(the opposite of hyperbole) intentional, often ironic, lack of emphasis.

MY MISTRESS' EYES ARE NOTHING LIKE THE SUN

My mistress' eyes are nothing like the sun;
Coral is far more red than her lips' red:
If snow be white, why then her breasts are dun:
If hairs be wires, black wires grow on her head.
I have seen roses damasked,* red and white,   5
But no such roses see I in her cheeks;
And in some perfumes is there more delight
Than in the breath that from my mistress reeks.
I love to hear her speak, yet well I know
That music hath a far more pleasing sound: 10
I grant I never saw a goddess go,—
My mistress, when she walks, treads on the ground.
    And yet, by heaven, I think my love as rare
    As any she belied with false compare.

—William Shakespeare (1564-1616)

11. **Alliteration**—the repetition of similar consonant sounds in the beginnings of nearby words.

He clasps the crag with crooked hands;
Close to the sun in lonely lands,
Ringed with the azure world, he stands.

The wrinkled sea beneath him crawls;
He watches from his mountain walls,
And like a thunderbolt he falls.

12. **Onomatopoeia**—the use of words whose sound closely resembles the sound of the event or object named

Examples: buzz, cackle, whir, sizzle, hiss, murmur, squish, slurp, slip

---

*of different colors

Contextual Analysis

The understanding of literature may be enhanced by venturing outside the work itself to see what genres and ethical viewpoints it embodies, to see what insights may be gained by examining the history of the times, or to see what information about the author's background may offer. These kinds of concerns are ways of looking at all art, and continue to be important. The historical milieu in which something is written often aids in seeing it in a more accurate perspective. Historical knowledge is especially helpful when the author's own background can be seen as a contributing factor in the creation of the literature. The insights available by examining an author's life have long been recognized as significant. Contextual analysis is, then, a series of analytical methods employed by students, teachers, and scholars which looks outside the work for help in understanding it.

Objectives;

After completing this chapter, you will be able to:
1. Identify the main elements of historical analysis.
2. Define the historical aspects of linguistic connotation.
3. Distinguish between biographical analysis and analysis based on broader historical context.
4. Analyze a short work for its generic characteristics.
5. Assess the contribution of authors' biographical data to their writing.
6. Evaluate a work's ethical considerations.

_____ 1. In reference to literature, didacticism means (A) to dictate (B) to teach (C) to analyze (D) to enjoy (E) to fool.

_____ 2. Serious literature achieves its status (A) through subtlety of expression (B) by teaching a moral lesson (C) by its association with a famous author (D) through uplifting characters (E) by being very popular.

_____ 3. The three main categories of literature are (A) short stories, novels, and fiction (B) short stories, plays, and prose (C) poetry, novels, and movies (D) fiction, poetry, and novels (E) prose, poetry, and drama.

_____ 4. Genre means (A) film types (B) ethical consideration (C) play casts (D) literary categories (E) poetic meter.

_____ 5. Linguistic connotation is concerned primarily with (A) today's meanings of the words in a story (B) the meanings of the words in a selection at the time they were written (C) the denotation of the words in a story (D) how emotional the words are in a selection (E) why certain words were chosen for a story.

_____ 6. In older works textual authenticity is often important because (A) we are not always certain we have all the words as the author wrote them (B) we want to test a work's impact upon the readers of its day (C) no one can tell what an author intended (D) the words are usually faded (E) we need to verify that the printers used the right manuscript.

MATCHING:

_____ 7. Connotation

_____ 8. Ethics

_____ 9. Linguistics

_____ 10. Universality

(A) the dictionary definition of a word

(B) the implied meaning of a word beyond its dictionary definition

(C) a system to investigate the validity and reasoning of arguments

(D) the study of speech and writing

(E) that which appeals to all people during all times in all places

(F) a set of values or principles by which human actions are judged

HISTORICAL ANALYSIS

Historical analysis is the critical approach of many library research papers. Prior to the 1930s, historical analysis seemed to be the *only* approach and led to an overemphasis upon the background of an author's life or the context in which a work was created. Later critics, reacting to what they viewed as the excesses of historical analysis, refused to consider anything outside the literature itself as relevant. By maintaining perspective, however, historical analysis can contribute considerably to your understanding of much literature.

Ethical Considerations

Of all the ways literature may be viewed in a context, ethical considerations are perhaps the oldest. From classical times (ancient Greece and Rome) scholars viewed literature's primary purpose as teaching ethics. These ethics may or may not be religious in precept, but they must instruct. Consequently, all good literature, early scholars felt, must teach some ethical lesson. The word that is used to characterize those works that teach is **didacticism**. It is taken from the Greek word *didaskein*, meaning "to teach."

As used in contemporary literature, however, didacticism often has a negative connotation. The term is generally used to describe those literary selections which attempt to teach in such an overbearing way that the enjoyment and art are diminished or lost altogether. For example, read the following didactic verse and poem:

Didactic verse —

"Early to bed and early to rise
 makes a man healthy, wealthy, and wise."

Didactic poem —

A PSALM OF LIFE
What The Heart Of The Young Man Said To The Psalmist

Tell me not, in mournful numbers,
  Life is but an empty dream!—
For the soul is dead that slumbers,
  And things are not what they seem.

Life is real! Life is earnest!   5
  And the grace is not its goal;
Dust thou art, to dust returnest,
  Was not spoken of the soul.

Not enjoyment, and not sorrow,
  Is our destined end or way;   10
But to act, that each tomorrow
  Find us farther than today.

Art is long, and Time is fleeting,
  And our hearts, though stout and brave,
Still, like muffled drums, are beating   15
  Funeral marches to the grave.

In the world's broad field of battle,
  In the bivouac of Life,
Be not like dumb, driven cattle!
  Be a hero in the strife!   20

Trust no Future, howe'er pleasant!
  Let the dead Past bury its dead!
Act,—act in the living Present!
  Heart within, and God O'erhead!

—*Henry Wadsworth Longfellow* (*1807-1882*)

43

While "Psalm of Life" was enjoyed in its day—1838—modern readers feel that Longfellow's purpose, to teach or preach, was obviously more important to him than the art of his poem. While it is true that great literature usually teaches, it achieves its greatness through subtlety of expression and form; the arrangement is fresh and the author does not overstate the point.

For example, the following poem (which you examined in Chapter One under Irony) might also be said to teach, or at least contain, a strong theme:

OZYMANDIAS

I met a traveller from an antique land,
Who said: "Two vast and trunkless legs of stone
Stand in the desert . . . Near them, on the sand,
Half sunk a shattered visage lies, whose frown,
And wrinkled lip, and sneer of cold command,   5
Tell that its sculptor well those passions read
Which yet survive, stamped on these lifeless things,
The hand that mocked them, and the heart that fed:
And on the pedestal, these words appear:
My name is Ozymandias, King of Kings: 10
Look on my Works, ye Mighty, and despair!
Nothing beside remains. Round the decay
Of the colossal Wreck, boundless and bare
The lone and level sands stretch far away."

—*Percy Bysshe Shelley (1792-1822)*

EXERCISE 2.1

In one or two sentences describe the point of the above poem.

_____

_____

_____

_____

_____

If you noticed a considerable difference between "Psalm of Life" (1838) and "Ozymandias" (1817), you have probably begun to see what didacticism is and how it detracts from an appreciation of literary art. The poet Shelley is obviously much more concerned with his poem's artistic impact on the reader in "Ozymandias" than is Longfellow in "Psalm of Life." Yet, Shelley's poem can be said to have an ethical lesson—a moral. But the poem's moral is discovered by the reader. Longfellow, on the other hand, states his ethical conclusions directly. Essentially, that is the difference between didactic writers and those who are not.

44

During the twentieth century, some writers have written novels so didactic that, while the story may be otherwise interesting, the propagandistic characterizations and plots detract from the other merits the works may possess. Some critics, for example, feel Frank Norris' *The Octopus*, an anti-railroad story, and John Steinbeck's *The Grapes of Wrath*, a story about the plight of depression era migrant farmers, to be didactic. Nonetheless, many readers find these to be moving and profound works.

EXERCISE 2.2

Define didacticism in the space below and explain why modern writers avoid it.

_____

_____

_____

_____

_____

_____

_____

EXERCISE 2.3

Compare the following two poems.

WHEN I HEARD THE LEARN'D ASTRONOMER

When I heard the learn'd astronomer,
When the proofs, the figures, were ranged in columns before me,
When I was shown the charts and diagrams, to add, divide,
    and measure them,
When I sitting heard the astronomer where he lectured with much
    applause in the lecture-room,
How soon unaccountable I became tired and sick,
Till rising and gliding out I wandered off by myself,
In the mystical moist night-air, and from time to time,
Looked up in perfect silence at the stars.

—Walt Whitman (1819-1892)

THE OAK

Live thy Life
   Young and old,
Like yon oak,
Bright in spring,
   Living gold;   5

Summer-rich
   Then; and then
Autumn-changed,
Soberer-hued
   Gold again.   10

All his leaves
   Fall'n at length,
Look, he stands,
Trunk and bough,
   Naked strength.   15

—*Alfred, Lord Tennyson (1809-1892)*

1. Which of the above poems might be considered didactic? _____

2. Explain the reasons for your choice.

_____

_____

_____

_____

_____

_____

    Didacticism aside, ethical consideration offers readers a vast mirror in which they may view the soul of humanity. Through literature we can all see the questions with which humans have struggled for centuries. Basic ethical-philosophical questions have remained virtually unchanged since the dawn of recorded history, and literature is but one avenue of discovery. When you read the dramas of ancient Greece, you will discover that ethical musings were the same then as they are today: *Are there gods or is there a god? If there is does he/she/they have control over the lives of humans? What happens after death? Why are we here? Why is there evil and suffering in the world?* These are all universal questions. It is fascinating to note that while the universality to these questions remains virtually the same, the answers differ among different peoples and different times.

    The ethical debate is the concern of not only literature but all the humanities. Painting, sculpture, music, dance and photography, as well as literature, offer answers to universal questions. It was through the postulating of ethical answers to the universal questions in the humanities, in particular literature, that classical

Greeks and Romans came to feel that good literature must teach. The ancient Greek philosopher Plato (427-345 BC) emphasized literature's morality and utilitarianism, and the Roman critic Horace (65-8 BC) stressed *dulce et utile* —delight and instruction.

Consider again Shelley's classic poem "Ozymandias" (on page 44). Contextual scholars who emphasize ethical consideration along the lines espoused by Plato and Horace are likely to point out the statement of excessive pride Ozymandias had inscribed upon his memorial. The delight is in the poetic irony— the fact that the old king asks us to look at all his accomplishments and to despair because we are so puny by comparison, yet nothing of his works remains. His accomplishments are in actuality puny in comparison with the forces of wind and sand. The lesson, of course, concerns human pride and one's influence in so short a span of time on earth as a lifetime—or even a time-span of a civilization.

Students and scholars of ethical considerations need not, however, neglect other aspects of literature, such as form, use of language, and artistic merit. Moreover, it is important to note that serious writers often struggle with ethical questions in ways that didactic writers do not. The didactic writer always has a definitive answer to ethical questions; for the serious artist the answer can be much more difficult. For example, Herman Melville was obsessed with many of the universal questions listed above throughout his literary career; his continuing struggles to come to terms with such questions are reflected in the highly charged symbolism of *Moby Dick*, as well as his other works.

EXERCISE 2.4

After each of the following selections write two or three sentences in which you list its major ethical consideration.

RICHARD CORY

Whenever Richard Cory went down town,
We people on the pavement looked at him:
He was a gentleman from sole to crown,
Clean favored, and imperially slim.

And he was always quietly arrayed,   5
And he was always human when he talked;
But still he fluttered pulses when he said,
"Good-morning," and he glittered when he walked.

And he was rich—yes, richer than a king—
And admirably schooled in every grace: 10
In fine, we thought that he was everything
To make us wish that we were in his place.

So on we worked, and waited for the light,
And went without the meat, and cursed the bread;
And Richard Cory, one calm summer night,   15
Went home and put a bullet through his head.

—*Edwin Arlington Robinson (1869-1935)*

MIRROR

I am silver and exact. I have no preconceptions.
Whatever I see I swallow immediately
Just as it is, unmisted by love or dislike.
I am not cruel, only truthful—
The eye of a little god, four-cornered.
Most of the time I meditate on the opposite wall.
It is pink, with speckles. I have looked at it so long
I think it is a part of my heart. But it flickers.
Faces and darkness separate us over and over.

Now I am a lake. A woman bends over me,   10
Searching my reaches for what she really is.
Then she turns to those liars, the candles or the moon.
I see her back, and reflect it faithfully.
She rewards me with tears and an agitation of hands.
I am important to her. She comes and goes.
Each morning it is her face that replaces the darkness.
In me she has drowned a young girl, and in me an old woman
Rises toward her day after day, like a terrible fish.

—Sylvia Plath (1932-1963)

TO THE STONE-CUTTERS

Stone-cutters fighting time with marble, you foredefeated
Challengers of oblivion
Eat cynical earnings, knowing rock splits, records fall down,
The square limbed Roman letters
Scale in the thaws, wear in the rain. The poet as well
Builds his monument mockingly;
For man will be blotted out, the blithe earth die, the brave sun
Die blind and blacken to the heart.
Yet stones have stood for a thousand years, and pained
    thoughts found
The honey of peace in old poems.

                        —Robinson Jeffers (1887-1962)

---

pity this busy monster,manunkind

pity this busy monster,manunkind

not. Progress is a comfortable disease:
your victim(death and life safely beyond)

plays with the bigness of his littleness
—electrons deify one razorblade
into a mountainrange;lenses extend

unwish through curving wherewhen till unwish
returns on its unself.

               A world of made
is not a world of born—pity poor flesh   10

and trees,poor stars and stones,but never this
fine specimen of hypermagical

ultraomnipotence. We doctors know

a hopeless case if—listen:there's a hell
of a good universe next door;let's go

              —e.e. cummings (1894-1962)

_____
_____
_____
_____
_____
_____

Lesson 2

Genre Characteristics

Each literary type, or genre, has particular standards by which it is judged. Before you can analyze any work, you first need to determine carefully into which category it might best be placed. Sometimes distinctions are difficult to make. Yet overall, literature has three genre categories: *prose, poetry,* and *drama*. Each of these types may be further divided into subtypes. For example, modern prose is usually characterized as either *fiction* or *nonfiction*. Poetry, even more than prose, has a plethora of forms: *lyric, narrative, dramatic, symbolic, epic, haiku, sonnet,* and *ballad* are but a few.

Each type has its adherents and each attempts to communicate according to a particular, predetermined structure. It is important, therefore, to establish accurately a selection's form in order to determine the standards by which it is to be analyzed. For example, in reading a poem like "Ozymandias" you should either recognize that its genre is a sonnet, or you should research the poetic types until you do recognize it. A sonnet is a fourteen line verse that in Old French means *little song*. Since "Ozymandias" fits this form, you should further research what special criteria might be employed in an analytical judgment of Shelley's poem as representative of the sonnet genre.

Genres differ in their qualifications. What makes a good ballad is not what makes a good sonnet, or consider the difference between the novel and the short story. It is not, for instance, a great defect for a short story to have weak character development, provided it has other strong elements. A short story is usually too brief to depict fully a human character. With the longer novel form, however, the failure of a writer to develop characters is a serious deficiency.

Although most literary works are readily classifiable by genre type and subtype, there are exceptions. For instance, the dramatic monologues of Tennyson and Browning employ both narrative and dramatic poetic elements, and some long prose poems—such as Robert Penn Warren's *Brother to Dragons* and Robinson Jeffer's *Roan Stallion*—have the characteristics of both fiction and poetry. You should be aware that you will encounter such merging of genres from time to time in your reading.

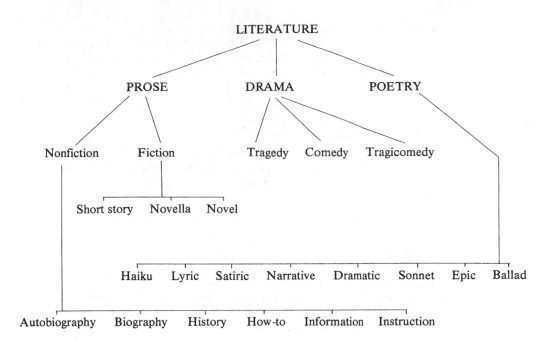

LITERATURE

PROSE   DRAMA   POETRY

Nonfiction   Fiction   Tragedy   Comedy   Tragicomedy

Short story   Novella   Novel

Haiku   Lyric   Satiric   Narrative   Dramatic   Sonnet   Epic   Ballad

Autobiography   Biography   History   How-to   Information   Instruction

EXERCISE 2.5

Analyze the following selection by emphasizing its genre characteristics. Use the library if you need to.

LORD RANDAL

"Oh where have you been, Lord Randal, my son?
Oh where have you been, my handsome young man?"
"Oh, I've been to the wildwood; mother make my bed soon,
I'm weary of hunting and I fain would lie down."

"And whom did you meet there, Lord Randal, my son?   5
And whom did you meet there, my handsome young man?"
"Oh, I met with my true-love; mother, make my bed soon,
I'm weary of hunting and I fain would lie down."

"What got you for supper, Lord Randal, my son?
What got you for supper, my handsome young man?"   10
"I got eels boiled in broth; mother, make my bed soon,
I'm weary of hunting and I fain would lie down."

"And who got your leavings, Lord Randal, my son?
And who got your leavings, my handsome young man?"
"I gave them to my dogs; mother, make my bed soon,   15
I'm weary of hunting and I fain would lie down."

"And what did your dogs do, Lord Randal, my son?
And what did your dogs do, my handsome young man?"
"Oh, they stretched out and died; mother, make my bed soon,
I'm weary of hunting and I fain would lie down."   20

"Oh, I fear you are poisoned, Lord Randal, my son.
Oh, I fear you are poisoned, my handsome young man."
"Oh, yes, I am poisoned; mother, make my bed soon,
I'm weary of hunting and I fain would lie down."

"What will you leave your mother, Lord Randal, my son?   25
What will you leave your mother, my handsome young man?"
"My house and my lands; mother, make my bed soon,
I'm weary of hunting and I fain would lie down."

"What will you leave your sister, Lord Randal, my son?
What will you leave your sister, my handsome young man?"   30
"My gold and my silver; mother, make my bed soon,
I'm weary of hunting and I fain would lie down."

"What will you leave your brother, Lord Randal, my son?
What will you leave your brother, my handsome young man?"
"My horse and my saddle; mother, make my bed soon,   35
I'm weary of hunting and I fain would like down."

"What will you leave your true-love, Lord Randal, my son?
What will you leave your true-love, my handsome young man?"
"A halter to hang her; mother make my bed soon,
For I'm sick at my heart and I want to lie down."   40

—Anonymous

EXERCISE 2.6

Haiku is a seemingly simple poetic genre that many find interesting to read and fascinating to write. Using the library, find three Haiku poems and copy them in the space below. (Or after studying the definitions and examples, write three Haiku poems of your own.)

_____

_____

_____

_____

_____

_____

_____

_____

_____

_____

_____

_____

HAIKU—Originally, a Japanese unrhymed poem in 17 syllables, usually arranged in three lines, often in a pattern of five syllables, seven syllables, and five syllables. In English, the Haiku may be either rhymed or unrhymed. Moreover, it need not adhere to the Japanese Haiku's rigidity in form.

Five by Gary Snyder

After weeks of watching the roof leak
            I fixed it tonight
by moving a single board

•   •   •

A great freight truck
            lit like a town
through the dark stony desert

•   •   •

Stray white mare
            neck rope dangling
forty miles from farms.

•   •   •

They didn't hire him
                    so he ate his lunch alone:
the noon whistle

•   •   •

over the Mindanao Deep
Scrap brass
                    dumpt off the fantail
falling six miles

----   ----   ----

Two by Richard Guches
A sleek sailing sloop
                    quiet as the dawn
slips past the green island

•   •   •

Candace counts cadence
                    numbers reel by
boat's at anchor, waiting to fly

Lesson 3

Textual Authenticity and Linguistic Connotation

Textual Authenticity

Textual authenticity, while quite closely related to linguistic connotation, is not primarily concerned with the connotation of a word. The first concern for the scholar interested in authenticity is whether or not contemporary readers have the word as originally penned by the author. Often in older works, and occasionally even in newer ones, the text which comes to the publisher is imperfect. Sometimes words are smudged, mis-copied, omitted, or in some way lost. Editors are then forced to repair or guess at an author's original intention. This practice makes the accuracy of an editor's choice debatable as new interpretations are placed upon the text, or as later evidence either confirms the editor's judgment or refutes it in favor of yet another view. For example, scholars are still debating what Andrew Marvell really intended in line 34 of his poem "To His Coy Mistress." As it is usually printed, lines 33 and 34 read as follows:

> "Now therefore, while the youthful hue
> Sits on thy skin like morning dew."

The problem is that the first edition has the last word as not *"dew"* but *"glew,"* a seldom used spelling of glue, a word that simply does not fit at all well in the context of the poem. Some critics have suggested that Marvell meant *"hew"* which means warmth; unfortunately, this term had drifted out of use and is, therefore, dubious as a choice. Originally some editor selected *"dew"* and the choice has become so well accepted that only critical texts footnote the word to point out that it was not Marvell's word.

54

With the advent of modern printing and reproduction techniques, fewer and fewer of these textual authenticity problems occur. However, some modern writers repeatedly revise their work. These revisions later become the focal point of study to determine not only which of a text's variations is the author's final intended version but also which is the best version.

In this age of the computer, new tools and new techniques are available for those interested in determining the authenticity of a work of literature. For example, a researcher recently discovered what some believe to be a previously unknown poem by William Shakespeare. Using a statistical study of Shakespeare's words that had been undertaken during the 1970s, statisticians were able to compare the new discovery with Shakespeare's known work. The previous study had determined that Shakespeare had used 31,534 different words. Some he used only once (14,376), some only twice (4,343), some three times (2,292), some four times (1,463) and so forth. Consequently, the statisticians were able to develop a formula of probability that if the 430 words in the new poem were actually written by Shakespeare it should contain 6.95 new words, 4.21 words he had used only once before, 3.33 words he had used only twice before, and so on. After analyzing the poem's words in comparison to those the bard used up to 100 times, the statisticians concluded that the new poem fits the pattern almost perfectly. (Of course, this does not prove that Shakespeare wrote the poem, only that it is statistically probable that he did.)

Linguistic Connotation

Linguistic connotation and textual authenticity, while related analytical interests, are distinct tools of criticism. **Linguistic connotation** concentrates upon the meanings of words *at the time they were written*. While it is usually not too difficult to determine the denotation (the definition of a word based upon dictionaries and other documents available from the period on interest) the word's connotation is the main interest of those who are concerned with linguistics.

Sometimes the meaning of a line may be lost or misinterpreted if you are unfamiliar with the connotation a word had at the time it was written. For example, in Shakespeare's tragedy *Hamlet*, Prince Hamlet, upset with his mother's hasty marriage after the death of her husband (Hamlet's father), takes out his bitterness upon Ophelia, a young woman of whom he is ordinarily quite fond. Seeing his mother's actions as indicative of all women, he tells Ophelia in Act III, Scene I,

> "Get thee to a nunnery. Why wouldst
> thou be a breeder of sinners?"

Some sources have suggested that the term "nunnery" means that Hamlet is suggesting to Ophelia that she remove herself from temptation. By entering a religious convent, she would not produce sinners as his mother has become, and what he feels he has become. The imagery of a "nunnery" as a convent is an effective way to explain Hamlet's growing misogyny, but it totally fails to impart the viciousness that has begun to cloud his thoughts. Nor will "nunnery," as a convent, explain Ophelia's obvious revulsion at such a suggestion. However, upon analysis of the slang of Shakespeare's day, you will discover that while the denotation of "nunnery" did mean convent, the common slang connotation of "nunnery" during Elizabethan times was that of a brothel.

Most people would agree that "nunnery" as brothel changes the imagery of the lines dramatically. This meaning is not only indicative of Hamlet's state of mind but is also in keeping with Hamlet's other comment that Polonius, Ophelia's father, is a fishmonger. In Elizabethan slang, a fishmonger is not a seller of fish but of women—a procurer. This imagery fits the play well if you see that Hamlet believes his mother's sin to be a sexual one—marrying without a suitable period of mourning. In fact, she waits only a few days after the funeral, and marries her brother-in-law, a union Hamlet regards as incestuous.

EXERCISE 2.7

Read the following poem.

SPRING

When daisies pied and violets blue,
   And lady-smocks all silver-white,
And cuckoo-buds of yellow hue
   Do paint the meadows with delight,
The cuckoo then, on every tree,   5
Mocks married men; for thus sings he
                "Cuckoo!
Cuckoo, cuckoo!" O word of fear,
Unpleasing to a *married ear!*

When shepherds pipe on oaten straws,   10
   And merry larks are ploughmen's clocks,
When turtles tread, and rooks, and daws,
   And maidens bleach their summer smocks,
The cuckoo then, on every tree,
Mocks married men; for thus sings he,   15
                "Cuckoo!
Cuckoo, cuckoo!" O word of fear,
Unpleasing to a *married ear!*

          —*William Shakespeare (1564-1616)*

As one interested in linguistic connotation, answer the following questions.

The poem ends each stanza by stating that the cuckoo is "unpleasing to the married ear."

a. What figure of speech is this phrase and why would the cuckoo bird's *behavior* be unpleasing?

_____

_____

_____

_____

_____

_____

b. Why should the *sound* the bird makes—"Cuckoo, Cuckoo, Cuckoo"—be unpleasing?

_____

_____

_____

_____

_____

_____

Lesson 4

Sociology

Sociological analysis, one of the oldest critical points of view, is concerned with the intellectual and social environment out of which literature is produced. Sociological critics do not think that authors create in an intellectual and social vacuum; consequently, even those who write in lonely isolation must be influenced by the world in which they live.

For critical purposes, the contextual sociological approach may be divided into two distinct areas of interest: (A) the immediate environment, **biography**; and (B) the larger environment, **history**.

A. The Immediate Environment—Biography

Authors' biographies are often quite helpful in attempting to understand their work fully because they usually write about what they know. For example, the knowledge that John Milton was blind is an invaluable aid to understanding his poetry, as is the knowledge that he was Latin secretary for Oliver Cromwell, the leader of the English Puritan revolution. Furthermore, a familiarity with other writings by the same author can offer insight. Characters and settings occasionally recur in subsequent works, and the fuller development that this practice occasions allows you to appreciate writers more fully by referring to previously written works. Both Kurt Vonnegut, Jr. and William Faulkner are famous for taking minor characters from one book and developing them into major characters in other books. John Steinbeck did this with a character from the short story, "The Snake," located on page 287 on this book.

Here is a part of a student paper that analyzes Steinbeck's other writing as it relates to "The Snake."

Born in Salinas, California, in 1902, John Steinbeck's early family history is outlined in his epic novel East of Eden as a subplot. Young Steinbeck grew up in California in the Salinas Valley and the Monterey Peninsula region, the settings of many of his works. The Long Valley, in which the short story "The Snake" first appeared, is the Salinas Valley. Another of his stories, "Flight," is set just south of Carmel on the Monterey Peninsula. Of Mice and Men is set in the farmland along the Salinas River. Finally, two novels, Cannery Row and Sweet Thursday, are set in the community of Monterey, California, the same locale as in "The Snake." The most important of these works in its relationship to "The Snake" is Cannery Row, for "The Snake," first published in 1938, introduces the character Dr. Phillips, who in 1944 becomes the central character Doc in Cannery Row.

The character of the doctor serves Steinbeck as a commentator for his philosophical view of life. Through the doctor in "The Snake," as well as the doctors in Cannery Row, In Dubious Battle, and The Moon is Down, he see life biologically. In fact, his view of human life is as though he were examining a seashore tide pool. With the objectivity of a scientist, he examines people in their environment, in their "tide pool." The living creatures, in this view, are independent but contained, and they are seen as subject to natural laws. Humans viewed in this respect take on the qualities of animals. Steinbeck seems to feel that humans must be understood first as animals before they can be understood as humans. In order to accomplish this, they must be examined objectively as biological specimens by observing both their physical and psychological reactions within their environment.

Steinbeck is indeed qualified to use a scientific frame of reference. Prior to entering upon a literary career, he studied marine zoology at Stanford University and later worked in a marine biology laboratory. Thus, in "The Snake" he is able to detail realistically the duties and functions of the marine biologist, Dr. Phillips. . . .

While some critics object to what they view as overdependence upon matters extraneous to the literature itself, it is hard to dispute the idea that some familiarity with an author's life, and other writing, can aid in the understanding of a particular piece of literature.

EXERCISE 2.8

Read the following poem.

WINTER

When icicles hang by the wall,
   And Dick the shepherd blows his nail,
And Tom bears logs into the hall,
   And milk comes frozen home in pail,
When blood in nipped and ways be foul,   5
Then nightly sings the staring owl,
          "Tu-whit, tu-who!"

A merry note,
While greasy Joan doth keel* the pot.

When all aloud the wind doth blow,   10
   And coughing drowns the parson's saw,
And birds sit brooding in the snow,
   And Marian's nose looks red and raw,
When roasted crabs** hiss in the bowl,
Then nightly sings the staring owl,   15
          "Tu-whit, tu-who!"

A merry note,
While greasy Joan doth keel the pot.

_____

*skim
**crab apples

1. What would you like to know about the above poem to enhance your understanding
   of it?

   _____

   _____

   _____

   _____

   _____

   _____

   _____

   a. When do you think it was written? _____

   b. Who do you think might have written it? _____

   _____

EXERCISE 2.9

Read the following poem.

THE WORLD IS TOO MUCH WITH US

The world is too much with us; late and soon,
Getting and spending, we lay waste our powers:
Little we see in Nature that is ours;
We have given our hearts away, a sordid boon!
This Sea that bares her bosom to the moon;   5
The winds that will be howling at all hours,
And are up-gathered now like sleeping flowers;
For this, for everything, we are out of tune;
It moves us not—Great God! I'd rather be
A Pagan suckled in a creed outworn;   10
So might I, standing on this pleasant lea,
Have glimpses that would make me less forlorn;
Have sight of Proteus rising from the sea;
Or hear old Triton blow his wreathed horn.

1. What personal statement is the author of the above poem making about life?

_____

_____

_____

_____

_____

2. When do you think this poem was written? Why?

_____

_____

_____

_____

_____

B. The Larger Environment—History

While the immediate environment or biographical data of authors is concerned with the personal information about their lives and their other writings, the larger sociological concern is with the historical context out of which authors germinate their ideas. In other words, many scholars are very interested in what influence the historical circumstances of a period might have either upon writers or upon the characters they create. For example, Charles Dickens' novel, *Bleak House*, concerns the fates of several families enmeshed in a court case that progresses with agonizing slowness through Chancery Court in London; your familiarity with the legal corruption and delay in mid-nineteenth-century England can greatly enhance your understanding of the book and the issues that Dickens is addressing. Likewise, your knowledge of the conditions in which books like Dickens' were produced (*Bleak House* first appeared in eighteen monthly installments) can help you understand some of the ways in which Dickens' characters are presented, and his close relationship with his readers, who waited eagerly for each installment.

Remember, no one creates in an intellectual or social void; all people, including writers, are influenced by the times in which they live. Of the many issues of the contemporary world, one might reflect upon the recent changes in attitude toward such issues as nuclear power, gun control, or feminism. It is difficult to see how any contemporary writer could write about those subjects and not be influenced by current attitudes and recent historical events.

Historical influences are particularly important for such works as *The Octopus*, by Frank Norris (railroad expansion); *The Jungle*, by Upton Sinclair (the meat-packing industry); or such propagandistic novels as *Uncle Tom's Cabin*, by Harriet Beecher Stowe (Slavery); and *The Grapes of Wrath*, by John Steinbeck (migrant farm workers). Sometimes the historical influence is more subtle, but it can offer insight nonetheless. Even such recent works as *Jonathan Livingston Seagull*, by Richard Bach, is more meaningful when viewed against the backdrop of the resurgence of interest in mysticism and parareligion.

EXERCISE 2.10

Read the following two poems:

THE MAN HE KILLED

Had he and I but met
By some old ancient inn,
We should have sat us down to wet
Right many a nipperkin!*

But ranged as infantry,   5
And staring face to face,
I shot at him as he at me,
And killed him in his place.

I shot him dead because—
Because he was my foe,   10
Just so; my foe of course he was;
That's clear enough; although

He thought he'd 'list, perhaps,
Off-hand-like—just as I—
Was out of work—had sold his traps—   15
No other reason why.

Yes; quaint and curious war is!
You shoot a fellow down
You'd treat, if met where any bar is,
Or help to half-a-crown.   20
    —*Thomas Hardy (1840-1928)*

---
*half-pint cup

DULCE ET DECORUM EST

Bent double, like old beggars under sacks,
Knock-kneed, coughing like hags, we cursed through sludge,
Till on the haunting flares we turned our backs,
And towards our distant rest began to trudge.
Men marched asleep. Many had lost their boots,   5
But limped on, blood-shod. All went lame, all blind;
Drunk with fatigue; deaf even to the hoots
Of gas-shells dropping softly behind.

Gas! GAS! Quick boys!—An ecstasy of fumbling,
Fitting the clumsy helmets just in time,   10
But someone still was yelling out and stumbling
And flound'ring like a man in fire or lime.—
Dim through the misty panes and thick green light,
As under a green sea, I saw him drowning.

In all my dreams before my helpless sight   15
He plunges at me, guttering, choking, drowning.

If in some smothering dreams, you too could pace
Behind the wagon that we flung him in,
And watch the white eyes writhing in his face,
His hanging face, like a devil's sick of sin,   20
If you could hear, at every jolt, the blood
Come gargling from the froth-corrupted lungs
Bitter as the cud
Of vile, incurable sores on innocent tongues,—
My friend, you would not tell with such high zest   25
To children ardent for some desperate glory,
The old lie: *Dulce et decorum est
Pro patria mori.**

—Wilfred Owen (1895-1918)

*Latin, from the Roman poet Horace, meaning, "It is sweet and becoming to die for one's country."

Write a paragraph explaining why one poem may be better understood through historical analysis than the other.

_____

_____

_____

_____

_____

_____

The following student paper is a contextual analysis of "What Happened Here Before" by Gary Snyder. See the poem on page 222-223.

Angela Turner

English 1-B TTH 9:15

Dr. Guches

21 October 1988

(Contextual Analysis)

Fooling with Mother Nature

People are creatures of habit. They arise at the same time every morning, eat the same breakfasts, and travel to work along the same routes. They rush through their lives as though chased by demons, scarcely stopping to admire the beauty and intricacy of the nature that surrounds them. And most people certainly do not pause to examine the repercussions that the drive toward progress has had on nature. In the eager acceptance of all that technology presents, people distance themselves from that which gives life--Mother Earth. Not so the poet-shaman Gary Snyder, who has "made himself spokesman for the most oppressed, taxed, and under represented of all classes: the grasslands, trees, and animals . . . "("Turtle Island" 195). In his poem, "What Happened Here Before," Snyder not only delivers a mini history lesson on the geology and people of the Sierra Nevada Mother Lode, but also illustrates his love of Earth and his belief that civilized humans, in their greed and insistence on progress, are laying waste the nature that they should be revering and preserving.

Almost half of "What Happened Here Before" is a description of the geologic processes which created the Sierra Nevada mountains. Through this discourse Snyder reveals his highly educated background. He took a degree in anthropology from Reed College in Oregon, and pursued graduate-level work at other colleges (Rothberg 28). Snyder writes with great understanding and feeling as he paints pictures with words:

> First a sea: soft sands, muds, and marls
>
> > -loading, compressing, heating, crumpling,
> >
> > > crushing, recrystallizing, infiltrating,
> >
> > several times lifted and submerged.

The imagery in his description of a lake that "tilted and the rivers fell apart" is strong and creates vivid impressions. Snyder does not neglect to mention how that alluring metal, gold, came to be deposited in rock

63

and streambeds, thus foreshadowing European immigrants future defacement
of the mountains that had taken nature millions of years to build.

Into this pristine wilderness of deer, bluejay, pine, and manzanita
come the Maidu Indians, a people with "basket hats, and "winter-houses
underground." This was a people who sang and told "songs and stories in
the smoky dark." It is not mere chance that Snyder includes the Indians
of the Gold Country in his poem. Snyder has been close to Native
Americans since his boyhood, when he grew disenchanted with "non-natives
who didn't even know the plants or where our water comes from" (Myths and
Texts viii.). His bond with the Indian strengthened the already deep
love for nature he had acquired growing up in eastern Oregon. From the
Indians, the poet gained insight into living harmoniously with nature
(Rothberg 27).

But the idyllic state that existed between the Indian and nature was
doomed.

> Then came the white man: tossed up trees and
>
> boulders with big hoses,
>
> going after that old gravel and the gold.

"Civilized" humans quickly rushed into the mountains and turned nature
"topsy turvy." The Indians, unable to cope with the upheaval, soon
perished, either through disease or political means. The miners brought
with them "card-games, pistol-shooting, churches, county jail," and that
most refined of institutions, the property tax. Snyder mocks this tax,
calling it "our body-mind, guest at the banquet Memorial and Annual."
Snyder sneers at the avarice of the people who spread their Manifest
Destiny across Turtle Island--the North American continent--with the
emphatic statement that "the land belongs to itself."

The '49ers were to Snyder symbols of the Judeo-Christian tradition,
"which he credits with the destruction and exploitation of the sacred in
man and physical nature by its alliance with and support of a predatory
capitalism" (Rothberg 34). Snyder is a student of Zen Buddhism, having
spent years in a Japanese monastery learning the Buddhist philosophy that
"the Universe and all creatures in it are intrinsically in a state of
mutual interdependence" (Earth House Hold 90). He sees modern Americans
as ignorant of this vital connection, and asserts that "the proper

attention must be given if the future is to be successful" (Huber). In "What Happened Here Before," Snyder's deep understanding and love for Earth is predominant. Fittingly, he ends the poem with bluejay, a symbol of nature, screeching

<u>WE SHALL SEE</u>

<u>WHO KNOWS</u>

<u>HOW TO BE.</u>

This ending makes it apparent that Snyder believes that it is nature that is right, and modern "civilized" humans who are wrong.

"What Happened Here Before," besides being an intriguing array of historical images, is a warning to humans to examine their attitudes toward Earth. By destroying nature, humanity is really destroying itself. The invisible umbilical cord that nourishes humanity may someday snap, or, more likely, humans will sever it through arrogance, and in so doing will obliterate the entire planet. Snyder, of course, wants to avoid the impending catastrophe. He wants modern humans, like the Indians, to live with the land rather than off it. Snyder sweeps aside the "bric-a-brac" of modern life,

> Revealing its essentially incidental nature, connecting
>
> us with the creeks, the mountains, birds and bears of
>
> North America that were here before it had that name
>
> and, nature prevailing, will be here after that name is
>
> lost, forgotten, destroyed" (McKenzie).

WORKS CITED

Huber, Dean. "Poet Gary Snyder--Seeking Anonymity." Sacramento Bee
     20 Nov. 1984: C1.

McKenzie, James. "Turtle Island." Library Journal 15 Nov. 1974: n. pag.

Rothberg, Abraham. "Passage to more than India; the Poetry of Gary
     Snyder." Southwest Review Winter 1976: 26-38.

Snyder, Gary. Earth House Hold. New York: New Directions, 1969.

---. Myths and Texts. New York: New Directions, 1978.

"Turtle Island." Western Humanities Review Spring 1975: 195+.

Analyzing Fiction

Of all the literary genres, fiction is the most widely read and enjoyed by modern readers. People read fiction—short stories and novels—to be entertained, to escape, and to learn. Occasionally fictional stories will seem to catch the imagination of nearly the whole reading public. These works become, almost overnight, "best sellers"; they sell out quickly, generate long waiting lists at libraries, and become conversation topics at parties and on television talk shows. All this attention, of course, catapults their sales into the millions. Beyond their popularity, or perhaps because of it, readers derive a great sense of satisfaction from reading fiction. It seems to appeal to some inner feelings—feelings that bring joy from vicarious experiences. To derive the most enjoyment possible from a work of literature, however, one needs to understand it. Fiction, like any other genre, has its characteristics, and to know them is to enhance one's understanding and appreciation.

Fiction is a literary genre that appeals both to casual readers and to serious students of literature alike. People who make the effort to learn the characteristics and techniques of fiction enhance their own critical, analytical skill.

Objectives:

After completing this chapter, you will be able to:
1. Define the basic elements of fiction.
2. Identify fictional elements in a literary work.
3. Distinguish between romanticism and realism, primitivism and naturalism.
4. Interpret a work's point of view and discuss its effectiveness.

67

5. Write an analysis of a short fictional work.
6. Relate the theme of a short story.
7. Assess the contribution of a story's setting to the plot, atmosphere, and ideas expressed.
8. Appraise the importance of foreshadowing in a story.
9. Evaluate a story's exposition, climax, and resolution for credibility.
10. Express greater confidence in your understanding of fiction.

Pre-Assessment

_____ 1. Romance may be characterized by an interest in (A) the true to life, (B) the cause and effect principles of science, (C) objective presentation, (D) fate determined by the environment, (E) nature and a return to the simple life.

_____ 2. Which of the following is not a characteristic of primitivism?
(A) Glorification of the primitive
(B) Celebration of natural beauty
(C) Emphasis upon scientific detail
(D) Idealization of childhood
(E) Desire to return to a simple life

_____ 3. Naturalists (A) revolted against romance, (B) believe all phenomena is a result of the cause and effect principles of science, (C) deny the existence of anything miraculous or supernatural, (D) feel that humans are controlled by their passions and by their environment, (E) all of the above.

_____ 4. Which of the following is NOT a basic area of conflict in fiction?
(A) The individual against nature
(B) The individual against history
(C) The individual against the individual
(D) The individual against self
(E) The individual against the gods

_____ 5. Foreshadowing can (A) prepare the reader for the final outcome, (B) substitute for a plot, (C) never be used in realistic fiction, (D) cause a story to lose probability, (E) make characters resemble real people.

_____ 6. In literature a *foil* is a character who (A) spoils the main character's plans, (B) duels constantly, (C) is a fool, (D) is intended to be contrasted with a main character, (E) functions as a listener.

_____ 7. Theme is concerned with (A) a story's plot, (B) a story's purpose, (C) propaganda, (D) the overemphasis of ideas, (E) entertaining diversions.

_____ 8. The omniscient point of view (A) gives the narrator god-like powers of seeing and knowing all, (B) gives the narrator no clear view of all the characters, (C) is objective, (D) tells only what characters look like and what they do, (E) is stream of consciousness.

_____ 9. A first-person narrator (A) sees all and reports what characters think, (B) reports what is on only one other character's mind, (C) refers to himself as "I," (D) is objective, (E) uses the pronoun "you" frequently.

_____ 10. Stream of consciousness (A) is omniscient, (B) is objective, (C) is a nineteenth century technique, (D) links thought patterns together subjectively, (E) refers to the setting.

Lesson 1

Literary Movements

When asked why they prefer fiction to other literary genres, modern readers often say that they feel fiction to be more realistic to read than either drama or poetry. This portrayal of the true-to-life in literature can be deceptive for the unwary, however. No short story or novel actually portrays truth or reality because the very nature of the printed word leads to some distortion.

Fiction can promote distortion in two obvious ways. The emphasis in the writing can be on the emotional aspects of experience or on the clinical aspects. When the fictional experience emphasizes the emotional, we refer to that experience as *romantic*; when the fictional experience emphasizes the clinical, we refer to it as *naturalistic*; when the emphasis is upon a balance between the two that attempts to mirror reality, we refer to it as *realistic*. Romanticism, Realism, and Naturalism are three ways that we can relate fiction to our lives. Each is a different perception of what is real, and each has, at one time or another, become so popular in literature and in art that whole periods of time have been called by these terms.

A. Romanticism

Romanticism is a term that has been applied to the principles and characteristics of the romantic movement (prominent from about 1770 to 1850). The main emphasis of the movement in both literature and art was the promotion of imagination, sentiment, and individualism in artistic expression. Since the Old French and medieval historical romances of the seventeenth century dealt exclusively with fanciful and far-fetched adventures that were distant from familiar and ordinary life, such as in tales of King Arthur and the Knights of the Round Table, the term romantic itself came to denote things that were unreal or opposed to fact. During the next century the term came to mean that which was extravagantly fictitious in creating scenes that are pleasing but deliberately far from an accurate depiction of truth.

The interests of the romantics were characterized by a concern for nature and a return to the simple life. Related to this was a renewed interest in the nostalgic past. As a result, writers chose subject matter for their fiction that was unfamiliar, remote, and out of doors. Passion and imagination, along with a great interest in the horrible and supernatural, were emphasized.

Some Characteristics of Romantic Fiction

1. Setting are often distant or in the past
2. Adventures among strange people
3. Mystery
4. Emphasis upon the unfamiliar
5. Unnatural and horrible situations or characters
6. The past

The huge popularity of romance stimulated writers to produce even more romantic fiction. Nathanial Hawthorne, for example, wrote of the puritans of the Seventeenth century from his vantage point in the mid-nineteenth century (e.g. *The Scarlet Letter*, 1850). Herman Melville's novels *Typee* (1846), *Omoo* (1847), and *Mardi* (1849), are all set in Eastern Polynesia among native peoples, and the books made their author extremely popular. Only later, after the publication of *Moby Dick*, a symbolic novel, did his popularity wane. The public loved him for his early romantic novels but did not seem to understand the symbolic quality of his later work. Perhaps they desired more passionate adventure with less serious intent.

A renewed interest in romanticism is flourishing among contemporary readers. Modern book companies have found financial success in publishing a plethora of new titles according to very strict romantic formulas. Names such as Georgia Bockoven (*Today, Tomorrow, Always*, 1985), Linda Ladd (*Moonspell*, 1985), and Victoria Pade (*Passion's Torment*, 1985) have become popular. Also, many new novels, as well as television programs and movies, have exploited a renewed interest in the past (e.g. *Clan of the Cave Bear*, 1980, and its sequels, by Jean Auel). Furthermore, horror and the unnatural, fundamental romantic subjects are ever popular as witnessed by the success of the novels (and the movies made from them) of Stephen King.

B. Primitivism

Primitivism, a subbranch of romanticism, is concerned with the idea that natural or very early conditions of society are the very best situations for human life. Those who subscribe to this view conclude that primitive humans, living close to nature in their tribal villages in the forests and jungles, do not suffer the evil influences of urban society. Primitive humans are, accordingly, more nearly perfect, thus nobler than civilized humans. Moreover, since gods reveal themselves more completely in nature, primitives are essentially moral; they are not confronted with the evils of self-imposed limitations on freedom that exist for city dwellers. Human behavior, the primitivists believed, is naturally prone to be good. Savages, by this reasoning, are quite superior—*Noble Savages*. Part of the enchantment with noble savages was created from the accounts of voyaging and by the discovery of the South Seas; consequently, primitive life became the theme of many romantic fictions.

Yet a note of tension often is discernible in accounts of civilized humans who confront primitive societies. A thin line between enthusiasm and abhorrence can be perceived in Melville's *Typee*, for instance. Tomo, the protagonist, is decidedly uneasy: are his Polynesian captors treating him well in order to initiate him into their midst (by tatooing his face and body) or are they planing to have him for dinner (cannibalism)?

Like savages, children were idealized in much romanticism as being closer than adults to divine beings. Children at birth are, of course, as close to nature as they can or will ever be. Thus the more educated and the more conformistic children become, the less natural they are and the farther they drift from a state of perfection. Civilization, in this view, is inherently unnatural and therefore evil. Pearl, in *The Scarlet Letter*, for example, is a primitive child who seems to be far more uninhibited and natural in the forest than when she is in the civilized, Puritan village.

Romantic Primitivism

1. Glorification of the primitive
   (*Typee*—Herman Melville)
2. Celebration of natural beauty and the simple life
   (*Walden Pond*—Henry David Thoreau)
3. Idealization of the child and childhood
   (*Uncle Tom's Cabin*—Harriet Beecher Stowe)

EXERCISE 3.1

Read the short story "The Masque of the Red Death" (Page 283) by Edgar Allan Poe and list the characterists of romance that appear in Poe's story.

1. _____

2. _____

3. _____

4. _____

5. _____

EXERCISE 3.2

Write a paragraph in which you contrast, in your own words, romanticism and primitivism.

_____

_____

_____

_____

_____

_____

_____

_____

_____

_____

_____

_____

C. Realism

After decades of romantic literature, writers became interested in achieving **verisimilitude**. Verisimilitude, a word of Latin roots, meaning true-like, represented a shift in the way people thought about fiction and the way writers treated it. Writers, like Stephen Crane in "The Open Boat" and *The Red Badge of Courage*, wished to incorporate within their work the semblance of truth by using realistic material. Beginning as a movement in the late nineteenth century, the emphasis in fiction became accuracy, especially in background information. Viewed in one way, the realistic movement was a reaction to the flights of imagination that characterized romantic writing. Realists wanted to portray an image of life as it really is.

The main emphasis of the realists became the presentation of events so specific that the details were nearly photographic. Quite the opposite of the romantics, with their imaginary conception of experience, realists became directly concerned with social and psychological problems. The characters in realistic fiction suffer frustrations from an environment which is often presented as sordid and depraved, as in Upton Sinclair's *The Jungle*, a novel set in the Chicago stockyards. While romance emphasizes beauty and order, realism emphasizes the actuality of life—including the ugliness and disharmony that exists in the world—thus, its themes differ markedly.

A scale from pure fantasy to factual history might look like this:

Fiction

| *Fantasy* | *Primitivism* | *Romance* | *Realism* | *Naturalism* | *History* |

While the differences between romance and realism seem quite substantial, they share important qualities when they are compared with history or journalism. What makes realists different from reporters is emphasis. A realist's actuality is still more generalized or typical than a reporter's factual account of actual events. Frequently, the realistic writer's fictional experiences are more vividly memorable than a newspaper account of a similar event. A comparison of Stephen Crane's newspaper account of his boat's sinking with his short story "The Open Boat" on the same subject is remarkably indicative of this difference in vividness.

Neither romance nor realism is, after all, absolute truth. Realism is closer to the romantic than to historical accounts, and, looking at the graph, one sees romance is closer to realism than pure fantasy. As a matter of fact, much of the most successful modern fiction is a very skillful merging of romance *and* realism. The works contain sufficiently accurate detail to give the reader the feeling of authenticity while the subject and characters are remote, exotic, adventurous, mysterious, deal with the unfamiliar, and emphasize the imagination. Such works as William Golding's *Lord of the Flies* or Anthony Burgess's *Clockwork Orange* demonstrate this combination of romance and realism.

D. Naturalism

Naturalism represents an extreme form of realism. In complete revolt against romance, naturalists take the philosophical position that all phenomena can and should be presented as the natural result of the cause and effect principles of science, especially those of chemistry and physics. Naturalists deny the existence of anything miraculous or supernatural. In art and especially literature, naturalists believe that the methods of scientific transcription of nature should be employed. Fiction should become, then, little more than a series of objective reports.

Particularly influenced by the theories of biological determinism espoused by Charles Darwin or the economic determinism of Karl Marx, literary naturalism strives for a treatment of natural humans with scientific objectivity. From the writer's or reader's point of view, then, naturalistic fiction includes more details and is less selective of these details than is realism. Humans, in this view, are largely controlled by their instincts and passions and by their economic and social environment. Accordingly, a naturalistic writer may make few or no moral judgments. Most naturalistic fiction is pessimistic, such as Norman Mailer's *The Naked and the Dead*.

Whereas romanticism was emphasized during the eighteenth and most of the nineteenth centuries, and primitivism reached its zenith in the late eighteenth century, realism was influential during the late nineteenth and early twentieth centuries. Naturalism has been a prominent literary movement during at least the first half of the twentieth century.

Leaders in the Naturalistic Movement

Scientists—Philosophers

Charles Darwin (1809-1882, British)
Thomas Huxley (1825-1895, British)
Herbert Spencer (1820-1903, British)
Karl Marx (1818-1883, Prussian)

Writers who have used Naturalism

Emile Zola (1840-1902, French)
James Joyce (1882-1941, Irish)
Theodore Dreiser (1871-1945, American)
William Faulkner (1897-1962, American)
Ernest Hemingway (1899-1961, American)
Robinson Jeffers (1887-1962, American)
Eugene O'Neill (1888-1953, American)
Henrik Ibsen (1828-1906, Norwegian)
Frank Norris (1870-1902, American)
Jack London (1876-1916, American)
John Steinbeck(1902-1968, American)
Norman Mailer (1923-   , American)

EXERCISE 3.3

Write a paragraph in which you contrast realism with naturalism.

_____

_____

_____

_____

_____

_____

_____

_____

_____

_____

EXERCISE 3.4

Read the short story "To Build a Fire" (Page 274) by Jack London and list the characteristics of realism and naturalism that appear in London's story.

_____

_____

_____

_____

_____

_____

_____

_____

_____

_____

_____

E. Existentialism

In contrast to the scientific restrictions of naturalism, existentialism asserts that human beings are totally free. This freedom, however, comes with the knowledge that all people are responsible for their own actions. Existentialist philosophy demands, therefore, a personal commitment from each person. This commitment is necessary to overcome the irrational nature of the human condition and to view it as the origin of a universal fear. The only way to overcome the feelings of anxiety, loneliness, and despair resulting from living in an absurd universe is the commitment to create meaning by taking some significant action.

The knowledge that people are totally free and completely responsible for themselves becomes a source of great anxiety. This anxiety has lead some literary existentialists to write of their feelings of utter hopelessness, a sense of nothingness. On a more positive side, existentialist philosophy does allow for the possibility for improvement. If human beings act authentically, act upon commitments only from within themselves, they can alter their human condition and repudiate the source of their despair: human nature.

As a literary/philosophical movement, existentialism began in the nineteenth century, became further defined and explored during the first part of the twentieth century, and achieved wide popularity after World War II. Existentialists have found literature to be especially useful as a medium for expressing themselves. Franz Kafka, for example, depicts beleaguered, lonely characters in conflict with absurd heartless bureaucratic systems in *The Trial* and *The Castle*. Albert Camus examines estrangement of the individual in an absurd world in *The Stranger*. Jean-Paul Sartre, writer of philosophical books (such as *Being and Nothingness*) as well as novels, plays, and short stories, writes of the alienation of modern humans in *Nausea* and describes the nature of freedom in *Iron in the Soul*. Many modern writers—Ernest Hemingway, for example—combine a naturalistic depiction of detail with an existentialist sense of free will at work in a meaningless or absurd world.

Philosophers and creative writers usually associated with existentialism

Søren Kierkegaard, Danish (1813-1855)
Martin Buber, Austrian (1878-1965)
Paul Tillich, American (1886-1965)
Martin Heidegger, German (1889-1976)
Samuel Beckett, French (1906-1989)
Eugene Ionesco, French (1912-1994)
Jean-Paul Sartre, French (1905-1980)
Albert Camus, French (1913-1960)
Franz Kafka, Czechoslovak (1883-1924)
Fyodor Dostoyevski, Russian (1821-1881)
Simone de Beauvoir, French (1908-1986)
Jean Genet, French (1910-1986)

EXERCISE 3.5

Write a paragraph in which you describe the elements of existentialism that are in the short story "A Clean, Well-Lighted Place" (page 271) by Ernest Hemingway.

_____

_____

_____

_____

_____

_____

_____

_____

_____

_____

_____

Lesson 2

Plot

Plot is probably the easiest element of fiction to observe. Many unsophisticated readers tend to see it as the whole story, failing, as a result, to see any of fiction's other rewarding elements. On the other hand, analyzing plot is a good place with which to begin understanding any fictional work. On its simplest level, plot may be only a sequence of action that embodies some sort of *conflict*, one force opposing another. The plot's action is composed of the changing balance of forces in the story's events. The reader's interest in a story is centered first on this struggle. Conflicts may be divided into four chief types:

1. The individual against nature—
   The Old Man and the Sea—Ernest Hemingway
   Jaws—Peter Benchley
   Moby Dick—Herman Melville

2. The individual against another individual—
   Hamlet—William Shakespeare
   The Three Musketeers—Alexandre Dumas
   (most stories of action and love)

3. The individual against self—
   Les Miserables—Victor Hugo

4. The Individual against the gods—
   Oedipus—Sophocles

EXERCISE 3.6

What is the conflict in the short story "To Build a Fire" (page 274) by Jack London?

_____

_____

_____

_____

_____

_____

The ancient Greek philosopher, Aristotle, stated that every story must have a beginning (before which nothing matters), a middle, and an end (after which nothing matters). Simple sounding though this is, it insures readers' interest, and it makes sense with regard to a story's plot. A story's beginning, called the **exposition**, introduces characters and their relationships to one another and to their environment. Even though they may be involved in actions or events with which we are unfamiliar, the situation quickly develops into a hint or promise of conflict. Once the conflict begins to develop, the largest section of a story begins: the **complication**. The complication continues until, at what is called the **climax**, it becomes apparent where the plot's action is headed. The final portion of the story indicates the conflict's settlement in the **resolution**. In some formulaic stories these plot elements are easily identified. For example, a typical tale of the old west might be organized as follows:

Exposition   Nearly seventeen-year-old Nell, planting seeds in her garden on her father's sheep ranch, is startled when several cattle crash through the barbwire fence to drink from the spring near the new corn, while Bart, the foreman from the neighboring cattle ranch, looks on without any visible concern for either the broken fence or the trampled corn.

Complication   Despite the fact that Dalton Bradley has vowed to wipe out every sheepherder in the valley, his son, Dalton, Jr., has fallen in love with Nell. She shyly returns his affection even though her father is organizing all the sheepmen to lead a raid on the cattle ranches.

Climax   The young couple, caught in the crossfire between the opposing sheep and cattlemen, are seriously injured by the hooves of stampeding cattle.

Resolution   The chagrined fathers, meeting outside the room where their children may be dying, agree to divide the valley between sheep and cattle and live peacefully together. The young couple recover and marry, thus uniting the two families and forever ending the conflict.

77

As trite and full of western cliches as the above plot outline is, it represents how a basic plot structure works. Sometimes simply understanding the plot's structure is all we want from a book or a movie; we only want some entertainment and escape. For analysis, however, plot structure does not tell you very much about the story, but it does give you a place to start a discussion or an analysis. What is helpful and leads toward a deeper understanding is an analysis of a story's probability.

You should note that some modern writers adapt an ironic attitude towards what they consider the artificial certainties of plot in a chaotic world. For an example see the short story "Lost in the Funhouse" where author John Barth makes this attitude explicit.

EXERCISE 3.7

In one sentence each, summarize the exposition, the complication, the climax, and the resolution of "To Build a Fire" (page 274) by Jack London.

Exposition _____

_____

_____

Complication _____

_____

_____

Climax _____

_____

_____

Resolution _____

_____

_____

Probability

Since we know that fiction is only a representation of life and not really life itself, we—the audience—demand that writers make their stories seem probable. We want to believe in the events and the characters. However, we are inclined to disbelieve anything that seems excessively fantastic or implausible. Nevertheless, as Samual Taylor Coleridge observed, writers can rely upon a uniquely human capability: **the willing suspension of disbelief.** This is our ability to pretend that the events we read in a book or view in a drama or a film are actually happening right there before our eyes. This phenomenon allows us to cry, to be horrified, to fear, or to love, in short, to be affected by what we read or view. We want to really care and fear for the characters. We want to fear for the young man as we wonder whether he will be able to rescue his love before the train crushes her on the tracks where the villain has tied her. Of course, we are likely to grant writers of romantic fiction somewhat more leeway than we would grant to realistic writers, but in either case, or even in fantasy, writers must take pains to create within their plots a feeling of truth. This may be accomplished through chronology, motivation, and foreshadowing.

Chronology

Chronology, the arrangement of events in time, is an important element for establishing a story's credibility. If the events seem to progress too swiftly, a story will not seem to portray truth. In actuality it is not the clock or calendar that is of most importance, but rather the effect of the passage of time. You may have seen thirty-minute situation comedies on television during which a young couple meet, fall in love, become engaged, survive an ordeal, and marry. These events might seem credible for a ninety-minute program, perhaps even sixty minutes, but thirty minutes leaves us not only breathless but unconvinced. The same situation is true in fiction. Sufficient time must *seem* to pass for the story's events to seem probable.

Several techniques for movement of time are available to writers. The most important of these is the manner in which the author unfolds the story. For example, simple narration—story telling—covers considerable ground swiftly; therefore, if a writer wishes to create the impression of the passage of time, some other writing style should be employed. Dramatized narration, which includes dialogue, moves a plot much more slowly; consequently, the reader, having to take more time to read the passage, feels that the story time has also been extended. The plot action of a story stops altogether when a writer employs pure analysis and description. Even though time stands still for these passages, typically the writer must engage in analysis sparingly lest readers find these sections tedious or irrelevant. The creative use of these delaying tactics "controls" the fictional chronology, thereby making the characters and events more probable.

A writer, skillfully employing all of the above techniques can control an ostensibly implausible passage of time in ways which become plausible within a particular work. For example, in James Joyce's *Ulysses* the author credibly devotes a very long novel to the events of a single day in Dublin, Ireland. This is accomplished by using a variety of fictional techniques, creating a sense of the richness and complexity of one day viewed through the exhaustively described thoughts and feelings of a variety of characters.

Motivation

Why do characters in a story behave as they do? Readers not only want to know what happens in a story but why it happens. Unless a story reveals the motivation behind its events and character's plausible behavior, it may seem improbable. There are several ways for writers to present motivation.

1. Analysis—the narrator tells readers the motives for actions.
2. Dialogue—characters themselves or other characters report motives.
3. Personality—characters act as we would expect people of their temperament to behave.

In any case, a character's motivation must come from within the story. The fiction must be an entity unto itself and not depend upon any outside justification for the motives inherent in the plot. If a reader must search for motivation outside the story, the story's power is diminished. To make the characters in a story resemble real people, their behavior must not be questioned: readers must feel that if they knew real people like the fictional characters, they would react and behave in a similar manner; otherwise, the story loses probability.

But, even so, you need to be aware that in fiction, as in life, motivation can sometimes be disguised or uncertain. In such cases, probability may be retained even when a story deals with the more bizarre or irrational forms of human behavior. In Truman Capote's *In Cold Blood*, Capote spins a web of objective, naturalistic detail around an ultimately unanswerable question of motivation: why were these murders committed? The fact that Capote employs the novel form to depict events that actually happened reinforces our awareness that probability can sometimes—paradoxically—be maintained even when characters' actions do not make sense.

Foreshadowing

Surprise, Samuel Taylor Coleridge concluded, is not nearly as satisfying as expectation. By this, Coleridge meant that readers sincerely enjoy the fulfillment of the expectation that a story has created, for example, when the main characters marry. Expectations, or suspense, is created by a plot device known as **foreshadowing**—hints about what will happen later in a story. If we have been led to expect something, we feel satisfaction when it occurs. Foreshadowing can be accomplished in several ways. In mystery stories, for instance, a knife introduced early in the story may play a crucial role in the later action. Foreshadowing can occur in more subtle ways, however. In Kurt Vonnegut's *Slaughterhouse Five* Billy Pilgrim, the protagonist, lives through the cataclysmic World War II bombing of Dresden, Germany, which creates a sudden, disastrous rupture in the everyday reality of life in that city. This sense of a sudden break in reality prepares us for the later leap into complete fantasy, when Billy Pilgrim, shattered by his wartime experiences, is transported seemingly without warning to the imaginary planet Tralfamadore. This result is satisfying to us not because of the characters' fate but because our expectations—even though stretched and challenged by seemingly fantastic events—are ultimately realized within the context of the story. A story's probability is enhanced when foreshadowing hints at the final outcome. Critical readers are those who are alert for foreshadowing hints and thus are the most rewarded by discovering them.

Another useful function of foreshadowing is the preparation of the reader for the final outcome. Without this preparation the conclusion to the story might be quite confusing. In *Moby Dick*, for instance, the mechanics of a whaleboat's operation are described early and in detail. This allows the reader to understand fully just what is occurring in the story's final chapters as Captain Ahab becomes tangled in the harpoon line. Without the earlier foreshadowing detail, either the action would have to be interrupted for explanation or readers might be confused about how Ahab confronts his fate. This foreshadowing in *Moby Dick* allows the action, at its most exciting point, to move forward uninterrupted and with complete probability.

EXERCISE 3.8

Summarize in two or three sentences the foreshadowing used in "To Build a Fire" (Page 274).

_____

_____

_____

_____

_____

_____

_____

_____

_____

_____

Lesson 3

Setting

The setting in fiction is the *place* where the events occur and the *time* or *era* of the action. But more than that, the setting establishes the atmosphere which helps create the mood. You might note, for example, how important setting is to certain types of stories. Ghost stories are often set in old castles or ancient houses, preferably located on cliffs overlooking barren and rocky shorelines. The atmosphere, established by the setting, plays a dominant role in the fiction of certain writers—for instance, "Heart of Darkness" by Joseph Conrad or many of the stories of Edgar Allan Poe.

Notice how the setting establishes an atmosphere of impending doom in the following excerpt:

> The room in which I found myself was very large and lofty. The windows were long, narrow, and pointed, and at so vast a distance from the black oaken floor as to be altogether inaccessible from within. Feeble gleams of encrimsoned light made their way through the trellissed panes, and served to render sufficiently distinct the more prominent objects around; the eye, however, struggled in vain to reach the remoter angles of the chamber, or the recesses of the vaulted and fretted ceiling. Dark draperies hung upon the walls. The general furniture was profuse, comfortless, antique, and tattered. Many books and musical instruments lay scattered about but failed to give any vitality to the scene. I felt that I breathed an atmosphere of sorrow. An air of stern, deep, and irredeemable gloom hung over and pervaded all.

"The Fall of the House of Usher"
by Edgar Allan Poe

In this next excerpt, the mood is again established by the setting. This time, however, the vivid description of a room results in feelings of security, fellowship, and warmth.

> Then Stevens was there, holding the door open, and a moment later I was inside. Down the mahogany-paneled hallway, through double doors standing three-quarters of the way open on their recessed tracks, into the library *cum* reading-room *cum* bar. It was a dark room in which occasional pools of light gleamed—reading-lamps. A brighter, more textured light glowed across the oak parquet floor, and I could hear the steady snap of birch logs in the huge fireplace. The heat radiated all the way across the room— surely there is no welcome for a man or a woman that can equal a fire on the hearth. A paper rustled—dry, slightly impatient. That would be Johnssen, with his *Wall Street Journal*. After ten years, it was possible to recognize his presence simply by the way he read his stocks. Amusing . . . and in a quiet way, amazing.
>
> "The Breathing Method" *Different Seasons* by Stephen King

Setting may also reveal to readers something about the fictional characters in a story. The details of setting can reveal their personality traits, their personal habits, their social status, and their interests. This subtle development of characters through the setting is especially effective because the traits and interests are implied rather than explicit. This makes the characters seem all the more real, since in life we gain opinions about people and their habits through impressions.

In some stories the setting is so closely related to the plot that the events appear to be a direct result of the setting. For instance, the Mississippi River governs many of Huckleberry Finn's actions. Likewise, stories that have a limited environment, such as *Robinson Crusoe* or *Aliens* are often inseparable from their settings. The setting may also take on a symbolic function that is much beyond simply a realistic description of where and when the story takes place. In "The Open Boat" by Stephen Crane, the great, impersonal, superior sea is a natural power that is objectively indifferent to the four men in a small dinghy who are desperately trying to reach shore after a shipwreck. The philosophical nature of the story is symbolized by the setting. Setting, then, may be simply where a story takes place, or the setting may relate to the characters, the plot, or the ideas on subtle symbolic levels.

EXERCISE 3.9

In two or three sentences describe how the setting in "To Build a Fire" (page 274) contributes to each of the following:

Plot _____

_____

_____

_____

_____

Atmosphere _____

_____

_____

_____

_____

_____

Ideas _____

_____

_____

_____

_____

_____

Lesson 4

Character

Characters are the people of fiction, the author's cast. Writers reveal characters to us in several ways, and understanding the techniques of revelation can show you not only how to look at characters but how the author intends for us to see them. Some characters are revealed through the same techniques that people are revealed in life:

1. We learn to know characters by what others say about them.
2. We make judgments about them based upon what they look like or mannerisms they exhibit.
3. We learn about them by what they say in the dialogue.
4. We learn about them based upon what they do or what they do not do.

We also learn about characters based upon what they themselves think. This is not a method by which we can learn about real people. It is a fictional technique only. Usually, writers reveal their characters through a variety of these devices, but the method or methods that are employed are determined to a large extent by the story's point of view. (see Lesson 6)

After you determine how characters are revealed in a particular story, it is important to understand each individual character's function. (What did each give the story? Why is each included in the story?) It is not difficult to answer these questions for main characters, but you need to ask the same questions of minor characters as well, since minor characters are there for a purpose also. Occasionally, minor characters are present in fiction simply to create the illusion of a populated setting. Often, they are important in successfully moving the plot forward. Sometimes minor characters serve an essential role in the environment because their presence can help shed light on the main character's personality. Once in a while, a character is the sympathetic *confidant* or *confidante* who listens and who is necessary to draw the main character into conversation, thereby allowing the reader to learn more about the plans or events of the story.

Another function of a minor character is that of a *foil*. A foil is a character who is intended to be contrasted either in behavior or attitudes to the main character. This term derives from the custom that dueling foils come in matched pairs that appear to be the same on the outside but may be quite different upon exceptionally close analysis. In Shakespeare's *Hamlet*, for example, the young Laertes is contrasted to Prince Hamlet. The personality and attitude of Hamlet are made all the more clear through the contrast.

EXERCISE 3.10

In a sentence or two, state how the main character is revealed in "To Build a Fire" (page 274).

Lesson 5

Theme

In fiction theme is the generalization, either stated or implied, that holds a story together. Sometimes referred to as a *controlling idea* or a *central insight*, theme is concerned with a story's purpose. Of course, not all stories have themes that pursue anything beyond attempts to intrigue, to frighten, or to excite—in short, to offer vicarious experience. Mysteries, horror stories, and adventures are entertaining, but they are not typically significant beyond what they are: entertaining diversions that are pleasurable but of little lasting importance. Theme is present in fiction only when there exists a serious effort on the author's part to create a unified work and to explore some significant truths with it. Occasionally, writers incorporate some life theory or concept as the central idea and construct a story that is designed to illustrate its truths as with Charles Dickens' novels *Bleak House* and *Hard Times*.

While it is informative to isolate a story's theme in order to examine and discuss it, theme is never the *only* meaning, for whole meaning is the sum total of all a story's elements. When writers dwell excessively on a theme in fiction, they run the risk of overemphasizing ideas: the result is a fiction that appears didactic—written solely to teach. Didactic fiction frequently preaches and, as you should remember, is often regarded as inferior literature. Moreover, didactic fiction typically enjoys a relatively short popularity. For example, Harriet Beecher Stowe's *Uncle Tom's Cabin* is today only a historical document, relating to the American Civil War; almost no one these days reads it simply as fiction. Even great writers may occasionally lapse into fiction that, because it is so concerned with a moral message, preaches rather than illustrates. Some critics believe John Steinbeck's famous *The Grapes of Wrath* will probably not be regarded by future generations as among his best works because it preaches excessively.

Theme and *moral* are not terms that may be employed synonymously. Their meanings are different. If you view the term "moral" narrowly, it becomes simply a value judgment about what you consider to be good or bad, right or wrong. Using this narrow definition of moral one might, for example, condemn a work's characters for "immoral behavior" and thus condemn the work as not being moral. Most critics, however, believe that any work of art, if it is worthwhile at all, is essentially moral. This apparent contradiction can best be understood by a broader definition of moral as applied in literature. Lacking the narrow, restrictive definition of what is right or wrong, moral in its broad sense is an expressed precept or general truth; consequently, if writers have been successful in accurately illustrating life—word-painting a true picture of life's condition—then their fiction is moral. In this broad sense, moral and theme, while still somewhat different, may be closely related, and no work may be pejoratively classified as lacking in moral content simply because we do not approve of the behavior of the characters. All serious works of literary fiction are essentially moral because the harmonious combination of the fictional elements of plot, setting, character, and theme attempt to illustrate life's truths.

Sometimes it is difficult to recognize a story's theme, but there are two obvious ways available to examine a work for the author's meaning.

1. Sometimes our estimation of a theme can be confirmed by reading an author's other writings.
   (This would be helpful, for example, in discovering Ernest Hemingway's recurrent theme of a man illustrating his virtue by facing death alone and bravely.)

2. More often, however, theme must be determined by closely analyzing the characters' conflicts—what they are and how they are resolved.

EXERCISE 3.11

Read the very short story "Birthday Party" (page 226) by Katherine Brush. In no more than two or three sentences, write out the theme of the story. Then, list the hints or clues which lead you to the theme.

_____

_____

_____

_____

_____

_____

_____

_____

_____   _____

_____   _____

_____   _____

EXERCISE 3.12

In no more than two or three sentences, state the theme of "To Build a Fire" (page 274). Then list the hints or clues that lead you to the theme.

_____

_____

_____

_____

_____

_____

_____

_____

_____   _____

_____   _____

_____   _____

Lesson 6

Point of View

Another way to begin to examine theme in fiction is to determine a story's point of view. In its technical sense, point of view means the way the story's narrator relates to the fictional characters and to the story. Sometimes referred to as a story's *angle* or *focus*, point of view is not an arbitrary method used by an author to reveal character or plot; it is, rather, a very carefully planned and special viewpoint. If a story is told completely in dialogue or we see a play, there is no one between the action and the viewer. However, if we read a play, or a story that contains any descriptive material whatsoever, that stage direction or story description has a point of view. For example, in "Birthday Party" we are told that the man has a "self-satisfied face," and his wife is "fadingly pretty." These are not objective qualities of people; they are subjective observations of the story's narrator. As a result, they are from a particular, biased point of view.

Since all stories, except those of pure dialogue, need a teller, a narrator from whose viewpoint a story's elements unfold, an author must choose the point of view carefully. This choice of point of view determines to a large extent a story's impact upon readers. As a reader you must be careful that you do not confuse the narrator's view with the author's view; they are not the same even when the narrator employs the first-person pronoun "I." No matter how well Hamlet speaks nor what opinions he may hold upon acting, it is not necessarily Shakespeare speaking nor his opinions.

Whenever we begin a story, we expect to be able to see clearly how narrators relate to the content of the story and into which characters' minds they can see. To accomplish this an author may choose from four basic points of view:

1. **First Person Narrator**—One of the characters tells the story. Referring to him or her self as "I," the narrator tells the reader what he or she thinks or feels about the events but can only speculate about the thoughts or inner feelings of any other character.

Character is Narrator

e.g. *Lord Jim*—Joseph Conrad
   The Stranger—Albert Camus (seems natural—character tells us what happened—very intimate)

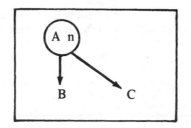

A variation of this technique has a narrator, who is completely outside the action, relate the events. Even though not a participant, the narrator, likewise, cannot see into the minds and true motives of anyone.

e.g. *Tom Jones*—Henry Fielding
     parts of *Huckleberry Finn*—Mark Twain

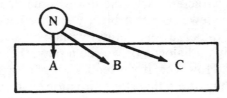

2. **Limited Omniscient**—Someone, other than a character in the story, tells the reader the tale. The narrator refers to the character with the pronouns "he" or "she" and can see inside characters' minds but chooses to reveal the inner workings of only one character; therefore, while the reader is told what one character thinks and feels and what the others say and do, the reader sees the events from only a limited viewpoint.

     e.g. *Barn Burning*—William Faulkner
          Madam Bovary—Gustave Flaubert

    Narrator, who is an observer, has knowledge of the inner mind of only one of the characters (concentrated subjectivity).

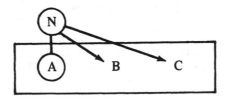

3. **Omniscient**—The narrator apparently has god-like powers of seeing and knowing all and chooses to tell everything to the reader. The omniscient point of view allows the reader into the minds of all the characters so that their thinking and feelings are understood.

     e.g. "The Bride Comes to Yellow Sky"—Stephen Crane
          Moby Dick—Herman Melville (after the first part, much of the novel)

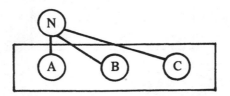

4. **Objective**—The narrator, who is outside the story, reveals the characters externally only. The reader is told what the characters look like and what they say but never what they think or how they feel. All matters of the subjective—thought and feelings—are impossible from the objective viewpoint.

   e.g. *The Killers*—Ernest Hemingway

Narrator, totally objective, reports only what is seen and what is said without revealing opinions in any way.

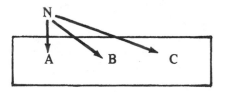

Occasionally, writers employ techniques that are different from these standard four points of view. One rare form is the second-person viewpoint. In this instance, the pronoun "you" is used throughout.

> "Early one morning, you walk along the winding trail overlooking the isolated beach when you notice a small, orange object just outside the crashing breakers. You tense as you realize that, just maybe, you have found the long missing life raft."

The "you" point of view is seldom used because it is not effective in involving the reader in the action.

Another fictional point of view, especially popular during the twentieth century, is **Stream of Consciousness**. This represents the greatest effort to involve the reader in fiction because it attempts to express a character's unexpressed, unspoken, and unstructured thoughts. A highly subjective writing style, stream of consciousness tries to link thought patterns in a way that reflects casual thought process. When the character, whose consciousness the reader is within, is incoherent or retarded, the words upon the printed page appear to be irrational, unfocused, and illogical. Moreover, it remains the reader's task to make sense out of the apparent jumble. But perseverance and close analysis will usually bring logical sense to it; the insights that you gain make the effort more than worthwhile. (e.g. *The Sound and the Fury* by William Faulkner; *Ulysses* by James Joyce.)

Sometimes, point of view shifts within a work. For example, *Moby Dick* begins with a first-person narrator beyond whose vision we cannot see: "Call me Ishmael." Later, after Ishmael is aboard the whaling ship *Pequod*, an omniscient narrator who is decidedly not Ishmael and who can see into the very heart and diseased soul of Captain Ahab takes over. Yet the work is effective; some critics consider it the greatest American novel.

EXERCISE 3.13

In two or three sentences, analyze the point of view of "Birthday Party" (page 226).

_____

_____

_____

_____

_____

_____

_____

_____

_____

EXERCISE 3.14

What is the point of view in "To Build a Fire" (page 274)?

_____

_____

_____

_____

_____

_____

_____

_____

Typical Lengths of Modern Literary Genres

Genre	Typical number of words	Typical number of pages*, length of performance times or number of lines
Short story	500-5,000	2-20
Novella	7,000-15,000	28-60
Novel	25,000-150,000	100-600+
Nonfiction book	20,000-200,000	80-800
TV script: ½ hour		25-40
TV script: 1 hour		55-70
Play: three act	20,000-30,000	1 ½-2 hrs playing time
Movie scenario	30,000-60,000	1 ½-2 hrs playing time
Poem	10-800	2-100 lines (most magazines prefer 4-16 lines)

* Double-spaced, typewritten

Formalist Analysis

Formalists assert that if a work of literature is worthwhile at all, it ought to be able to stand on its own merit. Readers should be able to enjoy literature without having to rely upon prior knowledge of an author's work, the history of the era during which it was written, or the psychological profile of the author. Readers should be able to understand, to analyze, and to appreciate a work without library research and without reading what critics have written about it. The real joy of reading comes through ones own critical abilities, developed through wide experiences in reading and through an understanding of literature as an art form—a structure that stands by itself. The formalist approach to the interpretation of literature is a method that emphasizes readers' critical abilities and encourages the acquisition of analytical skills even for casual readers.

Objectives;

After completing this chapter, you will be able to:

1. Describe the formalist approach to literary interpretation.
2. Define the literary terms that form the basic vocabulary of formalist analysis
3. Identify the views that are irrelevant to the formalist approach.
4. Follow a step-by-step procedure in planning a formalist analysis.
5. Write a formalist analysis of a literary selection.
6. Evaluate a story's use of formalist elements.
7. Assess the value of "New Criticism" for contemporary literature.

8. Express greater confidence in your ability to perform your own analysis of literature without assistance.

9. Evaluate a story's allusions and appraise their effectiveness.

Pre-Assessment

_____ 1. Which of the following is NOT a concern of formalists?
A) imagery B) irony C) metaphor D) biography E) symbol

_____ 2. Which of the following IS a concern of formalists?
A) the relation of a literary work to its era
B) the relation of the meanings of words in the story to the story's imagery
C) the relation of a literary work to other works of the same type
D) the relation of the work to other works by the same author
E) the relation of a literary work to the biography of the author

List five of the most important literary techniques of the formalist approach:

3. _____

4. _____

5. _____

6. _____

7. _____

_____ 8. The primary concern of the formalist critic is the viewing of a literary work as
A) a work of art
B) a work of social significance
C) a work of philosophical thought
D) a work of psychological importance
E) all of the above

_____ 9. The fomalist critic looks for
A) the anthropological significance of the recurring words
B) the important events from an author's life that may appear in his story
C) evidence that the work has or will become a "classic"
D) the unifying patterns that shape a work and give its parts a relevance to its whole
E) all of the above

_____ 10. Literature that is art differs from a newspaper story by
A) having wider appeal
B) having hidden meanings
C) avoiding profanity and violence
D) not being true
E) being written in a higher level of English

The New Critics

After World War I, a group of scholars gathered at Vanderbilt University where Professor John Crowe Ransom (b. 1888) was teaching. Ransom, along with three of his students—Allen Tate (b. 1899), Robert Penn Warren (b. 1905), and Cleanth Brooks (b. 1906)—developed a new philosophy of literary analysis that became known as **New Criticism.** During the decades of the 1930s and the 1940s the ranks of *New Critics*, as they became known, grew with the addition of Kenneth Burke (b. 1897), Yvor Arthur Winters (b. 1900), and Richard Palmer Blockmur (b. 1904). By 1941 Ransom had written *The New Criticism*, and what the New Critics called *formalist analysis* was launched. Formalist analytical philosophy is still popular in some circles, and the above-mentioned names remain the dominant writers on formalism in literature.

Examining the biographical information of an author and the historical context in which the writing took place is frequently rewarding. The New Critics took the position, however, that the really important or valuable information can be derived only from the text of the work itself. Everything else, according to their theories, is peripheral, extraneous, and distracting. For example, a reader who concentrates upon Herman Melville's extensive voyages throughout the South Pacific rather than reading, rereading, and closely examining the text of *Moby Dick* will never truly understand the fullest significance of Captain Ahab's conflict with the great white whale. It is through an examination of a work's *form*—the structure or pattern of a work such as the short-story form or the ballad form—that one may derive a deep understanding of it as a work of art.

The central focus of the formalist approach is, then, to discover what a work expresses and what it means without any other reference to the work such as biographical data on the author or the history of the times. One must examine a piece of literature closely enough to begin discovering its structure; one must look for the unifying patterns that shape the work and give its parts a relevance to the whole. Thus, a reader of an epic poem should begin an analysis by examining the text to discover how closely the poem is structured like other epic poems. This approach can lead one to different levels of meaning, which, in turn, leads to greater understanding. For example, William Golding's *Lord of the Flies* may be read as (1) a novel of adventure about the struggles of some English school boys to secure their rescue from an island; (2) a story about the passage of a group of youngsters from childhood toward maturity and adulthood; (3) an examination of guilt and responsibility between the rights of the individual and the power of the mob; (4) a criticism of world power politics and the use of force as an instrument for the settlement of disputes; or (5) an analysis of philosophical and ideological concepts in conflict with one another. How the different levels of meaning are interwoven and assist one another and how they are linked with the action in the story has to do with the work's structural form. Form is the concern of formalist analysis, and a formalist expresses what a work means by first considering how the work achieves meaning through its structure.

What Do Formalists Look For?

Formalist analysis emphasizes certain language devices as a means toward understanding form. Actually these language devices are many of the same ones considered important in other analytical approaches (see Chapter One), but the formalist concentrates upon them with an intensity that is not shared by the others. By way of review, the major language interests of formalist analysis follow:

1. Semantics

Semantics, the study of word meanings in language or the study of communication processes themselves, belongs at the head of any list of formalist interests. Semantics, for instance, is concerned with topics like the ritual use of language, fallacious reasoning, and connotation and denotation. Although formalists are interested in each of these semantic topics, they seem most interested in connotation, the meanings that words have in addition to their dictionary meanings.

A. Denotation

A word denotes that which the dictionary states. In other words, denotation is the dictionary meaning of a word. Formalists emphasize denotation primarily to establish the connotation of words.

Example: mother = a female who has borne a child

B. Connotation

Connotation is the meaning of a word beyond its dictionary meaning. Words acquire their connotations through their past histories, their associations, and the emotional responses they elicit.

Example: mother = beyond a female who has borne a child, mother may suggest security, affection, home, selflessness, and love.

2. Imagery

Imagery represents sense experience through language. Words or phrases that explain how something looks, feels, tastes, sounds, or smells appeal to the senses.

Example: golden poppies, cold showers, sour lemons, chirping birds, fresh bread.

3. Metaphor

Metaphor is an implied comparison between things that are essentially unlike. A metaphor implies that something *is* something else. The technique is particularly useful for its power of suggestion in explaining or clarifying people, objects, ideas, or occurrences.

Examples: He is a pig; The boat sliced through the bay's chop; Freedom should soar on a warm summer's thermal.

4. Symbolism

A symbol is anything in literature that means more than what it is. Often the meaning of an abstract idea may be represented in a story or poem by some object.

> Example: Youth and beauty are frequently pictured as a rose in poetry; In his novel *Moby Dick*, Melville used the whiteness of the whale to suggest many symbolic meanings.

5. Irony

Irony is an apparent contradiction between what is said and what is meant or between what is done and what was intended.

> Example: A snow storm in May—what great weather for water skiing; The revolution was fought to free the peasants from the oppression of the old dictators—now the peasants are oppressed by the those who led the revolution, the new dictators.

6. Allusion

Allusion is a reference, often brief, to other literature, previous history, mythology, or even an earlier part of the same work. Authors use allusion to make ideas more easily understood by calling something familiar to readers' attention. The most frequently used sources of allusions in English refer to Greek mythology, the King James translation of the Bible, and Shakespeare.

> Example: George discovered, much to his displeasure, that by continuing his romance with Dawn, he was reaching for forbidden fruit. (The allusion is to Genesis where Adam and Eve have been forbidden to eat of the fruit of the Tree of Knowledge.)

7. Tone

Tone represents a writer's or a speaker's implied attitude toward the subject, audience, or self. Tone is the writer's point-of-view; it expresses mood in a literary work.

> Example: See "Apparently With No Surprise" by Emily Dickinson on page 99.

EXERCISE 4.1

Place the letter of the correct choice in the space at the left.

_____1. The New Critics gathered together
A) after World War II
B) after the stockmarket crash of 1929
C) after World War I
D) after John Kennedy was elected president
E) after William Golding won the Nobel Prize for literature

_____2. The New Critics developed an approach to literature that became known as
A) symbolic analysis
B) archetypal analysis
C) structural analysis
D) traditional analysis
E) formalist analysis

97

3. The New Critics took the view that really important or valuable information in literature may be derived only from
A) the text
B) the author
C) the era
D) the psychological symbols
E) linguistic authenticity

4. For a formalist it is through an examination of a work's _____ that its art may be discovered.
A) religious significance
B) form
C) psychic aura
D) mood
E) irony

5. Which of the following is NOT a concern of new criticism?
A) semantics
B) imagery
C) metaphor
D) history
E) allusion

Identify the figure of speech or literary device used in each of the following lines:

6. "A tap at the pane, the quick sharp scratch and blue spurt of a lighted match . . . ."

7. "It is with words as with sunbeams—the more they are condensed, the deeper they burn."

8.   "In the garden there strayed
        A beautiful maid
    As fair as the flowers of the morn;
        The first hour of her life
        She was made a man's wife
    And was buried before she was born"

Anonymous

9. Some dirty dog took my parking place.

10. "When blood is nipped and ways be foul,
        Then nightly sings the staring owl . . . ."

Lesson 2

What Formalists Consider
and What They Do Not Consider

If you look closely at the analytical devices of formalist analysis, they are an attempt to understand and explicate a literary work's structure and texture by isolating its parts to see how they relate to the form of the whole. The complete emphasis is upon the work itself. Therefore, formalist analysis does not consider the following:

1. the relation of a work to its historical era
2. the relation of a work to any other works of the same type
3. the relation of a work to any other works by the same author

No matter how interesting authors' lives may be or how intriguing the social significance of their works, these details are irrelevant to the formalist. Thus, formalists deal solely with the work itself. Consequently, one who wishes to employ the formalistic approach should not be tempted to become sidetracked by dealing with the fact that, for instance, Kurt Vonnegut, Jr., author of *Slaughter-House Five*, was a prisoner of war in Dresden, Germany, when that city was firebombed by the Allies just as was the novels protagonist Billy Pilgrim. Samuel Clemens' boyhood along the Mississippi River is interesting, but hardly necessary to an understanding of his book, *The Adventures of Huckleberry Finn*. Likewise, the speculation that Samuel Taylor Coleridge was addicted to drugs or that Shakespeare's sonnets were written to some "dark lady" are interesting sidelights for speculation but without importance to any formalist explication of their writing. What is important is what can be found within the literature itself.

Appeal

Putting aside the esoterica of sociological, psychological, biographical, and historical information, the formalist concentrates upon the work—the poem, the short story, the drama, or the novel—as a pattern of words. Because they are set down on the page in a particular and precise way, they form a structure that has a meaning of its own. Unlike the newspaper story that simply reports an event in a functional form, the work of art has built into it the form that gives it an appeal that touches almost everyone who reads it—today as in the past and, undoubtedly, into the future.

Emily Dickinson's poems have many elements of wide general appeal. No journalistic report, "Apparently With No Surprise" appeals to almost everyone with its comment upon the apparent contradiction between faith and beauty and an approving, indifferent Almighty.

APPARENTLY WITH NO SURPRISE
Apparently with no surprise
To any happy flower,
The frost beheads it at its play
In accidental power,
The blond assassin passes on,
The sun proceeds unmoved
To measure off another day
For an approving God.
—*Emily Dickinson (1830-1886)*

Writing the Formalist Analysis

Before reading further, turn to page 287 and read "The Snake" by John Steinbeck. Do not proceed until you have read the story.

Reread "The Snake" several times—until you are familiar with all of its parts. Begin to ask yourself questions about the story as you become more and more familiar with the major events. Concentrate upon what happens and why. Think about the characters, the setting, and the language. Following are some questions that you might ask about Steinbeck's story.

1. What is Dr. Phillips' attitude toward his work?

Dr. Phillips sees himself as a scientist: objective, clinical, and unaffected by emotions. He has constructed for himself a little world of his own, isolated and separate from the world of human contact. He seems to feel that what he is doing is important; he seems to feel a bit superior to others. The story is clearly seen through his eyes.

2. Why does the woman come to the laboratory?

The woman wants to purchase a snake. Her reasons are ambiguous; at least we do not see her motives clearly because the story is not seen through her eyes. We only become acquainted with her through Dr. Phillips' perceptions of her.

3. Why is Dr. Phillips so irritated with the woman's visit?

Dr. Phillips has very carefully isolated himself from the world of humans; therefore, he finds any outside intrusion unwelcome. Moreover, his scientific, clinical, objective domain is challenged by his emotional reactions to the woman and her purpose. Dr. Phillips' emotions seem to be in conflict, for he is both attracted to and revolted by the events of the evening.

4. Why does not Dr. Phillips simply ask the woman to leave?

Dr Phillips seems uncertain of himself. He does not wish to be rude, yet he seems to lack the diplomatic social skills necessary to be either graceful as a host or polite in requesting her to return at a time more convenient for him.

5. How does Dr. Phillips treat the woman?

Dr. Phillips, unsure of his own feelings, attempts to shock his guest. He first impolitely lectures on the biological reproduction of starfish then prepares the cat he has just killed for examination by students in biology classes. He is plainly upset that his work neither disturbs the woman nor even interests her.

6. What is Dr. Phillip's reaction to the evening's events after the woman leaves?

Dr. Phillips has had his snug world disturbed. He has been unable to deal with his emotional responses to what has occurred, nor, for that matter, to the woman herself.

7. Why is Dr. Phillips so increasingly disturbed by his guest?

Dr. Phillips is apparently proud of his work and his knowledge. He is accustomed to awe filled, respectful treatment, and his guest's indifference bothers him. Furthermore, as the visit continues, he begins to notice certain physical peculiarities in the woman that cause her to look more and more reptilian in the doctor's eyes. This accelerating visual image reaches its most profound impact upon the doctor when he refuses to look at the woman for fear she is opening her mouth just as the snake is opening its mouth to consume the rat.

8. *Why are there repeated references to the sound of waves under the laboratory?*

First, the waves remind us of both the story's setting and of Dr. Phillips' physical and emotional isolation in the laboratory. Second, the sound of the water grows louder as the story's tension accelerates in intensity. After the tension of the immediate events subsides, the sound of the water is reduced to a gentle whisper.

9. *What language devices or techniques are used in the story?*

The answer to this question is that there are many. You should have discovered several by simply rereading and asking yourself questions about what is happening in the story. The following is not an exhaustive list of techniques you could find in the story. Rather, it is only a suggestion to start you on your analysis:

A. Imagery—Sound is an important element of the setting. The kettle on the stove hums; the rats scramble; the cats mew. Underneath, the waves lap against the piles while the snakes hiss. What other imagery can you find in the story?

B. Metaphor—"The person is the rat." People as animal metaphors are central to the theme of the story. Can you find other metaphors?

C. Symbolism—Dr. Phillips is himself a symbol of a modern scientific attitude of professional objectivity.

D. Irony—It is ironic that Dr. Phillips' clinical professionalism leaves him helpless in the presence of the woman.

E. Allusion—"If I knew—no, I can't pray to anything," alludes to the popular notion that scientists do not believe in any supernatural beings, such as gods; therefore, his scientific background leaves him without any emotional support.

F. Tone—The story is seen only through Dr. Phillips' eyes, and we share in his loneliness. We understand his philosophy and his professional bias. The tension that we feel as the mood of the story becomes uneasy, even fearful, is the doctor's fear and his mood. The tone, then, is one of fear; the doctor's attitude toward himself, perhaps even Steinbeck's attitude toward science, is revealed in "The Snake."

Identifying a Topic for Analysis

By now you should be quite familiar with the selection; consequently, you can begin to identify a topic for analysis that interests you. Here you should ask yourself if the topic you are considering is sufficiently interesting to be worth your effort. Once you are certain that it is worthwhile, you should choose a topic for analysis that grows out of the questions you asked about the literary selection. Some topics that might be considered for "The Snake" are as follows:

1. How the setting enhances and contributes to the tone.
2. How the woman challenges the doctor's philosophy.
3. The use of literary techniques to reveal the theme.

Dividing the Topic

Now you are ready to develop your elements into a *working* thesis, a thesis sufficiently well thought out to begin writing but which might need further editing later.

Once you have a working thesis, you can proceed promptly to the development of an outline. Beginning with your thesis, think about the paragraph division you want in your analysis. Then, when you have carefully considered what you want to cover, write out your potential topic sentences, in order, under your selected thesis.

> *Example:* "The Snake"
> 1. The use of symbolism
> 2. The use of imagery
> 3. The use of metaphor to develop theme

Possible Thesis Statements

> *Draft #1:* Steinbeck employs symbolism, imagery, and metaphor to develop his theme.
>
> *Draft #2:* The metaphoric connection between snake and woman is developed through the use of symbolism and imagery.

Still, for a short paper either one of these thesis sentences could go over 1,000 words; therefore, the thesis needs further narrowing.

> *Draft #3:* Although he uses several literary devices in "The Snake," Steinbeck relies heavily upon imagery to create a metaphoric connection between the woman and the rattlesnake.

The Outline

Once you have a working thesis, you can proceed promptly to the development of your outline. Beginning with your thesis think about the paragraph division you want in your analysis. Then, when you have carefully considered what you want to cover, write out your potential topic sentences, in order, under your selected thesis.

> *Example:*
>
> *Thesis*— Although he uses several literary devices in "The Snake," John Steinbeck relies heavily upon imagery to create a metaphoric connection between the woman and the rattlesnake.
>
> *Topic Sentence #1*—Close examination of the story reveals that no metaphors actually compare the visiting woman with the snake she buys, but the imagery and the implied comparisons make this relationship impossible to overlook.
>
> *Topic Sentence #2*—The movements of the snake and woman are also similar.
>
> *Topic Sentence #3*—Situations that would probably cause some sort of reaction in most people do not even make her blink.
>
> *Topic Sentence #4*—The woman's reptilian presence makes the doctor uneasy, which further reveals her serpentine connection.
>
> *Topic Sentence #5*—Even the snake seems to recognize the connection.

The Analysis

Now you should be ready to develop your full analysis. You have become familiar with the story's structure and after several readings you have asked yourself a number of questions about the story's situation and its structure. You have also developed a working thesis and carried it through several versions. The outline has been written; it is now time to write the first draft of the analysis. After revision, correcting for content and mechanical errors, and rewriting to correct any structural problems, you should be ready to write your final copy.

The following student paper was written after having carried out these steps:

B. J. Henning

English 1B 8 TTh

Dr. Guches

14 October 1987

(Formalist Analysis)

THE SNAKE CHARMER

John Steinbeck's short story "The Snake" has but two human
characters. One is a solitary, studious scientist who lives and works in
an old, rundown laboratory building. "Dr. Phillips climbed up the wooden
steps . . . and built a fire in the tin stove." His bedroom, "a book-
lined cell, containing an army cot, a reading lamp, and an uncomfortable
chair" indicates that he has only the barest of essentials. The words
"cell" and "uncomfortable chair" imply that he is not especially happy
and that living there is perhaps tedious. The second character, a woman
who is a stranger to the protagonist, comes to see the doctor about
acquiring a rattlesnake. She purchases one, feeds it a rat, then leaves,
never to be seen again. Although he employs several literary techniques
in "The Snake," Steinbeck relies heavily upon imagery to create a
metaphoric connection between the woman and the rattlesnake.

A close examination of "The Snake" reveals that no metaphors
actually compare the visiting woman with the snake she purchases, but the
imagery and the implied comparisons make this relationship impossible to
overlook. The physical features of the woman and the snake appear
remarkably similar. The snake has "dusty eyes that seemed to look at
nothing." The woman's eyes are mentioned several times; they "glittered
in the the strong light," much like a snake's would when under similar
lighting. "Her eyes came out of their dusty dream for a moment . . . her
dusty eyes . . . her black eyes were on him, but they did not seem to see
him." Dr. Phillips finds himself avoiding "the dark eyes that did not
seem to look at anything." A rattlesnake is slim in body. It has a flat
forehead, a small chin, a blunt nose, and virtually no lips. It is not a
colorful reptile. The woman has eyes with "irises (that) were as dark as
the pupils, there was no color line between the two." A snake has no
line between iris and pupil either. "The blunt dry head with its blunt
nose" describe physical characteristics of the snake that also pertain to

104

the woman. She is "a tall lean woman . . . [with hair] growing low on her flat forehead." Dr. Phillips notices "how short her chin was between lower lip and point." Sometimes "the beginning of a smile formed on her thin lips."

The movements of snake and woman are also similar. A snake seems to glide and move quietly and effortlessly. Usually it moves along unnoticed. "The snake moved out smoothly, slowly. The motion was so gradual, so smooth that it did not seem to be motion at all." The woman, too, is quiet. "The woman's motions could not be heard . . . He had not heard her get up from the chair; he could not hear her walk away on the pavement." Reptiles have low metabolic rates; they awaken and move slowly unless provoked. Dr. Phillips, in reference to the woman, thinks to himself that she has a "low metabolic rate, almost as low as a frog's." "She seemed to awaken slowly . . . The doctor wanted to shock her out of her inanition . . . She was completely at rest . . . The rest of her was in a state of suspended animation . . . She had not moved, she was still at rest."

What small movement the woman displays suggests a further comparison. "Her head raised . . . her head swung around . . . ." When a snake stalks its prey, its body stiffens for attack. "He keeps the striking curve ready." As the snake prepares to strike, the woman "crouched and stiffened " at the same time. The snake weaved slowly back and forth. "And while the woman watched the snake, she was weaving too." When the snake strikes to kill, it hits and then retreats quickly and quietly to watch. "The snake backed hurriedly into the corner from which it had come, and settled down," while "she relaxed, relaxed sleepily" after the snake struck. The woman uses her hands little and speaks without expression. While her hands are at rest in her lap, she almost seems to be a slim form lacking those appendages. "Her hands rested side by side on her lap. . . . Her two quiet hands did not move." The woman's voice is soft, much like one would imagine a snake's hiss would be--without expression. She spoke in a "soft throaty voice, . . . she said softly, . . . in her low monotone . . . she said in her soft flat voice . . . ."

Situations that would probably cause some sort of reaction in most people do not even make her blink. She has no qualms about putting her hand among the rattlesnakes to move one to another place. When Dr. Phillips jerks her away from the snakes, her only response is, "'You put him in the other cage then.'" The woman exhibits none of the characteristic curiosity over the doctor's experiments and microscope; "a lack of interest in what he was doing irritated him." Gore and death do not faze her; "she looked without expression at the cat's open throat."

The woman's reptilian presence makes the doctor uneasy, further revealing her serpentine connection. He talks more loudly than usual, which shows his discomfort: "he said rather loudly"; "he shivered" when she stares unconcernedly at the cat's open throat, as if evil were in his presence. Dr. Phillips is "drawn back" to the cage where the woman stands after he moves away to continue his starfish experiment. She makes him feel odd. He has fed many rats to many snakes, yet he feels it is sinful this time, and "he did not know why this desire [to watch the snake feed] sickened him."

When the woman and snake first see each other, it is strange that the snake's "tongue slipped out and hung quivering for a long moment" rather than flickering in and out rapidly. Even the snake seems to recognize the connection, which obviously pleases the woman. The woman shows a possessiveness towards the snake; rather than saying that she wants to feed him, she says, "I want to feed my snake." The only time she shows any emotion or expression is when she knows her snake is going to eat. When she asks to see the snake eat and the doctor says yes, "a beginning of a smile formed on her thin lips." When she knows the snake is going to eat the dead rat, "the corners of the woman's mouth turned up a trifle again." Dr. Phillips finally admits that he is in the presence of something revolting and incomprehensible when the snake is in the process of swallowing the rat. He says to himself, "'If she's opening her mouth, I'll be sick. I'll be afraid.'"

To make the connection between the woman and the snake that is the implied metaphor in the story, Steinbeck relies upon the use of imagery. From the outset, the similarity of woman and snake is obvious. Their appearance and movements mirror one another, and the woman's snake-like features make the doctor uneasy. Even the snake is aware of some sort of kinship with the woman. Ultimately, it is the effective use of imagery that establishes the woman's snake-like qualities and enriches the story's dramatic tension.

EXERCISE 4.2

For each of the following selections list two topics that might be developed into a formalist analysis.

1. "Kubla Khan" (page 207)

_____

_____

2. "To Build a Fire" (page 274)

_____

_____

3. "Patterns" (page 214)

_____

_____

4. "Hurt Hawks" (page 4)

_____

_____

Here is another formalist analysis student paper. Helga Erickson analyzes the Hemingway short story, "A Clean, Well-Lighted Place" (page 271).

Helga Erickson

English 1B 11:00 MWF

Dr. Guches

24 October 1988

(Formalist Analysis)

FEAR OF THE DARK

"A Clean, Well-Lighted Place" presents a view of an uneventful
evening shared by three unnamed characters at an ordinary cafe. Two of
the characters are waiters, who carry on a conversation inside the cafe,
while the other character, an elderly deaf man, sits alone on a terrace
drinking brandy. When the cafe is closed for the night, the old man and
one waiter leave. The other waiter continues the discussion by himself
for a time, then leaves the cafe and stops in at a bar before going home.
"A Clean Well-Lighted Place" deals primarily with old age and its
relationship to death, and symbolism is the most prominent literary
device used by the author to illustrate this theme. While many aspects
of the story can be interpreted symbolically, the weight of the theme
falls upon the meanings of light and darkness as the author, Ernest
Hemingway, uses them.

Light, as a major symbolic element in the story, is first introduced
in the title and remains a key image throughout the text. Light
represents youth and things which are associated with youth, such as
security, confidence, companionship, and faith. One of the waiters is a
young man who is anxious to close the cafe for the evening so that he can
go home. The older waiter and the old deaf man are reluctant to leave the
light of the cafe, but the young waiter is not afraid of the outside
world at night because he has an "inner light," his youth, to protect
him. The cafe, then, represents safety and comfort and protection from
the darkness outside, which is only threatening to those who recognize
it.

The significance of light to the theme of the story is accentuated
by the presence of darkness, or nothingness, as a symbol. Darkness is
suggestive of the unknown, and of the fears and doubts which come with
age. The old man sitting on the terrace is continually in shadow, even
though he is at a well-lighted cafe. He cannot escape the shadow because

he is old and too near death, but he can surround himself with light and borrow some strength from it. The shadow has not yet enveloped either of the waiters, but the older one feels it approaching him and finds the thought disturbing. After the young waiter and the old man have gone, the remaining waiter recites to himself a version of "The Lord's Prayer," replacing all words of religious importance with the word "nada," or nothing. This is indicative of his growing doubt, as he moves closer to death, in things which the Church has taught him to take for granted. He wonders what will become of his soul when he dies, if indeed he has a soul at all, and he realizes that religion will not provide answers which he can trust to shelter him from the unknown.

The young waiter symbolizes the ignorance of youth. He does not understand why the older waiter and the old man wish to stay longer in the cafe; he is unaware of the nothingness outside. In the initial dialogue between the waiters, it is revealed that the old man has recently attempted suicide. When questioned about it by the older waiter, the young one does not know why the old man tried to kill himself except that he was in despair about nothing. The statements of the young waiter demonstrate, ironically, that although darkness, or old age, contains what is known, ignorance can be found even in the light. The old man tried to commit suicide because he felt the nothingness, or the shadow, which was all around him; when the young waiter says that the cause was despair and about nothing, he speaks the truth, but does not even realize it.

Each of the main characters in "A Clean, Well-Lighted-Place" is in a different phase of life; one is old, one is young, and one is midway between the two. By comparing and contrasting these three men, the author makes a statement concerning the relationship of youth to age. The young man thinks that he has knowledge, when in reality he is ignorant; the old man knows that he does not have any answers. The difference in the way young people and old perceive the unknown is that the young are confident about the future but with age that confidence is replaced by increasing doubt. This perspective on youth and age is maintained throughout the story by the symbolic representations of light and darkness.

Analyzing the Performing Arts

"The purpose of playing [acting], whose end, both at the first and now, was and is, to hold, as 'twere, the mirror up to Nature."
Hamlet, Act III, Scene 2, *William Shakespeare (1564-1616)*

Drama is meant to be performed, to be seen and heard, not merely read. It is through the immediacy of the theatrical experience that drama takes on an aura that radically separates it from other literary genres. Playwrights visualize their work as a presentation to a group; novelists, modern poets, even essayists view their work as it affects the individual. Herein lies part of the fascination of the stage performance over the book, for the book's imagery is abstract, in the mind, while the play's imagery is present and alive. A play's imagery is effective since the actors convince the members of the audience that the acting that is transpiring before their eyes is both real and significant. If the members of the audience are convinced, they are transported to a level of consciousness that makes drama, for many people, the most thrilling of literary experiences.

Objectives:

After completing this chapter, you will be able to:
1. Identify the main elements of drama.
2. Define catharsis.
3. Distinguish between classical and modern tragedy.
4. Analyze a short play for its dramatic characteristics.

5. Assess the value of those techniques unique to film.
6. Appraise a film's use of ten cinematic techniques.
7. Evaluate a film's and a play's literary elements.
8. Distinguish among the component parts of tragedy.
9. Express more critical judgment in evaluating what you choose to view.

Pre-Assessment:

_____ 1. The most important difference between plays and other literary forms is that (A) plays are never read (B) plays are a group experience (C) plays cannot use metaphor and imagery (D) plays are not considered literature (E) plays are an individual experience.

_____ 2. Which of the following is NOT a convention of drama?
(A) Characterization is through speech and action.
(B) Tone is part of meaning.
(C) The playwright is outside the action.
(D) Characters' thoughts may not be suggested.
(E) Moods may be suggested by lighting.

_____ 3. A film maker uses symbols to (A) lengthen the film's dramatic impact (B) amuse the intelligent members of the audience (C) divert overemphasis upon the plot (D) make it similar to literature (E) stimulate feelings or thoughtfulness.

_____ 4. According to the Greek philosopher Aristotle, literature is (A) a lie, thus sinful (B) an imitation of reality (C) a fruitless waste of energy (D) a mere diversion for the wealthy (E) an escape into fantasy.

_____ 5. Which of the following is NOT part of tragedy?
(A) antecedent action
(B) suspense
(C) narration
(D) reversal
(E) catastrophe

MATCHING

_____ 6. Explains events that occur prior to the play's beginning

_____ 7. The emotional tension that sustains interest

_____ 8. Hints about the outcome

_____ 9. Point at which catastrophe becomes inevitable

_____ 10. The unraveling or untangling of the plot action

A. suspense
B. reversal
C. antecedent action
D. foreshadowing
E. dramatic irony
F. climax
G. catastrophe
H. denouement
I. narration

The Play

Although drama includes many of the same techniques other literary genres employ, some profound differences exist. While writers of short stories and novels and plays have stories to tell, writers of plays have somewhat fewer technical options at their disposal. Playwrights cannot typically tell audiences what characters look like, what they think, why they do what they do, or even what they are doing; all these must be shown, and they are shown through the interpretations of actors. Out of these limitations come the *central conventions of drama.*

1. The playwright is outside the action.
2. Characterization is through speech and action.
3. Tone is part of the meaning.
4. Characters' thoughts may be suggested by a line's content *and* its delivery.
5. Mood may be suggested by lighting.

Since a modern play usually lasts fewer than three hours, its action is often compressed. Even what seems to be minor action must contribute to the meaning of the whole. As a result, the playwright's use of metaphor and symbol are often less subtle than the novelist's. Consequently, their figures of speech seem more obviously attached to the play's meaning.

Unlike novels, a play, to be convincing, should be unified in time and space. This means that a play's subject matter typically commences near to the end of an action. In other words, since the audience wants to see the action at its climactic point, the action starts close to that point. *Hamlet*, for instance, begins with the sighting of the ghost of Hamlet's father, not with the elder Hamlet's death or even with the plot that led to his death. Rather, the action starts at the point where the ghost sets into motion the action that precipitates the climax. Therefore, playwrights often limit their plays to a realistic time span and as few setting changes as are absolutely necessary.

The most important difference between plays and other literary forms is that drama is a group experience. Most modern poems, novels, and short stories unfold within the mind of each individual reader; they appeal to individual emotions, relatively unaffected by outside stimuli. Plays, however, derive much of their response from the fact that members of the audience are affected by one another. Humor in a play, for example, may bring more intensified responses because the whole group is reacting not only to the humor but to the other members of the audience. Moreover, watching something happen, watching it along with others, makes it appear more realistic. Although the audience only watches, individual members participate in the action by identifying with the emotions being portrayed before them.

A play, then, is a very different kind of experience for its viewers than other forms of literature are for readers. However, although they are intended to be viewed, we do read plays. Readers of plays, consequently, need to assume a director's frame of mind. Through this process, readers can take the view that, while it is somewhat different from other reading, reading a play can be a richly rewarding experience. Furthermore, the rewards of reading drama are enhanced directly in proportion to readers' skills and experience in maintaining the director's point of view. Also, it should be remembered that a character's meaning is often indicated by the way a line is spoken: its tone. Therefore, the director's point of view requires readers to become alert to even very subtle shifts in tone, lest the meaning be either misinterpreted or lost.

Read *The Stronger* by August Strindberg, page 115.

THE STRONGER

Characters

MRS. X, an actress, married
MISS Y, an actress, unmarried
A WAITRESS

SCENE: *The corner of a ladies' cafe. Two little iron tables, a red velvet sofa, several chairs. Enter MRS. X, dressed in winter clothes, carrying a Japanese basket on her arm.*

MISS Y: sits with a half-empty beer bottle before her, reading an illustrated paper, which she changes later for another.

MRS. X: Good afternoon, Amelia. You're sitting here alone on Christmas eve like a poor bachelor!

MISS Y: (Looks up, nods, and resumes her reading.)

MRS. X: Do you know it really hurts me to see you like this, alone, in a cafe, and on Christmas eve, too. It makes me feel as I did one time when I saw a bridal party in a Paris restaurant, and the bride sat reading a comic paper, while the groom played billiards with the witnesses. Huh, thought I, with such a beginning, what will follow, and what will be the end? He played billiards on his wedding eve! (*MISS Y starts to speak*) And she read a comic paper, you mean? Well, they are not altogether the same thing.

(*A WAITRESS enters, places a cup of chocolate before MRS. X and goes out.*)

MRS. X: You know what, Amelia! I believe you would have done better to have kept him! Do you remember, I was the first to say ''Forgive him?'' Do you remember that? You would be married now and have a home. Remember that Christmas when you went out to visit your fiancé's parents in the country? How you gloried in the happiness of home life and really longed to quit the theatre forever? Yes, Amelia dear, home is the best of all—next to the theatre—and as for children—well, you don't understand that.

MISS Y: (Looks up scornfully.)

(*MRS. X sips a few spoonfuls out of the cup, then opens her basket and shows Christmas presents.*)

MRS. X: Now you shall see what I bought for my piggywigs. (*Takes up a doll.*) Look at this! This is for Lisa, ha! Do you see how she can roll her eyes and turn her head, eh? And here is Maja's popgun.

(*Loads it and shoots at MISS Y.*)

MISS Y: (Makes a startled gesture.)

MRS. X: Did I frighten you? Did you think I would like to shoot you, eh? On my soul, if I don't think you did! If you wanted to shoot *me* it wouldn't be so surprising, because I stood in your way—and I know you can never forget that—although I was absolutely innocent. You still believe I intrigued and got you out of the Stora theatre, but I didn't. I didn't do that, although you think so. Well, it doesn't make any difference what I say to you. You will believe I did it. (*Takes up a pair of embroidered slippers.*) And these are for my better half. I embroidered them myself—I can't bear tulips, but he wants tulips on everything.

MISS Y: (Looks up ironically and curiously.)

MRS. X: (*putting a hand in each slipper*) See what little feet Bob has! What? And you should see what a splendid stride he has! You've never seen him in slippers!

(*MISS Y laughs aloud.*) Look! (*She makes the slippers walk on the table. MISS Y laughs loudly.*) And when he is grumpy he stamps like this with his foot. "What! damn those servants who can never learn to make coffee. Oh, now those creatures haven't trimmed the lamp wick properly!" And then there are draughts on the floor and his feet are cold. "Ugh, how cold it is; the stupid idiots can never keep the fire going." (*She rubs the slippers together, one sole over the other.*)

MISS Y: (*Shrieks with laughter.*)

MRS. X: And then he comes home and has to hunt for his slippers which Marie has stuck under the chiffonier—oh, but it's so sinful to sit here and make fun of one's husband this way when he is kind and a good little man. You ought to have had such a husband, Amelia. What are you laughing at? What? What? And you see he's true to me. Yes, I'm sure of that, because he told me himself—what are you laughing at?—that when I was touring in Norway that brazen Frederika came and wanted to seduce him! Can you fancy anything so infamous? (*pause*) I'd have torn her eyes out if she had come to see him when I was at home. (*pause*) It was lucky that Bob told me about it himself and that it didn't reach me through gossip. (*pause*) But would you believe it, Frederika wasn't the only one! I don't know why, but the women are crazy about my husband. They must think he has influence about getting them theatrical engagements, but he is connected with the government. Perhaps you were after him yourself. I didn't use to trust you any too much. But now I know he never bothered his head about you, and you always seemed to have a grudge against him someway.

(*Pause. They look at each other in a puzzled way.*)

MRS. X: Come and see us this evening, Amelia, and show us that you're not put out with us—not put out with me at any rate. I don't know, but I think it would be uncomfortable to have you for an enemy. Perhaps it's because I stood in your way (*more slowly*) or—I really—don't know why—in particular.

(*Pause. MISS Y stares at MRS. X curiously.*)

MRS. X: (*thoughtfully*) Our acquaintance has been so queer. When I saw you for the first time I was afraid of you, so afraid that I didn't dare let you out of my sight; no matter when or where, I always found myself near you—I didn't dare have you for an enemy, so I became your friend. But there was always discord when you came to our house, because I saw that my husband couldn't endure you, and the whole thing seemed as awry to me as an ill-fitting gown—and I did all I could to make him friendly toward you, but with no success until you became engaged. Then came a violent friendship between you, so that it looked all at once as though you both dared show your real feelings only when you were secure—and then—how was it later? I didn't get jealous—strange to say! And I remember at the christening, when you acted as godmother, I made him kiss you—he did so, and you became so confused—as it were; I didn't notice it then—didn't think about it later, either—have never thought about it until—now! (*Rises suddenly.*) Why are you silent? You haven't said a word this whole time, but you have let me go on talking! You have sat there, and your eyes have reeled out of me all these thoughts which lay like raw silk in its cocoon—thoughts—suspicious thoughts, perhaps. Let me see—why did you break your engagement? Why do you never come to our house any more? Why won't you come to see us tonight?

(*MISS Y appears as if about to speak.*)

MRS. X: Hush, you needn't speak—I understand it all! It was because—and because—and because! Yes, yes! Now all the accounts balance. That's it. Fie, I won't sit at the same table with you. (*Moves her things to another table.*) That's the reason I had to embroider tulips—which I hate—on his slippers, because you are fond of tulips; that's why (*throws slippers on the floor*) we go to Lake Malarn in the summer, because you don't like salt water; that's why my boy is named Eskil—because it's

116

your father's name; that's why I wear your colors, read your authors, eat your favorite dishes, drink your drinks—chocolate, for instance; that's why—oh—my God—it's terrible, when I think about it, it's terrible. Everything, everything came from you to me, even your passions. Your soul crept into mine, like a worm into an apple, ate and ate, bored and bored, until nothing was left but the rind and a little black dust within. I wanted to get away from you, but I couldn't; you lay like a snake and charmed me with your black eyes; I felt that when I lifted my wings they only dragged me down; I lay in the water with bound feet and the stronger I strove to keep up the deeper I worked myself down, down, until I sank to the bottom, where you lay like a giant crab to clutch me in your claws—and there I am lying now.

I hate you, hate you, hate you! And you only sit there silent—silent and indifferent; indifferent whether it's new moon or waning moon, Christmas or New Year's, whether others are happy or unhappy; without power to hate or to love; as quiet as a story by a rat hole—you couldn't scent your prey and capture it, but you could lie in wait for it! You sit here in your corner of the cafe—did you know it's called "The Rat Trap" for you?—and read the papers to see if misfortune hasn't befallen someone, to see if someone hasn't been given notice at the theatre, perhaps; you sit here and calculate about your next victim and reckon on your changes of recompense like a pilot in a shipwreck. Poor Amelia, I pity you, nevertheless, because I know you are unhappy, unhappy like one who has been wounded, and angry because you are wounded. I can't be angry with you no matter how much I want to be—because you come out the weaker one. Yes, all that with Bob doesn't trouble me. What is that to me, after all? And what difference does it make whether I learned to drink chocolate from you or someone else. (*Sips a spoonful from her cup*) Besides, chocolate is very healthful. And if you taught me how to dress—tant mieux!—that has only made me more attractive to my husband; so you lost and I won there. Well, judging by certain signs, I believe you have already lost him; and you certainly intended that I should leave him—do as you did with your fiancé and regret; but, you see, I don't do that—we mustn't be too exacting. And why should I take only what no one else wants?

Perhaps, take it all in all, I am at this moment the stronger one. You received nothing from me, but you gave me much. And now I seem like a thief since you have awakened and find I possess what is your loss. How could it be otherwise when everything is worthless and sterile in your hands? You can never keep a man's love with your tulips and your passions—but I can keep it. You can't learn how to live from your authors, as I have learned. You have no little Eskil to cherish, even if your father's name was Eskil. And why are you always silent, silent, silent? I thought that was strength, but perhaps it is because you have nothing to say! Because you never think about anything! (*Rises and picks up slippers.*) Now I'm going home—and take the tulips with me—*your* tulips! You are unable to learn from another; you can't bend—therefore, you broke like a dry stalk. But I won't break! Thank you, Amelia, for all your good lessons. Thanks for teaching my husband how to love. Now I'm going home to love him. (*Goes.*)

August Strindberg (1849-1912)

EXERCISE: 5.1

In one paragraph describe how the tone of Mrs. X changes from the beginning of the play to the end.

_____

_____

_____

_____

_____

_____

_____

_____

_____

EXERCISE 5.2

Identify the literary techniques that you studied earlier in this book that Strindberg has written into his short play.

_____

_____

_____

_____

_____

_____

_____

_____

Tragedy

Many feel that the highest form of drama, and perhaps of all literature, is tragedy. From its earliest beginnings in ancient Greece down to today's tragic drama, tragedy has had wide appeal. Aristotle (384-322 B. C.), a Greek philosopher, postulated a philosophic theory regarding tragedy's appeal. Aristotle believed that literature (all art for that matter) is an imitation of reality. As such, literature presents a heightened and harmonious exercising of peoples' feelings. This exercising of feelings results in their enlargement and refinement which leads to the ability to form a more perfect total person, thus reconciling and integrating both emotions and intellect in art. This, according to Aristotle, has an ethically desirable effect upon the total well being of each individual. Part of this positive effect entails the purgation of emotions, a process which is called *carthasis* (katharsis).

Specifically, Aristotle believed catharsis purged the emotions of fear and pity. This purgation is accomplished in tragic drama, for example, by first exciting then tranquilizing emotions; it excites in order to tranquilize. The Greek view, as Aristotle expressed it, gave catharsis credit for the removal of disturbing, painful elements by purifying them in tragedy. This almost medicinal idea seems to fit well not only into Greek culture but into modern ideas of the arts as well. Part of the fascination of drama would seem to be that the audience identifies with the characters, fears for them as they proceed toward the inevitable, pities them as they plummet into the catastrophe.

Tragedy's Three Components:

Classical tragedy has three basic components at it proceeds:
1. a beginning (introduction; antecedent action)
2. a middle (suspense; climax; reversal)
3. an end (catastrophe; denouement)

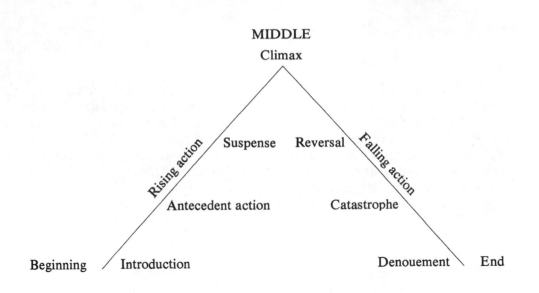

MIDDLE

Climax

Rising action   Suspense   Reversal   Falling action

Antecedent action   Catastrophe

Beginning   Introduction   Denouement   End

Beginning

1. *Introduction* (How to Start): Tragedy usually begins with one of five basic openings:
   a. a speech given by a major character
   b. small talk between minor characters
   c. a speech given by a chorus
   d. a recited prologue
   e. an exchange between major characters
   (*The Stronger* begins with e above)

2. *Antecedent Action:* In order to explain the present action of a play's characters, events that occur prior to the opening action must be explained. These events are the antecedent action. (In *The Stronger* we learn about the previous relationship of the two main characters and the relationship of each to Bob, the husband of Mrs. X.)

Middle

1. *Suspense:* As with any longer work of literature, something must be curious or sufficiently enthralling to maintain the self-discipline to read on or, as in the case with drama, to come back after the intermission. Without a doubt, one of the most effective methods of maintaining reader/viewer interest is through suspense. Suspense creates a tension and emotional involvement that rivets spectators to their chairs or makes it nearly impossible to put down certain books. Suspense requires somewhat more than simply passive involvement with the literature; its cathartic effect fulfills our expectations and so intrigues us that we feel cleansed afterward.

   In addition to heightening suspense by making the members of the audience experience curiosity, and uncertainty or excitement because they

120

do not know the outcome, the playwright may also increase suspense through the technique of *foreshadowing*. Foreshadowing hints at what the outcome will be without actually giving away the plot. Sometimes foreshadowing is accomplished by dwelling on something that will be important later. For example, the letter opener that will later become the murder weapon in a mystery play will be examined and commented upon early in the action. In the popular film *Jaws*, for another example, a picture of a shark destroying a small boat is shown relatively early in the film. This foreshadows the destruction of the boat by the giant shark at the film's conclusion. By letting an audience see hints that mirror later events their curiosity is stimulated and suspense is enhanced. Dramatic irony may, in addition, be used to stimulate suspense.

2. *Reversal:* The dramatic turning point (reversal) for the protagonist is that point at which it is discovered that the fate that was expected is not the fate that will transpire. Often during the beginning and the middle of a play, plans are made, character relationships established, and certain events are anticipated. Then, suddenly, a dramatic reversal reveals that the main character's expectations will not be fulfilled. For example, Romeo, thinking that Juliet is dead, kills himself. Hamlet, seeking vengeance and the throne, is himself the object of vengeance which results in his death. The reversal is sometimes an odd twist of fate and at other times a logical outgrowth of a character's personality; in any case, the technique is dramatic and contributes to cathartic value.

3. *Climax:* An often misunderstood term, the dramatic climax is not at the end of a play nor is it usually near the catastrophic events. Rather, the climax is that point at which the catastrophe becomes inevitable. Actually in many plays, such as in Shakespeare's tragedies, the climax comes during Act Three—directly in the middle of the play. For example, in *Hamlet's* rising action there are exposition, antecedent action, character introduction, and conflict. All these contribute to what Aristotle called "the complications" and results in mounting tension (suspense). The rising action peaks at the climax, after which begins the falling action. From this falling action or turning point, the tragedy proceeds rapidly toward disaster - again in *Hamlet*, when Hamlet mistakenly kills the King's chief counselor, the old fool Polonius.

End

Catastrophe and *Denouement:* Closely related in tragedy, the catastrophe and denouement come at or near the end of a play. The catastrophe is that point at which the protagonist, and often allies and loyal friends, dies. Denouement is a general term which means unraveling or untangling. The denouement is where the plot action ends and any unanswered questions are explained. A denouement is necessary to the achievement of a satisfying drama so that members of the audience do not leave the theater puzzled about any part of the dramatic story.

Modern tragedy, while similar to classic tragedy, has undergone certain shifts in focus. Contemporary emphasis has changed what the ancient Greeks called fate (the will of the gods) to a greater concern with social, cultural, or political milieu. In other words, the modern fates are "society" or "the system" or whatever playwrights believe controls people's destinies. Moreover, the characters in classic tragedy deeply care about what happens to tragic protagonists because their deaths change the fortunes of all people in a society. Modern protagonists, by contrast, do not usually have the fortunes of society resting upon their shoulders. In fact, their lives or deaths often seem to have little impact upon the societies in which they live. This change in focus has led to new directions in drama, such as the theater of the absurd (see Existentialism in Chapter 3, page 75).

Willing Suspension of Disbelief

The willing suspension of disbelief, while an awkward sounding expression, is of essential importance to the performing arts. Basically, it means that while you are in a theater watching a play or a movie you must, for that period of time, suspend your disbelief—that is pretend to believe that what you are seeing is actually taking place as you see and hear it. If you are not able to do this, then the play or movie fails. It fails because you, the audience, remain unmoved and untouched by what you see. If you do not willingly suspend your disbelief, then you can never be frightened, thrilled, excited, or brought to tears because throughout it all you know the actors are only pretending. The performing arts presuppose the ability to suspend disbelief willingly because without it people would not attend plays nor would they go to movies. Drama and film grip, excite, and intrigue us precisely because we believe, for a time, that reality is occuring on the stage or screen, as we see and hear it. We can, therefore, immerse ourselves in the performing arts and seemingly escape into another reality.

EXERCISE 5.3

Earlier in this chapter it was stated that we become acquainted with the characters in a play by how they look, what they do, what they say, how they speak, and what opinions others have of them. After listing some facts about either *Mrs. X* or *Miss Y,* (from *The Stronger*) write a description of one of them. (Submit on separate sheet.)

EXERCISE 5.4

A) In one paragraph describe Aristotle's view of what effect tragedy has upon those who view it. (Submit on separate sheet.)

B) In what ways does a play or a film you have seen recently meet the requirements of tragedy? (Submit on separate sheet.)

The following student paper is a formalist analysis of the ancient Greek tragedy, *Antigone,* by Sophocles.

Rosalba Sanchez
English 1-B MWF 10:00am
Dr. Guches
November 14, 2001
(Formalistic Analysis)

Passion Play

Sophocles' play, <u>Antigone</u>, translated by Elizabeth Wyckoff, tells of the final destruction of the ruling house of the city of Thebes. In <u>Antigone</u>, Oedipus' sons, Eteocles and Polyneices, have recently killed each other during a battle to determine who shall rule the city. Their uncle, Creon, formerly regent and now king of Thebes, declares Polyneices a traitor and decrees: "Leave him unburied, leave his corpse disgraced, / a dinner for the birds and for the dogs. / Such is my mind. Never shall I, myself, / Honor the wicked and reject the just." Creon's niece, Oedipus' daughter Antigone, feels she must defy the king and bury her brother. Creon's son, Haemon, is determined to dissuade his father from his chosen stance. The characters in the play <u>Antigone</u> are people compelled into tragedy by the largeness of their passions.

Antigone's passion is a fanatic devotion to the law of the gods. Her brother, Polyneices, is to be punished and not given the burial that divine law demands. But the Greek gods don't discriminate between friend and foe in death. "Death yearns for equal law for all the dead" Antigone tells her uncle, Creon, and she sets out to bury Polyneices: "...what greater glory could I find / than giving my own brother funeral?" Creon declares that defying his edict will result in her death, but Antigone's fervent belief makes her feel her spirit will die if she doesn't do what is right: "Who lives in sorrows many as are mine / how shall he not be glad to gain his death?" And it moves Antigone to denounce her sister, when Ismene fails to share her mission: "...I shall hate you first, / and next the dead will hate you in all justice." As Antigone is lead to her fate after burying Polyneices twice, she passionately calls upon divine retribution:

> I stand convicted of impiety,
> the evidence my pious duty done.
> Should the gods think that this is righteousness,
> in suffering I'll see my error clear.
> But if it is the others who are wrong
> I wish them no greater punishment than mine.

Creon is filled with a passion for power that overrides and fills him with arrogant pride: "The man the state has put in place must have / obedient hearing to his least command / when it is right, and even when it's not" although perhaps he has a sense of what is to come for he continues "...There is no greater wrong than disobedience. / This ruins cities, this tears down our homes..." Antigone accuses Creon of allowing his pride to overrule the will of the gods and warns him this passion will bring about his downfall:

> Nor did I think your orders were so strong
> that you, a mortal man, could over-run
> the gods' unwritten and unfailing laws...
> So not through fear of any man's proud spirit
> would I be likely to neglect these laws,
> draw on myself the gods' sure punishment.

The chorus, Creon's advisors, recognize his prideful passion and warn Antigone: "You showed respect for the dead.... / ...but power / is not to be thwarted so." And Creon becomes angry with them: "Unbearable, your saying that the gods / take any kindly forethought for this corpse." By making his edict above divine law, Creon brings about the end of his own heritage. And even after Teiresias prophesies his downfall and tells him, in disgust, "…you've confused the upper and lower worlds… / You rob the nether gods of what is theirs. / …The Furies sent by Hades / and by all gods will even you with your victims," Creon finds it "…hard, abandonment of my desire."

Haemon is filled with the dedicated and intense passion of youth. He recognizes his father's power, "Your presence frightens any common man / from saying things you would not care to hear," and tells Creon "…the whole town is grieving for this girl, / unjustly doomed, if ever woman was, / to die in shame for glorious action done." But Creon sees the people's desires as incidental to his will: "Is the town to tell me how I ought to rule?" Haemon brings reason to the discussion, attempting to sway Creon's decision to punish Antigone: "…yield your wrath, allow a change of stand. / …the ship that will not slacken sail, / The sheet drawn tight, unyielding, overturns. / She ends the voyage with her keel on top." But Creon becomes angry with this young man, his son, trying to change his decision. Their discussion becomes an argument. Haemon departs with passion: "… you will not ever lay eyes upon my face again." Creon does see his son once more, as the youth grieves in the tomb of his non-dead betrothed, Antigone. The passions of thwarted love and parental anger bring about Haemon's self-inflicted death:

The boy looked at him with his angry eyes,
spat in his face and spoke no further word.
He drew his sword, but as his father ran,
he missed his aim. Then the unhappy boy,
in anger at himself, leant on the blade.

With Antigone's death, Oedipus has no heirs. Eurydice, Creon's wife, passionately takes her own life upon hearing of her son Haemon's death, leaving Creon without an heir, or a wife to give him one. Carried away by passionate beliefs in the righteousness of their actions, the characters in Sophocles' play Antigone perpetrate their own downfall. Creon passionately defies the gods by exercising his kingly power, Antigone passionately defies secular law by devotion to divine law, and Haemon passionately defies his father and his king. These passions lead to the end of the family line.

Lesson 3

Film

Live theatrical productions are greatly admired and popular; however, most modern interest in the performing arts centers upon the medium of film. Film, whether in a movie theater or on the television screen, has a mass appeal and reaps financial rewards that can never be achieved by the necessarily more limited theatrical performance. Consequently, the movie, and its ability to stimulate emotional responses similar to those encouraged in stage productions, became the dominant performing art of the twentieth century.

While there are certainly similarities between film and other forms of literature, film is quite distinctive. Analyzing a film, for example, is strikingly different from analyzing a poem or a short story. Unlike the printed word, film exists on celluloid or magnetic tape; as a result, it is experienced by more of the senses. In addition, it must be viewed in a theater or on a television monitor. Since film viewing is usually a shared experience it is unlike a novel that we may independently lay down and return to at a later time. A film, like a play, is a continuous experience. Unless you attend another performance or start you VCR or DVD player from where you stopped, you cannot simply pick up again at the point you left off. Keep in mind, however that there is a distinct difference between seeing a film at home on a small screen in the company of a few friends and family and viewing it in a theater on a large screen in the company of an audience of perhaps several hundred strangers. Also, reading a film's script is a weak substitute to the multi-layered experience of viewing a movie because the script represents only a starting point, not a completed product. The difference might be likened to reading about a painting as compared to viewing it in an art gallery.

Writing an analysis of a film requires a good memory of what you saw in the movie, and an understanding of what to look for among the film's many images. You will not find writing this kind of analysis particularly difficult if you organize your preparation along a step by step plan.

Steps in Analyzing a Film

1. See a film (choose a significant movie and see it more than once).
2. Take notes (record your first impressions).
3. Analyze your reactions. (Looking over your notes, see if you can see any trends, themes, metaphors, symbols, setting and character impressions, etc).
4. Make special note of the technical aspects (camera and editing techniques, lighting, color, sound, direction, etc).
5. Evaluate the film's character development (give consideration to the actors' successes or failures to portray the characters plausibly).

   [By now you should have many notes on your observations and perhaps an outline of your overall impressions. Therefore, this is probably a good time to view the film again, just prior to the next steps.]

6. Identify the film's major symbols and metaphors (make special note of any allusions, irony, or imagery).
7. Examine the film's theme (make certain that you understand how each of the above concepts contributes to the theme).
8. Write the first draft of your film analysis. (Once the first draft is completed, treat this paper as you would any other composition: revise, rewrite, revise, revise, and revise—then type, proofread, correct, and submit your final draft).

An old truism states that popularity has little to do with critical acclaim. This is especially true with film. Only a unique film is both a critical success *and* a popular success with the general viewing public. Often, it seems a rare coincidence. The reason for this phenomenon should not be too difficult to understand, however. Critics want serious questions explored in works of art. In contrast, most people go to movies to be entertained. They want to laugh, to be thrilled, to be frightened, to live and enjoy in a way that they feel is absent from their own experiences, In other words, they rarely attend or rent movies for the purpose of exposing themselves to great truths. *However*, and this is an important "however," a good film—one that is both art and entertaining—employs the techniques of drama and other literature to ask the important (universal) questions and propose the tentative answers with which all serious literature is concerned.

The theme of a film, not the plot, is often discernible by a repetition of visual symbols and the use of metaphors. As with metaphor in any literature, a cinematic metaphor is achieved through an implied comparison of similar images. In *Passage to India*, for example, the metaphoric comparison is between civilizations—British and Indian; in the barroom scene in *Star Wars* the comparison is between a technologically advanced civilization and the American old west. In *Easy Rider* the comparison is between motorcycles and horses; in *The Gods Must Be Crazy* between modern society and that of the Kalahari bush people.

A film's symbols stimulate feelings and thoughtfulness. Consider, for example, the monoliths in *2001: A Space Odyssey* or the Statue of Liberty at the end of *Planet of the Apes*. Other film symbols have included the following: clocks (*High Noon*), a snow sled (*Citizen Kane*), a pair of ball bearings (*The Caine Mutiny*), a Coca Cola bottle (*The Gods Must Be Crazy*), a field of flowers (*The Color Purple*), and ubiquitous little Christmas tree-shaped odorizers (*Repo Man*).

Through an analysis of metaphors and symbols, the real subject or theme of a film may be determined, and the relationship of the theme to the experiences of the viewers may be explored. A way to reveal a film's real subject is to ask the following questions:

1. What is the theme of the film?
2. How does the theme relate to the plot?
3. How do the metaphors and symbols relate to the theme?
4. Do the technical elements (sound, photography, acting) of the film promote or interfere with the development of the theme?
5. How do the literary elements (setting, character, allusion) relate to the theme?

While most of the elements that are useful in analyzing other forms of literature are also indispensable in film analysis, some further elements are important to film. The total effect of a movie may involve some or all of the following; as a result, each should be considered for its individual contribution and effect upon the film as a whole.

1. Theme
2. Plot
3. Script
4. Acting
5. Setting
6. Costumes and makeup
7. Sound
8. Photography
9. Direction
10. Editing

THEME

The evolutionary journey (odyssey) of the human species is depicted through time and space.

The voyage of HMS *Bounty* leads to moral conflict between duty and freedom, between restraint and license in a clash of cultures.

PLOT

After the discovery of a long buried monolith on the moon, an expedition is launched to Jupiter to search out the destination of radio signals emanating from the monolith.

After a particularly difficult and hazardous voyage from England to Tahiti, the crew of the *Bounty* is confronted with a lifestyle so sensual and free when compared to what they have known in Victorian England that they mutiny rather than face the discipline and dangers of the return voyage home.

SCRIPT

Originally co-written by Stanley Kubrick and Arthur C. Clarke, Kubrick's final script is quite different from Clarke's novel because the initial concept continued to evolve during filming whereas the novel was based on one of the early drafts of their collaboration.

Based upon historical accounts and trial records (rather than upon the Nordhoff and Hall trilogy of novels: *Mutiny on the Bounty* -1932, *Men Against the Sea* -1934, and *Pitcairn's Island* -1934), the script is historically accurate and realistic, especially in its depiction of the relationship between First Mate Fletcher Christian and Captain William Bligh.

ACTING

Little dialogue is necessary as the script develops the theme through a series of visual images; therefore, gesture and expression are elevated in importance. Adding to the difficulty for the actors is that a major character is not a human being but a machine, the computer HAL.

As Captain Bligh, Anthony Hopkins gives a totally plausible performance as a proper British naval officer outraged at what he perceives as the degeneracy of his crew. Hopkins imbues his Bligh with realism and loyalty but with an unyielding certainty that he is right. Mel Gibson's Fletcher Christian is quiet and perceptive, a man of few words. He is driven to action only as a last resort.

SETTING

After the early scenes of primeval earth and the commuter flight to the space station and the moon, most of the action occurs inside the space ship which is on a deep space probe beyond Jupiter. The accuracy of the space vehicle and the technology of space travel were carefully authenticated by the film's director with scientists at NASA.

The exteriors were filmed on location on the island of Moorea, just north of Tahiti in Eastern Polynesia. The interiors were filmed in realistic appearing sets in New Zealand.

127

COSTUMES AND MAKEUP

The costuming and makeup are futuristic without being unrealistic. Based upon the then current practice in space flight, the clothing worn by the actors is projected forward to the kinds of clothing anticipated in the future.

Local Polynesian people, costumed in the dress of the era, lend a look of authenticity to the lush volcanic island local. Aboard ship and in court, the costuming and the makeup are consistent with Victorian English fashion.

SOUND

One of the most memorable sound tracks in film, the choice of music, (i.e. "The Blue Danube") clearly enhances the intensity of the film's images.

The sound is realistic and effective. The howl of the storm that prevented the *Bounty* from sailing around Cape Horn adds to the audience's anxiety for the ship's safety. Later, the gentle sound of sea breeze against coconut palms, accompanied by distant waves breaking upon the protective reefs, becomes part of the seductive quality of the islands.

PHOTOGRAPHY

The photographic techniques (special effects and camera angles) are designed to emphasize the mystery and immensity of space, while reminding the audience of humanity's relative insignificance.

The photography emphasizes the passionate colors and the lushness of nature. The emphasis is upon the cultural clash; therefore, the camera concentrates upon the symbols of each culture: the ship, the outrigger canoes, the modes of dress, tools, food, etc.

DIRECTING

Truly a director's film, *2001: A Space Odyssey* is constructed upon a series of imaginative situations which tell the story in a highly symbolic way:
1. pre-human life on earth
2. trip to the moon and an excavation site
3. space probe to Jupiter and beyond
4. birth of the starchild

The directing seems to have brought out fine performances from the principle actors. Even more effective, perhaps, are the realistic portrayals by the dozens of extras, who are not actors and who do not generally have many movies in their experience to guide them.

EDITING

While the editing might seem to be choppy, the result of the associative cuts suggest leaps of evolutionary progress. The first major evolutionary leap cuts directly from the ape, as it assimilates the discovery of the tool-weapon possibilities of a bone to the shuttle space ship on a routine trip to the moon. The second evolutionary leap involves the main human characters' "cosmic ride" beyond the infinite to the birth of the starchild.

The film editing illuminates the theme by juxtaposing contrasting cultural elements. However, after the mutiny, some puzzlement results from a confusing compression of time. This can probably be attributed to the fact that the film was originally planned as two movies, the first leading up to and including the mutiny itself and the sequel portraying the consequences of the mutiny—the long sail to safety by Bligh and those loyal to him and the escape to Pitcairn Island by the mutineers.

A Selection of Films to Consider for Analysis

The African Queen (1951)
Almost Famous (2000)
Amelie (2001)
Amistad (1997)
Angels and Insects (1996)
Apocalypse Now (1979)
Apocalypse Now (Redux) (2001)
Apollo 13 (1995)
At Play in the Fields of the Lord (1994)
Battleship Potemkin (1923)
Braveheart (1995)
Casablanca (1943)
Chinatown (1974)
Cinema Paradisio (1989)
Citizen Kane (1941)
A Clockwork Orange (1971)
The Color Purple (1985)
The Conversation (1974)
Das Boot [The Boat] (1981)
Daughters of the Dust (1991)
Dead Man Walking (1995)
Do the Right Thing (1989)
Dr. Strangelove (1964)
Driving Miss Daisy (1989)
Elizabeth (1998)
The Emerald Forest (1985)
La Femme Nikita (1990)
Fly Away Home (1996)
The 400 Blows (1959)
Gandhi (1982)
Ghost World (2001)
Girl, Interrupted (1999)
Hearts in Atlantis (2001)
Heavenly Creatures (1994)
Henry V (1989)
High Noon (1952)
Hoop Dreams (1994)
I Am Sam (2001)
Indochine (1992)
The Insider (1999)
The Joy Luck Club (1993)
Kagemusha (1980)
Kundun (1997)
The Last Emperor (1987)
Lawrence of Arabia (1962)
Leaving Las Vegas (1995)
Like Water for Chocolate (1992)
Lone Star (1995)

Mi Familia [My Family] (1995)
Michael Collins (1996)
The Mission (1986)
Mississippi Masala (1992)
Moulin Rouge (2001)
Mountains of the Moon (1990)
The Navigator: A Medieval Odyssey (1994)
Nell (1994)
Never Cry Wolf (1983)
Once Upon a Time in the West (1969)
Once Were Warriors (1994)
One Flew Over the Cuckoo's Nest (1975)
Philadelphia (1993)
The Piano (1993)
Platoon (1986)
Pollock (2000)
The Postman (Il Postino) (1994)
Quest for Fire (1982)
Repo Man (1984)
Richard III (1995)
Rob Roy (1995)
Rosencrantz and Guildenstern are Dead (1990)
Saving Private Ryan (1998)
The Scent of Green Papaya (1994)
Schindler's List (1993)
The Searchers (1956)
Searching for Bobby Fisher (1993)
The Secret of Roan Inish (1994)
The Seven Samurai (1955)
The Seventh Seal (1957)
The Shawshank Redemption (1994)
Silkwood (1983)
Songcatcher (2001)
Sophie's Choice (1982)
The Spanish Prisoner (1998)
Stand by Me (1986)
The Straight Story (1999)
Taxi Driver (1976)
To Kill a Mockingbird (1962)
The Truman Show (1998)
The Usual Suspects (1995)
12 Angry Men (1957)
Ulee's Gold (1997)
What's Eating Gilbert Grape (1993)
The Wild Bunch (1969)

EXERCISE 5.5

Write a short evaluation for each of the categories listed for one of the films on the previous page. (Submit on separate sheet.)

The following student paper is an analysis of the film *Apocalypse Now Redux*.

S. J. Choudhury
English 1-B TTh 7:00pm
Dr. Guches
January 8, 2002
(Eclectic Analysis)

Surfing Toward Apocalypse

To surf well, the aficionado learns how to become as one with the flows of water, reflecting that particular environment. Surfers project a legendary stereotype of almost mystically being "in-the-moment." The character Lance, portrayed by Sam Bottoms in Francis Ford Coppola's *Apocalypse Now Redux* (2001), is a famous, world-class surfer, an archetype of the blond nature boy, an innocent in the ways of war yet happy to be on the water. Captain Willard comments: "To look at him, you'd think he never fired a weapon in his life." Throughout the film, Director Coppola draws heavily on water imagery, especially the river. He presents traveling up the river as a metaphoric journey from civilization into savagery, Lance embodying this backward progression.

The civilization afforded by the U. S. Military Central Command in Vietnam is left behind as the crew of the patrol boat departs the Texaco fuel dock. Heading down the coast, the crew finds civilization slightly awry at the river entrance. The commanding officer here, Lt. Kilgore, chooses the entrance location based on the potential surfing conditions and forces his men to surf at low tide while under fire. This battle is a rite-of-passage for Lance. He finds himself separated from his immediate superior officer on the patrol boat, sitting in a foxhole with Captain Willard, the driving force behind the river expedition, and a charismatic lieutenant who wants Lance to following his inherent nature, to surf, albeit in less than ideal conditions. Lance is clearly afraid but passively willing to comply. Willard quickly leads Lance away from the beach and onto the patrol boat so the journey up the river can begin.

Little civilization is to be found while on the river and the men in the patrol boat learn this quickly: Chef and Willard encounter a tiger in the jungle; Lance and Clean react thoughtlessly, shooting violently at nothing discernable. However, a vestige of military civilization appears. Fuel is available in drums. The atmosphere is like an old fashioned American carnival with a hoochy-kooch sideshow. Lance celebrates, reflecting the off-kilter and nearly out-of-control seamy side of civilized humanity. It's a party atmosphere, and music on the radio keeps the boat crew giddy as they continue up the river. Lance brings both technology and indifference into nature. While water skiing behind the boat, his wake swamps locals fishing from their dugout canoes.

Civilization falling apart is presented as a military camp deep in rainwater with no commanding officer. Men run naked without discipline, and Lance grapples in the mud with his comrades from the patrol boat. Willard barters the boat's fuel for time with women the men clearly see as priestesses, earthy representatives of a nature goddess. This is Lance's initiation into "the mysteries" of disassociation from the world, perhaps into the realms of Hades. The *Playboy* Playmate of the Year whines disconnectedly and a naked dead body rests in a tumbled box. Lance paints the woman's face like a doll and then paints his own face with camouflage for the first time. He is merging himself into a part of the jungle, through which the river runs.

Civilization is in chaos at the last military outpost on the river. There is no fuel here, only more ammunition. Men are disassociated from their surroundings and actions, behaving as though crazy. Those in authority are far separated from the men in the trenches. Lance takes LSD, perhaps seeking a vision as the Huichol Indians of Mexico do when imbibing Peyote. He becomes mentally distant from all action, passive, watching and waiting, unable to lead himself, separated from his self-authority. Traveling on the beautiful river, he compares it to Disneyland, but his distraction contributes to Clean's death in an ambush. Further up the river, in the cultured but crumbling outpost of a French plantation homestead, Lance eats without civilized manners, wolfing his food and knocking over a glass while reaching across the table.

Still further up the river all civilization ceases to exist. The patrol boat is deluged with "toy" arrows and a well-flung spear kills the Chief. Lance becomes even more disassociated, mostly watching the world go by. He acts silently as a shaman might, performing loving last rights on Chief's body: camouflage painting the corpse's face and sending it to float down the river. Through the night the boat passes burning buildings and skulls displayed on stakes. Dawn at Colonel Kurtz's refuge, surrounded by towering pagan idolatry, a dead body is cut from a tree and splashes by the patrol boat's bow where savage-like Lance crouches clutching a spear. Face still painted, he follows Willard, staring in wide-eyed innocence at the dead bodies and silent men. Kurtz tortures Willard and beheads Chef, but Lance, no threat, is left alone. He has become a savage, leaving civilization completely behind him down the river, just as Kurtz's troops appear to have done. Wearing only a loincloth and a dazed smile on his painted face, Lance dances like a barbarous tribesman during a ceremony that climaxes in the slaughter of a water buffalo. When at last it is time to leave, to return down the river and to civilization, Willard leads the nearly catatonic, non-resistant young man onto the boat, just as he initially led Lance from the beach to the journey up the river.

Apocalypse Now Redux portrays civilization's deterioration during war. The more distant the troops from central command, the more barbaric become both military operations and the environment. Director Coppola uses the patrol boat's journey up the river, with frequent stops, to illustrate this point. The further from civilization the boat travels, the less control the men have over themselves and the world around them. Lance is only fully realized as a character in the Redux version of this film. Yet the deterioration of civilization and personnel is well characterized by following the personal journey of the nature-attuned surfer-dude, Lance.

EXERCISE 5.6

Write a paper that analyzes some aspect of film. You may use one of the suggested topics or propose one of your own and submit it for your instructor's approval.

Suggested topics for critical analysis papers of film comparison.

1. Contrast the portrayals of Captain William Bligh and Fletcher Christian in the three major film adaptations of the Bounty mutiny.

Captain Bligh	*Fletcher Christian*
Charles Laughton	Clark Gable
Trevor Howard	Marlon Brando
Anthony Hopkins	Mel Gibson

2. Compare and contrast the short story "Occurrence at Owl Creek Bridge" with the film of the same name. In particular, emphasize the written imagery with the film imagery. How are the theme, the symbols, metaphors, irony, etc. altered in transforming the story to film?

3. Compare and contrast the short story "To Build a Fire" with the film by the same name (see #2 above).

Other composition topics for film; compare/contrast:

4. The theme of mental illness or mental deficiency in the films *What's Eating Gilbert Grape*, and *Nell*, or *Girl, Interrupted*, and *Pollock*.

5. The film *Apocalypse Now* with the Joseph Conrad story "The Heart of Darkness."

6. The film *The Color Purple* with Alice Walker's novel.

7. The films *Dr. Strangelove* and *Failsafe* (perhaps also with the novel *Failsafe*).

8. The cultural, ethnic, or racial clashes in the films *Mississippi Masala*, and *Lone Star*.

9. The image of the old west in *Heartland*, *Once Upon a Time in the West*, *Shane*, and *The Good, the Bad, and the Ugly*.

10. The satiric symbols and ironies in *Repo Man* and *Dr. Strangelove*.

11. The role of the reporter (photo/journalist) to historical events as depicted in the film.
    - *The Year of Living Dangerously*
    - *Under Fire*
    - *Apocalypse Now*

12. The theme of "coming-of-age" in films such as *Almost Famous*, *Ghost World*, and *Hearts in Atlantis*.

Psychological Analysis

After Sigmund Freud had probed the inner workings of the human mind and began to publish his psychoanalytic discoveries, writers and literary critics began to view the nature of literature in new and strikingly different ways. Critics re-examined previous literature, all the way back to the ancient Greeks, for clues to the inner motivations of both the writers and their characters. Writers, meanwhile, created new types of characters, characters who could be understood fully only in light of Freud's theories. The psychoanalytic approach to literature grew from the belief that, while Freud certainly made a profound psychic breakthrough, what he discovered was not something new at all but may be likened to discovering gold in the American River in California in 1848. Both the human psyche and the gold were always there; it merely took Sigmund Freud and James Marshall, respectively, to make their discoveries. Consequently, if the inner psyche has always been there, then its evidence will surely exist in previous literature. While most literature published prior to Freud's work has been reanalyzed psychologically, the literature that has been written with the most familiarity with his theories was published during the first half of the twentieth century. Consequently, any serious reader needs at least a rudimentary understanding of Freud's basic tenets to be at all perceptive about literature written during that period.

Objectives:

After completing this chapter, you will be able to:

1. Describe the psychological approach to literary interpretation.

2. Define the literary terms that form the basic vocabulary of psychological analysis.

3. Write a psychological analysis of a literary selection.

4. Relate a story's psychological elements.

5. Assess the contributions psychology has made upon contemporary thought.

6. Evaluate how the id, ego, and superego affect current thinking.

7. Interpret a story's reliance upon psychology.

8. Assess the effect of the unconscious mind upon literature.

9. Express greater confidence in your understanding of human nature in literature.

10. Explain the dangers of an over emphasis upon psychology in literary analysis.

Pre-Assessment:

Place the letter of the correct answer in the space at the left of each question.

_____ 1. Which of the following might lead to psychological problems? (A) a person who allows the id to dominate the superego, (B) a conflict between the pleasure principle and morality (C) a person who represses id drives, (D) a frustrated Oedipus stage of development, (E) all of the above.

_____ 2. The zone of the human psyche that lacks any rational logic is (A) id, (B) ego, (C) superego, (D) libido, (E) preconscious.

_____ 3. Freud asserted that dreams are the expressions of (A) the conscious mind, (B) the conscience, (C) the ego, (D) the unconscious mind, (E) the anima.

_____ 4. Psychological analysis is based upon the work of (A) Carl Jung, (B) Charles Darwin, (C) Sigmund Freud, (D) Rollo May, (E) Leo Buscaglia.

_____ 5. Which of the following is NOT a characteristic of psychological analysis? (A) dream symbols, (B) erogenous zones, (C) repressions, (D) fixations, (E) the collective unconscious.

_____ 6. The part of the psyche called the id contains (A) the ego, (B) the superego, (C) reality, (D) guilt, (E) less pleasant aspects of the personality.

_____ 7. The superego represents the (A) bestial elements, (B) conscience, (C) conscious, (D) shadow, (E) desire for idleness.

_____ 8. The superego of a psychologically healthy, mature person (A) protects society, (B) mediates between the ego and the id, (C) promotes amoral behavior, (D) is the source of aggression, (E) reflects the collective unconscious mind.

_____ 9. Freud viewed dreams as (A) premonitions of what was about to happen, (B) symbols of the unsatisfied desires of the id, (C) reflections of past lives, (D) unsettled images of the ego, (E) unimportant to psychoanalytic technique.

_____ 10. One of the main aims of psychological analysis is to (A) examine characters' behavior, (B) discover mythic themes, (C) find metaphors and allusions, (D) show the relationship of theme to history, (E) ascertain the original meanings of terms.

PSYCHOLOGICAL ANALYSIS

The Psychoanalysis of Sigmund Freud

The implications of psychology have long been recognized as important to writers, who have perceived in human behavior certain forces, certain drives or needs that are significant motivators of human nature. Some of the world's most respected writers have supplied psychologists with such penetrating case histories of mental functioning in their literature that their works have been cited as particularly significant in understanding human mental processes. Among many others, Sophocles, Shakespeare, Dostoevsky, Melville, and Hawthorne have contributed much insight into the human psyche through their literature. (Sigmund Freud wrote that it was "not I, but the poets [who] discovered the unconscious.") While psychologists have been searching through literature for authentication of their discoveries, writers and critics have been busy reading the works of such psychologists as Alfred Adler ("will to power" and "the inferiority complex"), Otto Rank ("the will and human personality"), Carl Jung ("introversion/extroversion" and "the collective unconscious"—see Chapter 7), and B. F. Skinner ("stimulus response" and "behavior modification through positive reinforcement"). The psychologist who has been the most influential in stimulating a psychoanalytical approach to literature, however, is Sigmund Freud (1856-1939).

Emphasizing individuals' conflicts, anxieties, and frustrations, psychoanalysis, as postulated by Freud, is primarily concerned with disturbed or abnormal people because it is a therapeutic science rather than a purely experimental discipline; it seeks to diagnose, treat, and cure. As a result, not all of Freud's theories are amenable to literary study, but the following assertions have been sufficiently influential to alter the style of much analytical thinking about literature during the first half of the 20th century.

Freud asserts that

1. the unconscious mind is pre-eminent,
2. the psyche is organized into three zones: id, ego, and superego,
3. dreams are manifestations of the unconscious mind,
4. infantile behavior is basically erotic,
5. neurosis is closely related to creativity.

1. *The Unconscious Mind—*

Freud's underlying, major presupposition is that *most of the mental processes of human beings take place in the unconscious mind.* He asserts that even the most conscious processes quickly become latent although they may later become conscious (active). Grouped in what he calls the "preconscious," these processes, Freud asserts, are differentiated from those in the "unconscious," which are brought to the conscious mind only with the greatest of difficulty or never at all.

Freud demonstrated through his researched and recorded case studies that human actions are controlled by a psyche over which there exists only the most limited control. He likens the human mind to an iceberg: only the smallest portion of the whole iceberg is above the water's surface as only the smallest portion of the human psyche is accessible to consciousness. As the great mass of an iceberg is out of sight, below the surface of the water, so most mental processes lie below the surface of consciousness.

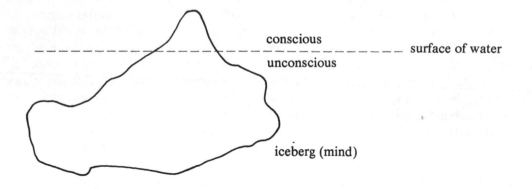

2. *The Psychic Zones: Id, Ego, Superego* —

Freud asserts that the human mind contains three psychic zones. These zones control the mental functions from which come motivations.

A. *ID*—The id is totally submerged in the unconscious, and its function is to fulfill what is called the primordial life principle - or as Freud referred to it, the *pleasure principle*. Contained within the id is the *libido* from which comes the individual's psychic energy. Freud describes the id as totally lacking in rational logic since mutually contradictory impulses may exist simultaneously and not cancel out each other. Consequently, the id knows no ethics or values; it knows no good or evil; it encompasses no morality. The id, moreover, is the source of human aggression and of all basal desires. Since the id is both amoral and lawless, it demands gratification without regard for any religious or legal ethics, social conventions, or moral constraints. Concerned solely with instinctual, pleasurable gratification, the id would drive the individual to any lengths for this pleasure, even to self-destruction, for self-preservation is not an id impulse. Prior to Freud, these instincts toward excessive pleasure were attributed to outside, often supernatural, forces. In many ways, for instance, the old Puritan concept of the devil fits well into the id psychic zone. Small children, not yet imbued with the restraints of society, operate on pure id impulses. They are egocentric, selfish, and solely interested in their own gratification. Occasionally, one hears the old phrase that a child who is misbehaving is "full of the devil." An id character in literature is often one of mystery who tempts protagonists to act against their "better judgment" with an offer that they find difficult to refuse. The temptation for some pleasurable reward is often nearly irresistible. (For examples, see *The Stand* by Stephen King and "Young Goodman Brown" by Nathanial Hawthorn).

B. *EGO*—The ego is usually thought of as the conscious mind; however, it resides equally in the unconscious as well. Referred to as the *reality principle*, the

136

ego's function is to govern the id and channel the id's drives into socially acceptable outlets. Since the id's pleasure demands are often not immediately obtainable, the ego postpones or even alters the demands into drives that are realistically obtainable. The ego's function is, then, to determine when, where, and how the id's demands might best be gratified in ways that are acceptable for the well-being of the individual within the culture. In a normal, well-balanced person the ego and the id work harmoniously together; when the two are in conflict, repression and neurosis result. (See the conclusion of "Young Goodman Brown," p. 263)

C. *SUPEREGO*—If the id is the source of the drive for pleasure and the ego is reality, then the superego is the source of ethics, the *morality principle*. As a moral, censoring agency, the superego is the home of the conscience and of pride. If a society regards a particular id impulse toward pleasure as socially unacceptable and the ego cannot divert the impulse to a satisfactory substitute, then the superego blocks its fulfillment by forcing it back into the unconscious, *repressing* it. Overt aggression, unacceptable erotic desires, and Oedipal instincts (see Part 4, "Infantile Behavior" page 138) are the kinds of impulses that are repressed; since the superego is responsive to its own society, however, its inhibitions vary from culture to culture. What is proper and moral in one culture can be improper and immoral in another. Allowed to become overactive, the superego can create a *guilt complex*: an unconscious, brooding sense of guilt. The initial and by all accounts most influential source of superego is a child's parents. They are the first to impart to the child their moral, ethical values, which is accomplished more by their example than by their instruction. These ethical influences are assimilated and internalized by children early in life (before school age); later, the outside influences of school, church, and peer group have an effect, but they are not nearly as influential as are parents early in a child's life. (See the character Faith in "Young Goodman Brown," p. 263)

OVERVIEW

ID—Pleasure Principle
 —the source of energy
 —impulse toward satisfaction
 —no logic
 —amoral
 —source of aggressions and desires
 —theologically similar to the devil

EGO—Reality Principle
 —rationality
 —regulates id's drives
 —mediating agency of psyche

SUPEREGO—Morality Principle
 —protects society
 —censors or represses the id
 —source of conscience and pride
 —theologically similar to angels

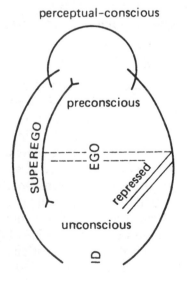

Choosing from short story, play, novel, poem, film, or television program, identify characters that in your opinion mirror Freud's psychic zones. Write a paragraph on each in which you explain these character's roles and psychological functions.

3. Dreams—

Since the unconscious is not directly observable by examination, the id is revealed only through deep hypnosis, during unintentional expressions ("Freudian slips"), and by an analysis of dreams. Unfortunately, even during dreaming the inhibiting power of the superego is functioning; consequently, Freud viewed dreams themselves as only symbols of the unsatisfied or the repressed desires of the id. If a dream's symbolic function comes too close to reality, then the dreamer awakens and is unable to recall the dream's content. Since dreams are expressions of the id, and the id is the source of erotic desires, dreams are, Freud believed, best interpreted in terms of those repressed sexual desires. This theory has led many psychoanalytical critics to examine literature for images that are concave - calling them female or womb symbols (e.g. ponds, cups, rings, caves, wells), and for images that have greater length than diameter - calling them male or phallic symbols (e.g. swords, knives, towers, snakes, arrows, keys). Still other images are seen as erotic (e.g. flying, walking up stairs, dancing, riding). Using dream theory, psychological critics see significance, for example, that in Henry James' *The Turn of the Screw* the narrator of the story within the novel consistently sees a male spirit upon a tower and a female spirit standing in a pond.

The major criticism of psychological analysis results from the overuse of erotic symbolism by psychoanalytic critics. These symbols, while they may help to suggest directions for further analysis, are, in reality, far too simplistic for serious analytical work. Freud himself argued that dream images are too personal to use for general interpretation because an individuals dreams are not sufficiently universal; they employ only the individual dreamer's symbols. Many critics, however, have used dream symbol analysis to examine literature, and some continue to claim insights into human and character motivation through its use.

4. Infantile Behavior—

At one time, general opinion held that children simply did not have erotic development until puberty; Freud asserted that childhood is, in fact, a period of intense erotic experience. (However, Freud's broad use of terms demands that readers understand his definitions rather than rely upon meanings from general usage.) During the first years of their lives, children pass through phases of erotic growth that are centered in erogenous zones, portions of the human body where physical pleasure is most intense. Freud identified three erogenous areas upon which children focus as they move toward maturation: oral, anal, and genital.

Erogenous zones are connected with those id functions that demand gratification (and that are capable of giving pleasure since they are associated with such vital needs). The gratification and pleasure come through eating, eliminating, and eroticism. If children are unable to gratify a need, they may become fixated in that phase of development and this may result in an adult personality with some distortions. For example, early weaning may result in oral fetishes such as cigarette smoking, fingernail biting, or compulsive pencil chewing. Excessively strict toilet training may lead to fastidiousness and obsessive orderliness. During the early genital phase, all children pass through an Oedipus complex (a boy's unconscious rivalry with his father for love for his mother) or an Electra complex (a girl's unconscious rivalry with her mother for love of her father); consequently, a frustrated rivalry with a parent may bring resentment toward parental authority and may later manifest itself in an unreasonable hostility toward all authority. A classic psychological analysis of Shakespeare's *Hamlet*, for example, asserts that the primary source of Prince Hamlet's predicament is not so much moral quandary as Oedipal repression: according to Freudian theory, Hamlet's antisocial behavior may be attributed to repressions, fixations, and complexes.

EXERCISE 6.2

Choosing from short story, play, novel, poem, film, or television program, discuss in one or two paragraphs a theme that in your opinion reflects Freud's ideas about the Oedipus or Electra complexes.

5. *Neurosis and Creativity*—

Sigmund Freud was interested in both psychology and literature. Indeed, he often expressed his indebtedness to literature as the laboratory wherein one could observe psychological phenomena in operation. Moreover, Freud's interest in these related fields led him to speculate about the nature of creativity. Freud believed that writers are people suffering from introverted personalities who write as a form of therapy to escape from their repressed erotic desires, much like in dreams. Consequently, writers express their neuroses in ways that are socially acceptable.

Freud's ideas about the relationship between neurosis and creativity are used in three distinctly different ways by literary analysts. (1) The first way concentrates upon psychoanalyzing writers by viewing their works as expressions of neurotic tension produced by frustrated and repressed id drives. (2) The second way concentrates upon the psychological result of characters' infancy and childhood problems. While these problems are not themselves described in the literature, the problems' existence is clearly suggested by characters' actions. Emphasizing unconscious motivation for characters' actions, this style of criticism attempts to analyze characters' mental turmoil, fixations and repressions, and social or antisocial behavior. (3) The third, and most recent way, concentrates upon the repressions and complexes of society that writers are able to reveal. The emphasis here is upon the unconscious of a society rather than upon the unconscious of individual writers or their characters.

Today, most critics and writers have moved beyond classical Freudian psychoanalysis. The current disaffection for Freudian theory may be attributed to two circumstance: first, the excesses of psychoanalytic critics who in their search through literature to find phallic and womb symbols have tended to trivialize literature as nothing more than manifestations of repressed erotic fantasies. While erotic desire is certainly a powerful source of human motivation, the zeal of Freudian critics to attribute all motivation to this phenomenon offends most casual readers and indeed oversimplifies Freud's observations. Second, since Freud's death in 1939, research has continued and modern psychology has moved beyond Freud's findings. Besides, many people are distrustful of Freud's quasi-scientific approach which emphasizes analogies to the empirical sciences of biology and chemistry. Modern readers are less concerned with therapy and more interested in literature as speculative, philosophic, and universal in its appeal; consequently, some readers are more curious about literature's relationship to anthropology, to religion, and to mythology. It is this that has led to the fascination for the observations of one of Freud's early colleagues—Carl Jung (see Chapter 7).

EXERCISE 6.3

Read "Young Goodman Brown" (p. 263) and answer each of the following questions.

1. What represents the unconscious?

_____

_____

_____

_____

_____

2. Who or what among the characters or setting represent psychic zones?

_____

_____

_____

_____

_____

3. What are the dream symbols?

_____

_____

_____

_____

4. What is the psychological significance of the fact that Brown dreams the story?

_____

_____

_____

_____

_____

Archetypal Analysis

As innovative and astounding as the results of Freud's research are regarded, his work has become dated. Recent research makes it clear that Freud's theories only just began to tap the hidden recesses of the human psyche. Moreover, another psychologist, Carl Jung,—an associate and later an adversary of Freud,—went far beyond Freud in his assertions and research and founded a psychological school that has greatly influenced writers and critics of modern literature.

Many contemporary theorists and critics believe that the significance of a work of art may well lie in its universality—its appeal to all peoples regardless of time or culture. Certain images or situations, these critics assert, create similar emotional responses in nearly everybody. Consequently, both visual artists and writers may evoke those experiences that create the most striking responses. Particularly in literature, the origins and range of this appeal is a critical puzzle. Critical readers should at least be able to identify what this school of thought considers a literary selection's universal elements. The identification of such archetypal elements can lead to a much deeper understanding of a work's value.

Archetypal analysis, sometimes referred to as *myth criticism*, is a method of analysis that enhances readers' critical abilities by requiring them to probe the mythic origins of symbols, imagery, and situations that suggest recurrent human circumstances.

Objectives:

After completing this chapter, you will be able to:

    1. Describe the archetypal or mythic approach to literary interpretation.

2. Define the literary terms that form the basic vocabulary of archetypal analysis.
3. Illustrate the relationship between the archetypal point of view and religion, anthropology, and mythology.
4. Write an archetypal analysis of a literary selection.
5. Relate a story's archetypal elements.
6. Assess the contributions mythology has made to contemporary life.
7. Appraise the effect of the archetype of creation upon humans.
8. Evaluate how the shadow, anima, and persona affect your daily life.
9. Interpret a story's reliance upon the archetype of the hero.
10. Assess the effect of the collective unconscious mind upon literature.

Pre-Assessment:

Place the letter of the correct answer in the space at the left of each question.

1. Archetypal analysis is based upon the work of (A) Sigmund Freud, (B) Carl Jung, (C) Charles Darwin, (D) C.P. Snow, (E) Rollo May.

2. Which of the following is NOT a characteristic of archetypes? (A) primordial, (B) universal, (C) recurrent, (D) contemporary (E) part of the collective unconscious.

3. Groups of mythic situations that together make up a larger, universal story are referred to as archetypal (A) motifs, (B) images, (C) shadows, (D) animus, (E) initiation.

4. Which of the following is NOT an archetypal image of women? (A) earth mother, (B) the temptress, (C) the working mother (D) soul-mate, (E) the platonic ideal.

5. The archetypal hero (A) usually achieves a victory over a king or a wild beast, (B) never becomes the king, (C) loses the beautiful princess, (D) has a happy childhood with his parents, (E) has the good graces of the gods throughout his life.

6. The part of the pyche called the shadow contains the (A) ego, (B) the psycho-motor responses, (C) initiation urge, (D) situations, (E) less pleasant aspects of the personality.

7. The anima represents the (A) bestial elements, (B) life force, (C) desire for idleness, (D) shadow, (E) male impulse.

8. The persona of a psychologically healthy, mature person must be (A) rigid, (B) satisfied, (C) rational, (D) arbitrary, (E) flexible.

9. Archetypes are found in the human psyche in the (A) personal unconscious, (B) subconscious, (C) collective unconscious, (D) spirit, (E) conscious.

10. Myths are (A) the beliefs of primitive people who do not know any better, (B) untrue stories, (C) whatever a people believe in, (D) created to fool the people, (E) not taken seriously by educated people.

Lesson 1

Archetypes

Archetype is a word with Greek roots (*arche - tupos*) that means "first type": the original pattern from which all other copies are made. The closest modern synonyms are "prototype" and "model." From this definition you may wonder how an analytical approach that emphasizes first patterns or models fits into the study of literature. Archetypal analysis shares some of the basic concepts of other analytical approaches but completely rejects others. As with formalist analysis, archetypal critics emphasize an intensively close, analytical reading of literature. Unlike the formalist, however, the archetypalist rejects the idea that nothing outside the printed page is relevant. As with psychological critics, archetypal critics search the unconscious mind, but their interest is with the collective unconscious, those similarities in the unconscious shared by all humans, rather than with the unconscious of the personal or individual psyche. While this approach is certainly indebted to Sigmund Freud, it is not restricted to Freud's version of psychological analysis. The form of analysis based upon archetypes was developed by one of Sigmund Freud's associates—Carl Jung (1875-1961), a Swiss psychologist. Archetypes, according to Jung, represent images or thematic patterns that are repeated so frequently in mythology, religion, and literature that they have taken on a universally symbolic power.

After working closely with Carl Jung for several years, Freud bitterly broke from the younger man over their differences in theory. While Jung agreed with Freud that all humans have deep within their psyches an unconscious which is unique to each individual, Jung further asserted that one aspect of the unconscious mind exists which is the same for each individual in the human species. As each person's unconscious is the result of personal, environmental experience, Jung suggested that the *collective unconscious* is the mental record of all the experiences of those who have existed previously.

In his book *Contributions to Analytical Psychology*, Jung writes that there are three basic qualities that characterize archetypes. These archetypal qualities are *primordial, universal*, and *recurrent*.

Primordial Characteristics

The most fundamental quality that characterizes archetypes is that they are **primordial**; that is, they represent primeval original concept that have existed from the dawn of the species. Located within the preconscious, that area of the mind from which information can be recalled ("re-membered"), they are not present in the conscious mind. As a result, these are sometimes thought of as expressions of human's instinctual nature.*

---

*You must be careful, however, about attributing instinctive motivations in humans. Little agreement exists about the importance or extent of human instincts or even what they may be. Most behavioral scientists concur that a human baby is born knowing how to suck and possessing a fear of falling. If you suggest almost anything else as instinctual, however, you will find argument and controversy.

Although also preconscious, the inborn behavior patterns that characterize most species of lower animals - such as whales migratory habits, birds nesting, bees ritual dances, or chickens fear of hawks—is only partly related to Jung's concept of archetypes in humans. Human archetypes are based, as with animals, upon the same kinds of deep-rooted behavior that results from encoded patterns. In humans, the experiences of the past that are so important for the species' survival, such as the fear of falling, are the result of countless numbers of experiences of the same kind, experiences that literally began before the development of consciousness. They are innate images of experiences which have been repeated so often that they have formed deep, lasting impressions upon the human psyche. These experiences have a cumulative effect much like what happens to unprocessed photographic film passed through airport x-ray machines. One trip through an x-ray machine is probably not noticeable on the photographs, but when the film passes through the machines several times, as it does on a trip that requires several flights, a haze begins to appear. The more trips through the machine, the deeper the haze becomes. The film "remembers" each x-ray and is affected by it; the human psyche remembers each experience and is cumulatively affected by it until it becomes codified into an archetype, buried deeply within the collective unconscious and passed on by the species generation after generation. While this process has never been satisfactorily explained,—Is it genetic? Is it "cultural"? Is it mystical? —these experiences represent those formed earliest in the development of the human species. Primordial experiences, therefore, are fundamental, original occurrences, repeated so many millions of times that they are mentally imprinted. Consequently, since Jung viewed them as models or prototypes of universal behavior, he named them archetypes.

Universal Characteristics

The second fundamental quality of archetypes is that they are **universal**; they are unaffected by time or situation, community or culture. They are now as they were in the past; they are as significant to tribal people, so isolated in dense jungles or on remote islands that they think their few members are the only human beings in existence, as they are to engineers striving to solve the complex problems of space travel. The ancient Greeks battling over Helen at the walls of Troy were as affected by archetypes as politicians today who are trying to calculate the interests and moods of the people so that successful election campaigns may be waged. From this perspective humans have changed little in the past 4,000 years of recorded history, a period which is itself only an instant when compared with the backdrop of evolutionary time. The psychoneurological functions of the modern mind remain essentially unchanged from the minds of Neolithic peoples. As a result, we all share similar experiences, emotions, drives, needs, and archetypes with each other and with our ancient ancestors. Archetypes are, therefore, truly part of the human universal experience.

Recurrent Characteristics

The third fundamental quality of archetypes is that they are **recurrent**. Those who have conducted research in the fields of anthropology, comparative religion, and mythology have tended to confirm the similarities among peoples, while demonstrating that what differences do exist are attributable mostly to local adaptations. It makes little difference, for example, where people are on the earth or when they exist; all people have been concerned with their creation and the meaning of their existence. These concerns are universal, therefore, archetypal. The most fascinating aspects of any comparison, however, comes with the realization that the explanations of human origin and worldly creation are strikingly similar.

For example, compare the following explanations of creation.

1. *Ancient Hebrew*

The First Book of Moses, called

GENESIS

1 In the beginning God created the heaven and earth.

2 And the earth was without form, and void; and darkness *was* upon the face of the deep. And the spirit of God moved upon the face of the waters.

3 And God said, Let there be light: and there was light.

4 And God saw the light, that *it was* good: and God divided the light from the darkness.

5 And God called the light Day, and the darkness he called Night. And the evening and the morning were the first day.

6 And God said, Let there be a firmament in the midst of the waters, and let it divide the waters from the waters.

7 And God made the firmament, and divided the waters which *were* under the firmament from the waters which *were* above the firmament: and it was so.

8 And God called the firmament Heaven. And the evening and the morning were the second day.

9 And God said, Let the waters under the heaven be gathered together unto one place, and let the dry *land* appear; and it was so.

10 And God called the dry *land* Earth; and the gathering together of the waters called he Seas: and God saw that it *was* good.

11 And God said, Let the earth bring forth grass, the herb yielding seed, *and* the fruit tree yielding fruit after his kind, whose seed *is* in itself, upon the earth: and it was so.

12 And the earth brought forth grass, *and* herb yielding seed after his kind, and the tree yielding fruit, whose seed *was* in itself, after his kind: and God saw that it *was* good.

13 And the evening and the morning were the third day.

(On subsequent days God [Yahueh {or Jehovah} Elohin] created the sun and moon, the living creatures, and the first humans, Adam and Eve.)

—from *The Bible*, Authorized King
James translation (1611)

2. *Ancient Greek*

In the beginning Earth, Sea, and Air were all mixed together in a formless, jumbled mass called Chaos.

God and Nature, growing weary of the dead weight, at last put an end to the confusion by separating earth, sea, and heaven from one another.

The brightest, lightest part of Chaos was formed into the sky; the air separated sky from earth, which because she was heaviest sank below buoyed by the water.

God and Nature then divided the earth by forming rivers, raising mountains, carving valleys, creating woods and fields and prairies.

The air, now cleared, let stars shine through; fishes ruled the sea, birds dominated the air and beasts prowled the land.

But not all the gods were satisfied, a nobler animal was desired, so Prometheus, the creator, took some of the earth and carefully mixing it with water made man. He made man in the image of the gods so that among all the animals that must walk face downward, man walked upright, facing heavenward.

3. Ancient Polynesian

In the beginning everything was nothingness and void.
Slowly, ever so slowly Darkness began to emerge and
Darkness conceived something even greater—night.

Night, after eons of time conceived thought which enlarged to Thought-Conception, then to Breath until it finally evolved to Thought in Immensity.

After more eons passed Spirit and Breath of Life combined into the creator, Tangaloa, the Supreme.

Tangaloa dwelt within the breathing space of Immensity.

The universe was in darkness, with water everywhere.

There was no glimmer of dawn, no clearness, no light.

And he began by saying these words,

That he might cease remaining inactive.

"Darkness, become a light-possessing darkness."

And at once light appeared.

(Later Tangaloa—[or Ta'aroa as he was known in Tahiti and Kanaloa in Hawaii] took clay and molded the first man, Tiki.)

4. Ancient Mayan

Popol Vuh

There is not yet one person, one animal, bird, fish, crab, tree, rock, hollow, canyon, meadow, forest. Only the sky alone is there; the face of the earth is not clear. Only the sea alone is pooled under all the sky; there is nothing whatever gathered together. It is at rest; not a single thing stirs. It is held back, kept at rest under the sky.

Whatever there is that might be is simply not there: only the pooled water, only the calm sea, only it alone is pooled.

Whatever might be is simply not there: only murmurs, ripples, in the dark, in the night. Only the Maker, Modeler alone, Sovereign Plumed Serpent, the Bearers, Begetters are in the water, a glittering light. They are there, they are enclosed in quetzal feathers, in blue-green.

Thus the name, "Plumed Serpent." They are great knowers, great thinkers in their very being.

And of course there is the sky, and there is also the Heart of Sky. This is the name of the god, as it is spoken.

And then came his word, he came here to the Sovereign Plumed Serpent, here in the blackness, in the early dawn. He spoke with the Sovereign Plumed Serpent, and they talked, then they thought, then they worried. They agreed with each other, they joined their words, their thoughts. Then it was clear, then they reached accord in the light, and then humanity was clear, when they conceived the growth, the generation of

148

trees, of bushes, and the growth of life, of humankind, in the blackness, in the early dawn, all because of the Heart of Sky, named Hurricane. Thunderbolt Hurricane comes first, the second is Newborn Thunderbolt, and the third is Raw Thunderbolt.

So there were three of them, as Heart of Sky, who came to the Sovereign Plumed Serpent, when the dawn of life was conceived:

"How should it be sown, how should it dawn? Who is to be the provider, nurturer?"

"Let it be this way, think about it: this water should be removed, emptied out for the formation of the earth's own plate and platform, then comes the sowing, the dawning of the sky-earth. But there will be no high days and no bright praise for our work, our design, until the rise of the human work, the human design," they said.

And then the earth arose because of them, it was simply their word that brought it forth. For the forming of the earth they said "Earth." It arose suddenly, just like a cloud, like a mist, now forming, unfolding. Then the mountains were separated from the water, all at once the great mountains came forth. By their genius alone, by their cutting edge alone they carried out the conception of the mountain-plain, whose face grew instant groves of cypress and pine.

And the Plumed Serpent was pleased . . . .

—from *Popol Vuh: The Mayan Book of the Dawn of Life* translated by Dennis Tedlock (1985)

While these explanations are remarkably similar, they serve also to illustrate human concern for self-definition. All peoples seem to thirst for an understanding of how the universe began and how humans fit into the great creation. Creation is, then, a fundamental recurrent archetype. Since stories of creation involve so much more than simply an image or single situation, all the stories of a particular people's explanation of creation combined form what is called a motif—in this instance, the archetypal motif of creation. There are many other universal motifs.

Other Recurrent Archetypal Motifs

A. World destruction by -
    1. Flood
        a. Greco-Roman
        b. Hebrew
        c. East Indian (India)
    2. Famine
    3. Plague
    4. Earthquake

B. Immortality
    1. Escape from time—beyond death
        a. Rewarded for "good" deeds—e.g. Valhalla; Elysian Fields; Heaven; Dream Time; Happy Hunting Ground.
        b. Punished for "bad" deeds—e.g. not permitted into the underworld; condemned to the lowest region (such as Hades' realm); Hell.
    2. Submission into nature's eternal cycle.
        a. Endless death and rebirth, e.g. the Phoenix bird.
        b. Loss of self into timeless (cyclical) merging with the godhead, e.g. Hinduism.

C. Hero (Savior or Deliverer) Tales
  1. The Call
  2. Separation
  3. Initiation
  4. Return
D. Oedipus Legends
E. Slaying of Monsters
F. Incest Stories
G. Virgin Births

EXERCISE 7.1

Research another culture's creation motif—one not mentioned in this chapter—and relate it to the stories of creation told in this lesson.

EXERCISE 7.2

Examine a hero tale and compare it to the recurrent motif of the hero.

Mandala

Lesson 2

Images, Characters, and Situations

The possible number of potential archetypes is limited only by the number of recurrent human experiences. Deep within the collective unconscious may well lurk archetypes of which we are not even remotely aware, or perhaps we know of them only in our dreams, for dreams are thought to be fogged windows through which we can catch a fleeting view of an inner archetypal world. The archetypes with which we are most familiar seem to fall naturally into three groups: images or symbols; characters; and situations.

Images or Symbols

Viewed one way, archetypes are universal in their symbolism. In other words, certain images seem to have universal appeal. These images call from within us certain responses and associations that appeal to us in emotional ways quite apart from our intellect. Test your own responses to the list of archetypal images below to see how closely you are in tune with the responses of others. Think about where you have read these images or seen them often repeated. (Here is a hint for No. 1 below (the sun setting). Think how old movie westerns always seem to end.)

EXERCISE 7.3

On the line beside each image (or symbol), write what you think it symbolizes and cite an example of each. For example: a ship

Example #1   The *Pequod*—The ship from *Moby Dick* symbolizes the conflict between humans and nature.

Example #2   The *Bounty*—The ship from the famous mutiny symbolizes the connective link between the rigid Victorian culture of England and the permissive Polynesian culture of Tahiti.

Example #3   The *Discovery*—The spaceship from *2001: A Space Odyssey* symbolizes the inexorable human quest for knowledge, even into the depths of the unknown.

1. sun

    rising _____

        example_____

    setting _____

        example_____

2. colors

    white _____

        example_____

    red _____

        example_____

    green _____

        example_____

    black _____

        example_____

    (choose another color)

        color _____

        symbol _____

           example_____

3. water

    rivers or lakes _____

        example_____

    ocean_____

        example_____

4. circle (or egg, yin-yang, ouroboros, mandala)

    _____

        example_____

5. garden

        example _____

6. desert

    example _____

7. numbers (3, 4, and 7)

    example _____

In checking your responses with others, do you find similarities? If so, to what do you attribute them?

Some of a culture's most common cliches may well have an archetypal origin. For example:

> pure as snow
> good as gold
> fast as the wind
> green with envy
> black as night

Jung's archetypal images of women are sometimes criticized because they are male-dominated. These images of women only view females as they relate to men, not as individuals. As a result, few female characters in Jung's studies achieve the emphasis that males receive. [Subsequent studies, however, have revealed the presence of major female archetypes.] Women, according to Jung's studies of images, can be grouped into four basic categories. Any one female character may, however, have the characteristics of more than one category.

1. The *earth mother* is associated with birth, warmth, and protection. She is every man's beloved "mom," representing growth, abundance, and fertility. This image has within it those good feelings of home, family, and heritage (roots).

2. The *temptress* is associated with danger, fear, and death. She is the evil witch, the siren, the wicked "step-" mother, the domineering wife, the seductress.

3. The *soul-mate* is associated with inspiration and fulfillment, both physical and spiritual. She is the princess, the beauty, the damsel-in-distress, the "girl next door," lover, mistress.

4. The *platonic ideal* is associated with inspiration and the spiritual ideal on an intellectual level, not on the level of physical attraction.

During his career, Jung seriously neglected the importance of female archetypes. In more recent studies, Jungian analysts have suggested that women, in fact, hold positions of incalculable significance in the archetypes of human beings. Female characters (rather than merely images) are as profound as male characters. (See next section on "Characters")

EXERCISE 7.4

Read the indicated selections and list the archetypal images in each.

"Stopping by Woods on a Snowy Evening" (page 212)

_____

_____

_____

_____

_____

"To Build a Fire" (page 274)

_____

_____

_____

_____

_____

"Young Goodman Brown" (page 263)

_____

_____

_____

_____

_____

Characters

A number of recurrent, archetypal characters make up the cast in many works of literature, as well as in mythology and in religion. These characters possess such remarkably similar experiences and behave in such a predetermined manner that their lives appear almost ritualistic in their predictability. Probably the most common such character is the **hero.**

The hero's life revolves around adventures that are so familiar you should be able to identify several heroes as you read the following list of their lives' major events.

a. A hero's conception is typically unusual, and often by tradition his mother is a virgin.

b. Frequently, the hero must escape a plot to kill him soon after his birth.

c. Although little is known about his childhood, the hero grows to maturity in the home of foster parents after a narrow escape from death.

d. As a young man, the hero feels a longing for something other than what he has and begins a journey of "initiation."

e. Along the way the hero encounters temptation, is assisted by mystical beings, and usually travels a road of trials that brings him close to death.

f. The hero finds that for which he has searched and returns victorious.

g. Settling down, the hero often marries a beautiful princess, and becomes king.

h. After a long, and often uneventful rule, the hero finds himself no longer in the good graces of the gods, is driven from his kingdom, and mysteriously dies.

i. Although not officially buried, the hero typically has one or more holy graves.

While not all of these events occur in the life of each hero, the following heros clearly embody these ritualistic events:

King Arthur	Moses	Hercules
Jesus Christ	Perseus	Beowolf
Dionysus	Romulus	Siddhartha Gautama (Buddha)
Robin Hood	Siegfried	Mohammed
Oedipus	Theseus	Lao-tse
Jason	Superman	Osiris

The story of Oedipus follows the pattern of the archetypal hero. Identify the predictable events in the hero's life.

Oedipus

Shortly after the birth of their first child, Laius and Jocasta, King and Queen of Thebes, travel to Apollo's sanctuary, the Oracle at Delphi, to ask about their infant's destiny. The happy parents are horrified when the Oracle indicates that the child's fate is to murder his father and marry his mother. Feeling that they can not allow the god's prediction to occur, the parents decide that their child must not be allowed to live. To avoid the wrath of the gods, however, they can not actually kill him themselves. Rather, they order a servant shepherd of the palace to abandon the baby up on the mountainside: there he can die either from exposure or from wild animals, but the King and Queen can not be accused of murder.

155

In order to seal his fate absolutely, the child's feet are pinned together. This mutilation prevents the baby from crawling to safety, keeps him from coming back to haunt his parents after his death, and, they believe, makes him undesirable to save.

The shepherd who is ordered to abandon the child upon the mountain has no stomach for his assignment, however. He chances upon a shepherd from the neighboring city of Corinth and persuades him to take the injured child. This shepherd happens to be employed by the King and Queen of Corinth, Polybus and Merope, who are childless; consequently, when the mutilated infant is presented to them, they are happy to treat his wounds and adopt him as their own. He is the child for whom they have prayed to the gods for years.

Polybus and Merope name their new, adopted son Oedipus, which means swollen-foot, and pretend that he is their natural son, thus heir to the throne of Corinth.

As a young man Oedipus hears persistent rumors that he is adopted. Although his "parents" try to assure him that he is not, he journeys to the Oracle at Delphi to learn the truth from Apollo—the god of truth. The Oracle, in response to Oedipus' question about his parentage, states that he is destined to murder his father and marry his mother. Stunned, the young man immediately determines never to return to Corinth. Upon leaving Delphi he decides to travel to Thebes.

At a narrow crossroads on the Corinth, Delphi, Thebes highway he meets a cantankerous old man on a chariot who will not let him pass. The old man is Laius, King of Thebes, on his way to the Oracle at Delphi to ask Apollo's assistance in ridding the City of Thebes of a terrible monster, the Sphinx.

(The Sphinx, who has the body of a lion, the wings of an eagle, and the head of a woman, stands outside the city gates and asks travellers to answer her riddle—what walks on four legs in the morning, two legs at noon, and three legs in the evening? Anyone who cannot correctly answer the riddle is devoured.)

Old Laius attempts to run down Oedipus in the crossroads, but Oedipus quickly jumps aside and, as the chariot charges by, strikes Laius a killing blow with his staff. Infuriated after killing the old man, Oedipus subdues and kills all but one of King Laius' guards and attendants. The one man escapes to return to Thebes to tell of a whole band of robbers who have ambushed the group and assassinated the King. The city, however, has greater worries because the Sphinx is still on the edge of town killing whosoever fails to answer her riddle.

After the slaughter at the crossroads, Oedipus proceeds toward Thebes. Upon arriving at the city's outskirts, the Sphinx leaps out at him and demands that her riddle be correctly answered or she will devour him. She states her riddle and the wise Oedipus quickly and easily answers it—man crawls upon hands and feet in the morning of life, walks upright on two legs in the noon of life, and walks with the aid of a cane in the evening of life. Her riddle successfully answered, the Sphinx kills herself, and Oedipus is treated to a hero's welcome by the grateful citizens of Thebes. He is given wealth, made king, and given Queen Jocasta, widow of King Laius, in marriage.

Oedipus rules uneventfully for several years, but as his oldest children approach adulthood, a great plague that kills young things strikes the city. Again it is necessary to take some action to save Thebes. Therefore, Creon, Jocasta's brother, is sent to the Oracle at Delphi to find the source of this calamity whereupon a solution might be found.

(The play—Oedipus by Sophocles—unfolds at this point as the audience learns, along with Oedipus, this history.)

After the truth is discovered, Jocasta hangs herself; Oedipus blinds himself and is sent into exile. After many years of wandering in the desert, led about by his youngest daughter, Antigone, the gods feel that he has suffered enough. Consequently, they decide to take him directly into the underworld, to the land ruled over by Hades, without having to pass through death. Thus, the earth opens up and Oedipus is taken directly down; he does not die but joins the dead without the unpleasantness of death. The site where the ground opened up to accept him became his holy grave.

You should have noted that the traditional patterns of a hero's life are nearly all present in the story of Oedipus.

Other archetypal characters, like the hero, can be identified by what happens to them. Their experiences too are varied and are important in literature and mythology.

1. The *hero* (see above)
2. The *outcast* is a character who is condemned to wander after committing some crime against society. (e.g. Cain; The Ancient Mariner; Clare Walker in "The Loving Shepherdess"; Moses and the tribes of Israel)
3. The *devil* character is the personification of evil. He often offers fortune, fame, or power in return for a soul. (e.g. Lucifer; Mephistopheles; Satan; Beelzebub)
4. The *scapegoat* is a person whose death in a public ritual expiates the community's sins. (e.g. The victim in "The Lottery" by Shirley Jackson; Jesus; the Wickerman)
5. The *star-crossed lover's* relationship ends with the tragic death of one or both of them (e.g. *Romeo and Juliet*; *Antigone*; Psyche and Eros)
6. The *intellectual* (mathematician, astronomer, scientist, computer whiz)
   a. Anti-social - wicked or mad scientist. (e.g. Dr. Frankenstein)
   b. Neutral - Dr. Strangelove
   c. Pro-social - Mr. Spock of *Star Trek*
7. The *medicine woman*—Possessor of the knowledge of the healing powers of nature (Ayla & Iza in *Clan of the Cave Bear*; Morgan la Fay in the legends of King Arthur; Witches)
8. The *Shaman*—Holyman, possessor of the knowledge of the healing powers of the spirit world, guardian of the traditions and rituals of the people (Mogar in *Clan of the Cave Bear*; don Juan in the books of Carlos Castaneda; the witch doctor)
9. The *Trickster* is an ambiguous figure who is a fool and a cheat. He assumes many guises, both animal and human, to perform cruel tricks and practical jokes. (Old Man, Coyote, Raven, Maui, Br'er Rabbit, Hermes [Mercury], Cupid)

Still other archetypal characters you may wish to investigate:

10. sage	14. warrior	18. guru or disciple
11. artist	15. giant	19. the double
12. fool	16. king	20. the father
13. wise fool	17. child or innocent	

EXERCISE 7.5

Identify the archetypal characters in the following selections:

"Young Goodman Brown" (page 263)

_____

_____ _____

_____

"Ulysses" (page 224)

_____

_____

_____

A selection of your choice

_____

_____

_____

_____

Situation

Several recurrent archetypal *situations* have been identified in the world's literature through the use of Jung's analytical techniques. These situations are what the images suggest (page 151) and what the characters pursue (page 155). In one sense, the situation forms the basis for plot in the literature of the mythic story. Some of the most common situations are the *initiation*, the *task*, the *quest*, the *fall*, and *death and rebirth*.

Initiation situations are usually concerned with the passage from childhood to maturity or from maturity to the wisdom of old age. The initiation forms a ritual introduction into adult life. The initiation often symbolizes an increased awareness, a deeper perception, or an awakening to life, its meaning and its consequences. The initiation itself may be symbolic of those events in a culture that mark one's passage to maturity. In contemporary American society these symbolic acts involve such situations as acquiring a driver's license, graduating from high school or college, having the first date, voting the first time, and drinking the first "legal" alcoholic beverage. (For examples in literature see *The Adventures of Huckleberry Finn, Catcher in the Rye, Look Homeward, Angel*, and Stephen King's "The Body.")

Although the task and the quest are closely related, a difference does exist. In the task, a hero must perform some extraordinary, difficult feat in order to reassert his authority, marry the beautiful princess, or save the kingdom (e.g. Odysseus

158

strings the great bow after all others have failed, and Arthur pulls the great sword Excaliber from a stone). The quest, on the other hand, involves a great search for someone or something that will bring about returned fertility to the land or a lost rightness and order to the world. The quest is in reality a large task - so large that often many of the participants cannot comprehend the end goal (e.g. the quest for The Grail; the quest for the great white whale, Moby Dick; Jason's quest for the golden fleece).

The archetype of "the fall" describes a loss of power, status, or innocence. Accompanying the fall is, typically, a banishment from paradise, a state of pure happiness or bliss, to some less desirable locale. Resulting from moral misbehavior or disobedience, the punishment sometimes lasts for generations (e.g. Adam and Eve; Prometheus; Tantalus).

One of the most popular archetypal situations with mythmakers and writers involves the cycles of death and rebirth. A close relationship exists between nature and life and their similar cycles. For example, death imagery suggests fall and winter because the natural environment's vegetation appears to die. Spring and summer, on the other hand, bring new life, a kind of rebirth; therefore, these seasons represent birth (or rebirth) and youth. Fertility rites, anthropologists suggest, are springtime activities because nature appears to support the ritual. Literature is filled with the close association of death with winter and birth with abundance. Frost's "Stopping by Woods on a Snowy Evening" set in winter, suggests death; Cummings' "in Just—" set in spring, suggests rebirth.

EXERCISE 7.6

Look again at the short story "Young Goodman Brown." Identify which archetypal situations exist in the story and write two or three sentences summarizing each.

_____

_____

_____

_____

_____

_____

_____

_____

_____

_____

Shadow, Anima, and Persona

On a much deeper plane than images, characters or situations, archetypal analysis is also concerned with the individual human psyche. Unlike Freud, however, Jung's approach is to probe the characters' psyches in literature in order to understand better the characters themselves, not to probe the psychological problems that may have confronted the author. As a result, you may find this approach somewhat more useful than Freud's therapeutic psychological analysis.

Shadow

Jung believed that, in addition to the collective unconscious, the mind has a personal subconscious. The darker part of this region he referred to as the **shadow**. In the shadow reside the less pleasant aspects of the personality. This dark part of the personality, often dangerous, belongs to the primitive, uncivilized, pre-evolutionary past of the species. The shadow holds emotions such as jealousy and repressed desires such as avarice, which most people would prefer not to recognize as part of their being. In literature, the shadow is represented by such characters as Iago in Shakespeares's *Othello*, Kurtz in Conrad's "Heart of Darkness," and the Lord of the Flies in Goldings's novel of the same name. In old Hollywood westerns the villain is the shadow character; in the movie fantasy *Star Wars* it is Darth Vader.

Anima (Animus)

While the shadow exists in everyone and is not a part of the personality we like to admit to, the **anima** is the element that sets humans apart from other animals. The anima is the *life force*, the vital energy within everyone; it is the part of people that is living and causes life. Jung asserts that without the anima people would deteriorate into pathological idleness. The anima figures are central to most literature because this is the most interesting part of the human personality.

One of the anima's functions is to mediate disputes within the personality, between consciousness and the unconscious. Moreover, the anima is a bisexual characteristic which mirrors in man a feminine image. In other words, within every man resides a female image that reveals herself in dreams or projections upon others in the environment. In women, this life force is referred to as the **animus** and is a masculine part of her psyche. For example, in the Hollywood western the anima is represented by the heroine. In *Star Wars* it is Princess Leia. According to Jung, the anima is responsible for feelings of love because when a man finds a woman who closely mirrors his anima, he will come to love her. The more closely she resembles his anima the more likely love will grow quickly. This, Jung believes, explains the phenomenon of love at first sight. Operating in the same way as the anima, a woman who finds a man who mirrors her inner animus will fall in love with him. The anima (animus) is the life force, the center of ambition and creativity.

The anima (animus) generally represents a background of the psyche close to the unconscious. Any person who dwells within his or her contrasexual self (male living in his female self or female living in her male self) lives in his or her psychic background and takes on some of the outward cultural characteristics of the other gender (e.g. an effeminate man or a masculine woman). However, our society often views as undesirable some of the traits that develop from living within one's contrasexual self. While women have a reputation for deep sensitivity and feelings, men who live in the anima are often characterized by undisciplined and irrational feelings. While men have a reputation for rational and independent thinking, women who live in the animus are often characterized as autocratic and aggressive. Each of these characteristics, in this view, is a distortion of each gender's major attributes. In recent years, however, cultural attitudes have been changing. The idea that the "whole person" will ideally develop some sort of androgynous mix between animus and anima characteristics has gained increasing acceptance. The conflict between the conscious and unconscious may represent the beginnings of neuroses, and it helps in the analysis of many literary characters (e.g. Willy Loman in *Death of a Salesmen*; Piggy in *Lord of the Flies*).

Some of the Characteristics Attributed to the Anima/Animus

ANIMA	*ANIMUS*
Yin	Yang
female principle	male principle
(dark, water, earth)	(light, fire, air)
1. passive	1. ego-centered
2. affected by environment	2. separated from environment
3. non-aggressive	3. aggressive
4. peaceful	4. prone to violence
5. conservative	5. inventive
6. irrational	6. rational
7. intuitive, emotional	7. logical, analytical
8. undisciplined, chaotic	8. disciplined, ordered
9. cooperative, communal	9. independent, individualistic
10. possessive	10. autocratic, hierarchical
11. democratic	11. authoritarian
12. subjective	12. objective

Persona

The **persona** is a concept that is perhaps more familiar. Simply put, the persona is the social personality or actor's mask that everyone puts on to face the world. Ofttimes, the persona is perceived as quite different from one's true self. The chief function of the persona is to mediate between the ego and the world outside. A personality that is psychologically healthy and mature must possess a persona that is flexible. The healthy persona is represented by the hero in the Hollywood western. In *Star Wars* it is Luke Skywalker. If, on the other hand, one's persona is too rigid, too inflexible, problems of personality and symptoms of neuroses may begin to develop, as with the character, Dr. Phillips, in "The Snake."

The persona is, then, the face we all put on to show the world (hero); the anima (animus) is the vital life force that gives us creativity and makes us human (heroine); the shadow is the darker side of the personality wherein reside the elements we often wish to suppress (villain).

Granted, many literary characters may be better understood by comparing their behavior with the principles of archetypal analysis, but in using the archetypal approach one must strive to remember that first and foremost, literature is art. It is much more than a clever medium for conveying mythic rituals and archetypes.

EXERCISE 7.7

From the short story "Young Goodman Brown," (page 263) identify the shadow, the anima, and the persona. In two or three sentences, explain how each of your identifications fits Jung's theory.

Shadow _____

explanation

_____

_____

_____

_____

Anima _____

explanation

_____

_____

_____

_____

Persona _____

explanation

_____

_____

_____

_____

_____

Mythology

A popular misconception about mythology is that it is synonymous with the word false, something that is believed only by the naive, the uneducated, or the primitive. (e.g. If, for instance, upon leaving its burrow on February second a groundhog casts a shadow, six weeks more of winter can be anticipated; if, however, it has no shadow, anticipate an early spring.) In contrast to the popular notion that they are untrue, myths make no comment whatsoever on whether or not a belief is literally true or not. What, then, is myth?

Some Definitions of Myth

1. "Myths are original revelations of the pre-conscious psyche, involuntary statements about unconscious psychic happenings . . . ." *Carl Jung*
2. "Myth [is] a dramatic presentation of the moral wisdom of the race. The myth uses the totality of the senses rather than just the intellect." *Rollo May*
3. "Myth is the secret opening through which inexhaustible energies of the cosmos pour into human cultural manifestations." *Joseph Campbell*
4. "Myths are things which never happened but always are." *Carl Sagan*
5. "Myth . . . is the distilled essence of human experience, expressed as metaphoric narrative." *John Alexander Allen*
6. "Myth is metaphor." *Joseph Campbell*
7. Myth is whatever a people believe or behave as though they believe.
   Richard Guches

Joseph Campbell, the foremost contemporary scholar of the world's mythologies, suggests that mythology has four essential functions:

Essential Functions of Mythology

1. Mythology awakens and perpetuates for each individual a sense of wonder and participation in the mystery of the universe. If mystery is manifest through all things, the universe becomes a holy picture. Myth evokes the experience of mystery and of awe.

Myth (Pima Indian—Southern Arizona)

In the beginning there was only darkness everywhere—darkness and water. And the darkness gathered thick in places, crowding together and then separating, crowding and separating until at last out of one of the places where the darkness had crowded there came forth a man. This man wandered through the darkness until he began to think; then he knew himself and that he was a man; he knew that he was there for some purpose.

The man put his hand over his heart and drew forth a large stick. He used the stick to help him through the darkness, and when he was weary he rested upon it. Then he made for himself little ants; he brought them from his body and put them on the stick. Everything that he made he drew from his own body even as he had drawn the stick from his heart. The stick was of greasewood, and of the gum of the wood the ants made a round ball from the stick and put it down in the darkness under his foot, and as he stood upon the ball he rolled it under his foot . . . . So the world was made. And now the man

163

brought from himself a rock and divided it into little pieces. Of these he made stars, and put them in the sky to light the darkness. But the stars were not bright enough.

So the man made Tau-muk, the Milky Way. Yet Tau-muk was not bright enough. Then he made the moon. All of these he made of rocks drawn forth from himself. But even the moon was not bright enough. So he began to wonder what next he could do. He could bring nothing from himself that could lighten the darkness.

Then the man thought. And from himself he made two large bowls, and he filled the one with water and covered it with the other. He sat and watched the bowls, and while he watched he wished that what he wanted to make in very truth would come to be. And it was even as he wished. For the water in the bowl turned into the sun and shone out in rays through the cracks where the bowls joined.

When the sun was make, the man lifted off the top bowl and took out the sun and threw it to the east. But the sun did not touch the ground; it stayed in the sky where he threw it and never moved. Then in the same way he threw the sun to the north and to the west and to the south. But each time it only stayed in the sky, motionless, for it never touched the ground. Then he threw it once more to the east, and this time it touched the ground and bounced and started upward. Since then the sun has never ceased to move. It goes around the world in a day, but every morning it must bounce anew in the east.

Interpretation

As discussed under Recurrent Characteristics (page 146), all peoples have myths of the origin of the universe. While they serve the first function of mythology - as the above story inspires a sense of wonder and participation in the mystery of the universe for the Pima Indians—they often, in addition, function as *aetiological myths*, those which explain the origins of objects or customs. In this fashion, the Pima tale explains not only the beginning of the universe but why it contains the stars, the Milky Way, the moon, the sun, even why the sun traverses the sky from east to west.

2. Mythology gives a deeply mystical importance to whatever image of the universe a people share. Myth shows one what the shape of the universe is, the larger order of the physical universe of which one's particular life and culture is a part. This is the dimension with which science is concerned, but science provides answers only in one dimension. Science can tell one how certain aspects of life work, but cannot answer the fundamental questions of what life really is and why. Myth addresses these questions.

Myth (Greek)

In the beginning, there was chaos. Chaos divided into two deities, Uranus (overhanging heavens) and Gaea (Mother Earth). Among their children, one group, the mighty Titans, became the rulers of the Universe. Chief among these early gods was Cronus (Father Time) who feared a child born to his wife Rhea (Mother Goddess) would become sufficiently powerful to rise up and usurp his rule. Consequently, he swallowed each of his children at birth (Hestia, Demeter, Hera, Hades, and Poseidon). Eventually, Rhea, tiring of his treachery, concealed a newborn from her husband, substituting in its place, a stone which Cronus swallowed believing it his child. The child, Zeus, was spirited away to Crete where he was reared and taught to master the thunderbolt, a formidable weapon. Upon reaching maturity, he returned to confront his father, and in the ensuing conflict for power, he mortally wounded Cronus, forcing him to vomit out the swallowed children. Zeus and his brothers and sisters became the first of the Olympian gods of Greece.

164

Interpretation

For the Greeks, one of the most important images of the universe was the mystical concept of fate, represented by the passage of time. Yet, only mortals are subject to time; the gods are immune. The story of Cronus (Father Time) swallowing his children is an image that demonstrated for the Greeks, in a visually understandable way, how each individual is ultimately "swallowed up by time." The Olympian gods were not subject to the forces of time, however, because Zeus had fought Father Time (Cronus) and defeated him. Consequently, the gods were immortal, free from the entrapment of time, free from the threat of being swallowed up by time. Through this story the image of the universe, of which time is an integral part, is given mystical importance.

3. Mythology supports and validates a particular social order, providing the basis for a moral system, customs, and ethical laws - the laws of life as they "should" be in a *good* society. Here is where the myths vary enormously from culture to culture and era to era.

Myth (Hebrew)

1 And Adam knew Eve his wife; and she conceived, and bare Cain, and said, I have gotten a man from the Lord.

2 And she again bare his brother Abel. And Abel was a keeper of sheep, but Cain was a tiller of the ground.

3 And in process of time it came to pass, that Cain brought of the fruit of the ground an offering unto the Lord.

4 And Abel, he also brought of the firstlings of his flock and of the fat thereof. And the Lord had respect unto Abel and to his offering.

5 But unto Cain and to his offering he had not respect. And Cain was very wroth, and his countenance fell.

6 And the Lord said unto Cain, Why art thou wroth? and why is thy countenance fallen?

7 If thou doest well, shalt thou not be accepted? and if thou doest not well, sin lieth at the door. And unto thee shall be his desire, and thou shalt rule over him.

8 And Cain talked with Abel his brother: and it came to pass, when they were in the field that Cain rose up against Abel his brother and slew him.

9 And the Lord said unto Cain, Where *is* Abel thy brother? And he said, I know not: *Am* I my brother's keeper?

10 And he said, What hast thou done? The voice of thy brother's blood crieth unto me from the ground.

11 And now *art* thou cursed from the earth, which hath opened her mouth to receive thy brother's blood from thy hand;

12 When thou tillest the ground, it shall not henceforth yield unto thee her strength; a fugitive and vagabond shalt thou be in the earth.

Interpretation

The myth of Cain and Abel reinforced the moral code of the Hebrew people by dramatizing how easy it is to fall into the sin of envy and pride. Sin, this story suggests, is waiting to attack, thirsting to destroy the unwary. And the punishment for those who fail to obey the will of God is banishment from both land and God.

4. Mythology harmoniously conducts individuals through the cycles of their lives—birth and the dependency of childhood, the responsibilities of maturity, old age and the passage into death. Myths teach one how to live. They serve to guide one through all the passages of life, to recognize where one is on the journey, and how to keep going. They do the same for the society as a whole.

Myth (Australia)

In the great night before people, there was only Sky and Earth. In the earth dwelt Ungud, in the form of a great snake; in the sky dwelt Wallanganda, the Milky Way. Wallanganda dropped water on the earth, and Ungud made it deep. In the night Ungud and Wallanganda dreamed and life arose on the earth in forms from their dreams. From Wallanganda's dreaming came images that he projected onto rocks and into caves, where the red, white, and black paintings may be seen to this day. Once painted, Wallanganda multiplied the forms in the shape of living beings, the animals of the earth. The paintings are the spiritual center of the animals. They are the fathers while the living beings of each kind are brothers.

Ungud's dreaming created spiritual germs on earth, and he will not let his creations die. At the bottom of the water he discovered Wondjina (anthropomorphic beings that personify rain represented in cave paintings). Wherever Wondjina went they brought rain, and while the rocks were still wet, they lay down upon them periodically and sank into the earth, leaving impressions behind that remain today as rock paintings. Each lake, river, or spring is owned by a specific Wondjina whose image is nearby and who dwells under the water that lies beneath the earth under the painting. These Wondjina create child-germs (which are part of the Wondjina, consequently, part of Ungud). During dream, a man will find one of these child-germs, which, in a subsequent dream, he projects into his wife's dream where it assumes human form. The germ is that portion of the spirit that returns at death to the waterhole to await reincarnation.

The rightful inhabitants of a region are all those who are descended from the same Wondjina. The oldest in a region is considered the Wondjina incarnate. During Dream Time (annually), it is his duty to renew (repaint) the cave images before the rainy season. When the painting is done, he fills his mouth with water and blows it onto the image. Later, when rain comes, it is regarded as the Wondjina's, therefore a gift from Ungud.

Interpretation

Dream Time is that time when the people, in ritual and ceremony, re-enact the local founding drama. In so doing, each individual draws upon the creative power of the Dreaming (especially useful in times of sickness, death, or need) to celebrate the continuity of life. During Dream Time people re-establish their connections with their spiritual lives, "remember" their origins, celebrate their progress along life's journey, and anticipate their reunion with their individual creator (Wondjina) as they await reincarnation. They are conducted harmoniously through their lives.

As varied as different people's mythologies appear, they all seem to serve these four essential functions. Myths accomplish this through the poetic technique of analogy, a comparison of two objects or ideas. In analogy, an unfamiliar concept is compared to a familiar one in order to explain it. In literary terms, a simile is an *expressed* analogy while a metaphor is an *implied* one (see pages 19-21). Many mythic, archetypal analogies are recurrently recognized (death and sleep; sunlight and consciousness; caves and wombs; waning and waxing of the moon and celestial death and rebirth; snakes shedding their skins and earthly death and rebirth) while others are culturally specific, applicable to only one group of people (the elephant as an earthbound cloud in Hindu myth; the seven days of a seven day week as the Creation and God's Rest in monotheism (Judeo-Christian-Islamic myth). Mythology is, then, the principal analogy that interprets the mysteries of life and the universe and as such is as applicable to the lives of people now as to all peoples in the past.

EXERCISE 7.8

Find and rewrite in your own words two old myths, interpreting in a paragraph or two how they fit Joseph Campbell's essential functions. (Name the country or people and give the myth a title.)

Myth #1

Name of people _____

_____

Title _____

Myth #2

Name of people _____

_____

Title _____

EXERCISE 7.9

Find and rewrite in your own words two contemporary myths, interpreting in a paragraph or two how they fit Joseph Campbell's essential functions.

(Name the country or people and give the myth a title.)

Myth #1

Name of people _____

_____

Title _____

Myth #1

Name of people _____

_____

Title _____

Read the following two papers for archetypal analysis in practice.

Margaret Harbridge

English 1B MWF 9:00

Dr. Guches

2 June, 1988

(Archetypal Analysis)

"Home is the Sailor . . ."

In his poem "Ulysses," Alfred, Lord Tennyson speculates on the
nature of human existence. After preparing to set sail, Ulysses is ready
to embark on his final voyage, a journey from which he will never return.
The mood of the poem is so stirring, the spirit of Ulysses is so noble
and admirable that readers may easily overlook the aspect of escapism.
Ulysses is actually a man well past his prime who abandons his aged wife,
his responsibilities, the people under his rule, and leaves his son to
"make mild a rugged people, and through soft degrees/Subdue them to the
useful and the good."

Ulysses, King of Ithaca, is a legendary Greek hero. He is a major
figure in Homer's Iliad, the hero of Homer's Odyssey, and a minor figure
in Dante's Divine Comedy. After ten years at the siege of Troy, Ulysses
set sail for home. Having incurred the wrath of Poseidon, god of the
sea, however, he is subjected to many storms and difficulties. He is
forced to wander for another ten years, having many adventures and seeing
most of the Mediterranean world before again reaching Ithaca, his wife
Penelope, and their son Telemachus. But once home, he still wishes to
travel and "to follow virtue and knowledge like a sinking star." As
Tennyson presents him, Ulysses is a combination of two archetypal
characters: the hero and the outcast.

Just as with the traditional hero, Ulysses is the ruler of a kingdom
and renowned in battle. At the same time, however, he may be regarded as
an outcast. Although he has not committed a crime against his countrymen
(except, perhaps, one of neglect) and he is not driven from his kingdom,
Ulysses is condemned to wander by his very nature. Despite his
responsibilities and duties as ruler of Ithaca, he speaks of himself as
an "idle king" and refers with contempt to the "common duties" which face
him. Ulysses' sense of alienation from his surroundings is not only a

common Tennysonian motif but is also present throughout much of literature.

Tennyson's dramatic monologue may be divided into three parts. Lines one through thirty-two are mainly concerned with Ulysses' previous exploits. Lines thirty-three through forty-four describe his uneventful present. Finally, in lines forty-five through seventy, Ulysses resolves to set forth once again on his quest for a "newer world" and an eternal rest. Together these make up the entire range of all people's experience. The past, the present, and the future of people's lives represent the extent of their beings - the cycle or wholeness of their lives.

In his description of Ulysses' experiences, Tennyson presents him as a larger-than-life character. The poet gives to him an intensity and capacity to live far beyond that of any ordinary man. Ulysses says, "All times I have enjoyed/Greatly, have suffered greatly." These qualities possessed by Ulysses are the very attributes which make him a legendary character. He speaks in grandiose terms like other literary egotists, such as Macbeth and Othello. "I am become a name . . . Much have I seen and known . . . Myself not least, but honored of them all . . . I am a part of all that I have met." Perhaps that which is most noble (or audacious) in Ulysses, and distinguishes him from his countrymen, and even his mariners, is his aspiration to be like the gods. He wishes to "follow knowledge like a sinking star/Beyond the utmost bound of human thought," and to undertake "some work of noble note . . . Not unbecoming men that strove with Gods."

In this poem, it is interesting to note that the archetypal soulmate of Ulysses is not his wife, but rather his fellow mariners. Ulysses feels no affinity with his agèd wife, Penelope. His comradeship with his mariners is the source of his spiritual inspiration and fulfillment. He speaks lovingly of these mariners as "Souls that have toiled, and wrought, and thought with me--/That ever with a frolic welcome took/The thunder and the sunshine. . . ." In his old age Ulysses abandons his wife and his homeland to be with his mariners. "You and I are old/Old age hath yet his honor and his toil."

The symbolic significance of the poet having Ulysses, at last, sail

169

westward can be explained in two ways. This ancient hero wishes to free himself from the limitations of his present life, and the reader at once envisions the unknown lands that await an adventurous spirit. Also, in traditional literary imagery, a journey westward suggests the conclusion or death of something which once existed. Ulysses' ship and the water imagery present in the poem symbolize his voyage through life which is at last coming to an end. With his nobility and greatness of character, it is especially fitting that Ulysses would exit with an assertion or challenge to "strive, to seek, to find, and not to yield."

Theresa A. Moravec

English 1B   MWF 11:00

Dr. Guches

5 June 1989

(Archetypal Analysis)

Blood and the Hunt

The mystery of death will forever grip the hearts of human beings. Is death the culmination of the existence known to humans or the continuance of life in a different form? In his short story "The Old People," William Faulkner speculates naturalistically on the universal question: is there life after death? The story exists in parallel form: a young boy's journey to manhood by making his first kill on a hunt and secondly, a more universal story that likens life to an ongoing hunt with the kill representing death. The archetypal motif of immortality is explored throughout Faulkner's story with symbolic images of blood and forest representing life and the symbolic image of the hunt representing death.

The symbolic imagery of blood is vivid, recurring, and runs throughout the story to emphasize the symbol of life. Sam Fathers, the hunter, was born with "the blood of slaves and warriors and chiefs" flowing in his veins while Boon Hogganbeck's blood ran "white." The "hot smoking blood," of Isaac's freshly killed buck is wiped across his face. Isaac dreams of his first kill when ". . . he would draw the blood, the big blood which would make him a man, a hunter. . . ." The deer's blood represents its life force. Blood is the gift of life. Jesus Christ shed His blood and died so that the unrighteous might repent and live everlasting lives. Menses is the flow of blood from the uterus of females that occurs monthly, yet it is an integral part of the breeding life cycle of men and women. Faulkner's symbolic use of blood is inherent to the archetypal motif of immortality.

Faulkner's forest represents humankind's life environment. Isaac had ". . . an unforgettable sense of the big woods - not a quality dangerous or particularly inimical, but profound, sentient, gigantic and brooding. . . ." Although the forest bears representation of the positive life symbols through water images of rain, dew, and

condensation, it also presents a symbolic image of death as the place of
the hunt (death), the slaughterhouse of deer and bear. However,
Faulkner's forest is replenished with ". . . bear and deer, hunter's
meat. . . ." The naturalistic life/death cycle of Darwin's survival of
the fittest reinforces the concept of life renewal.

The hunt is symbolic of death. "Once each year, in the late fall,
in November, the boy would watch the wagon . . . being loaded . . . and
go into the big bottom of the Tallahatchie where the deer and bear were,
to be gone two weeks." Sam Fathers hunted with Isaac ". . . in the
November or December woods." In traditional literary motif, a hunt in
the fall or waning months of the year represents the conclusion or
impending death of something that once was living. It is interesting to
note that the preparatory hunting skills taught to Isaac by Sam Fathers
occur in the summer and spring months. The two would ". . . sit beneath
the close fierce stars on a summer hilltop while they waited for the
hounds to bring the fox back. . . ." And they were ". . . fireless in
the pitch dark and heavy dew of April mornings while they squatted
beneath a turkey-roost." As the calendar year completes its annual
cycle, the living mourn the deterioration of fall yet rejoice in the
approaching rejuvenation of spring.

"The Old People" represents the archetypal motif of immortality.
Faulkner uses the blood and forest as positive life symbols. He
represents death by the hunt. These symbols demonstrate that life and
death are cyclical and unending. The answer to the universal question
about immortality, however, remains an individual quest, a quest sought
by millions of human beings through centuries of time.

172

Feminist Analysis

Analytical approaches, like literature itself, evolve, adapt, or fall from popular esteem. The ones discussed in the preceding chapters have been or are consistently prominent. One relatively new approach that seems to be increasingly important is *feminist analysis*. While it borrows from other analytical points of view, its main thrust is somewhat different. For instance, feminist critics challenge the traditional view that other analytical perspectives are objective and free from bias. The fact is, they assert, a sexist point of view has dominated the thinking of those who would closely examine the world's literatures. Claiming that most previous criticism has emphasized a male-dominated point of view, feminist analysis condemns any critical perspective that strives for universality while neglecting feminine consciousness. An outgrowth of the contemporary women's liberation movement, begun during the 1960s, feminist analysis grew rapidly in scope and influence during the 1970s and continues to influence social and literary scholarship today.

Objectives:

After completing this chapter, you will be able to:

1. Identify the major elements of feminist analysis.
2. Assess the political goals of feminist writers.
3. Distinguish between realistic and sexist literature from a feminist perspective.
4. Analyze a literary selection for its androgynous characteristics.
5. Differentiate between female and male perspectives.

6. Evaluate the influence of Jung on feminist analysis.
7. Recognize feminist objections to other critical approaches.
8. Demonstrate critical but unbiased judgement in evaluating reading and viewing choices.

Pre-assessment:

_____ 1. Feminists challenge the idea that previous analysis shows universality while ignoring, (A) the images of women, (B) feminine consciousness, (C) women's political history, (D) women's roles as mothers, (E) the feminine mystique.

_____ 2. Many feminist critics feel that the primary objective of feminist analysis should be, (A) political and social, (B) social and sexual, (C) only descriptive, (D) psychosexual, (E) social Freudianism.

_____ 3. Previous analysis needs to be reevaluated because, (A) there is little new literature to analyze, (B) it's good experience, (C) previous analysis is male-dominated, (D) few women can relate to male writers, (E) it relies too little on Freud.

_____ 4. The ideal literature to feminists is, (A) female dominated, (B) when each sex is in its prescribed role, (C) erotic, (D) androgynous, (E) romantic.

_____ 5. Feminists feel that the archetypal analysis of Jung, (A) is preferable for its emphasis of the sexes, (B) is most chauvinistic of all analytical perspectives, (C) is without logical foundation, (D) undervalues the roles of women, (E) neglects the contributions of the housewife.

_____ 6. Feminist critics condemn the Great Works because they, (A) are Freudian, (B) were selected from Europe, (C) combine approaches, (D) do not include any literature from a female perspective, (E) they emphasize sociology.

_____ 7. Feminist analysis is, in part, an outgrowth of, (A) the anti-war movement, (B) women's liberation movement, (C) the anti-nuclear movement, (D) the movement to secure the right to vote for women, (E) all of the above.

_____ 8. Feminist critics feel that formalists are, (A) most sympathetic to feminism, (B) most objective, (C) least prejudicial, (D) eclectic, (E) not objective.

FEMINIST ANALYSIS

During the turbulent social upheavals of the 1960s and 1970s, several new analytical perspectives surfaced. The struggle for racial equality created new interest in the literature of the black experience. The liberation movement for homosexuals stimulated an interest in the literature of homosexual writers and its criticism. Considering the depth of the turmoil, the protests, the multiple demands for change, however, no social crusade has stimulated as much new literature, as much new publication of previously neglected writers, nor such sustained new criticism as that of the women's liberation movement. Consequently, although feminism is over 200 years old, in the space of only two decades feminist criticism has achieved a position that demands that modern readers give it serious consideration.

As with any general protest movement, those interested in the liberation of women have the opinion that the contemporary values of the society are inherently unfair. In particular, members of this movement feel that the patriarchal (male-dominated) society is dehumanizing to over half, if not most of the population. Feminists, whose ranks include both men and women, assert that society must be reoriented toward a system that eliminates the dominance of a male-oriented power structure. Out of this struggle for liberation and equality has developed new feminist literary perspectives which challenge the view that analysis is genderless. For example, feminists question any critical perspective, such as formalism, that professes universality while excluding even the acknowledgement of the existence of a feminine consciousness.

Although feminist analysis may lack some of the unity of a traditional criticism because it is still an emerging perspective, three main points of emphasis among feminist critics are identifiable:

1. Feminist analysis should be principally social and political.
2. Literature that has been previously analyzed should be reanalyzed.
3. Literature and analysis should strive to achieve an androgynous perspective.

1. *Political and Social*—Feminist scholars who adopt the political/social focus challenge the claim of "mainstream" analytical criticism that it is objective, for too much analysis ignores literature's social environment. These feminists assert that the supposed objectivity of formalists, for example, is specious: formalists not only neglect a primary explanation for motivation (discrimination within the environment) but actually perpetuate discrimination by undervaluing the role of females in the social setting of the literature. Likewise, contextual analysis lacks objectivity by promoting literary sexism in undervaluing the literary contributions of women writers. In contrast to these views, feminist analysis strives to acknowledge the social context of literature and asserts a political viewpoint by emphasizing the roles of women within the historical context of the writer and the literature.

To accomplish these ends, feminist analysis is often not merely descriptive, but also prescriptive, describing a situation and suggesting an appropriate formula for change. The prescriptive view accepts the relevance of a social context to the analysis itself. Feminists suggest that it is through this prescriptive analysis that the women's liberation movement may best be served, awareness increased, and attitudes changed. Making no claim of final objectivity, feminists and feminist critics wish to be instruments of change—toward the ideals of liberation and equality. Literature, in this view, can become a central focus for an increasing awareness of oppression, thus inspiring political involvement.

2. *Reanalyzing Literature*—Many feminists suggest that since previous analysis is so male dominated, previously analyzed literature must be reevaluated from a feminist perspective. Feminists are often particularly critical of the psychological theories of Sigmund Freud. Freud's theories are attacked for their general disregard for the feminine psyche, including grossly inaccurate views of feminine anatomy and erotic experience. Moreover, such critics assert that Freud failed to consider the implications of a social environment's oppression of women and, as a

175

result, erred in his diagnoses of the source of his women patient's neuroses. Worse, they charge, Freud generalized from his experiences with psychotics to describe the female population at large. These generalizations and errors subsequently led to simplistic theories regarding the experience of the female psyche, such as male envy and immature parenthood. Many feminists conclude that the preference for Freud, among any number of practicing psychologists of his day, constitutes a further extension of political oppression against women—coming as it did at the very time when women were achieving the right to vote, developing the beginnings of effective birth control, introducing the Equal Rights Amendment (1923), and, for the first time, being granted custody of their children in divorce settlements. They feel Freud's psychological views overly influenced literary analysis in ways that were, and continue to be, detrimental to the interests of women.

Feminists also often criticize theories of Carl Jung for his failure to recognize and include a feminine consciousness, and assert that this omission has led to mistaken literary analyses. Basically, feminists suggest that archetypal analysis fundamentally undervalues the roles of women, a point which even Jung admitted late in life. This underemphasis of women may be readily observed by comparing the many archetypal male characters with the few archetypal images of women. Although a traditional patriarchal value system will naturally privilege males, feminists believe that any society that strives for equality must look beyond rigid, stereotypical views of people in order to value all human beings—male and female—by emphasizing their equal importance. Many feminists critics, however, employ Jung's archetypal analysis of male characters, but they adapt and extrapolate from his theories to provide better understanding of female characters. This involves emphasizing females in literature as archetypal characters, rather than merely images. Consequently, many feminist critics are concerned with the images of women as they have persisted in the work of male writers who have a male bias, and with the analysis of women writers whose work has previously been analyzed with the same bias or, perhaps worse, not reviewed at all.

Another goal of feminist scholars is to expose cultural circumstances that narrowly prescribe the function and the role of the female. History, they suggest, is only the record of the authoritative male experience, written primarily by men from a male perspective. This results in a seriously distorted history that ignores the female experience and neglects the female past. Likewise, those who have "canonized" certain *Great Works* by claiming that they are superior because they represent universal human truths simply demonstrate their adherence to a male bias. Feminists, therefore, wish to engage in a complete rereading and reanalyzing of the entire literary inheritance.

In addition to reanalysis, feminist critics argue that a major effort is also needed to recover and analyze the work of those women writers who were neglected by the literary establishment. In search of a female literary tradition, feminist scholars have noted themes, images, metaphors, and situations unique to women writers. Since the values of the male culture were different, all too many of the works by women have been lost. As a result, female literary tradition is incomplete and in need of rediscovery and the kind of analysis that reflects women's experience. The short story "The Yellow Wallpaper" (page 253) is an example of one such previously neglected work.

3. *An Androgynous Perspective*—Many feminists emphasize that in both analysis and literature the ideal to be achieved is an androgynous (from the Greek *andros* = man + *gyne* = woman) perspective, which stresses a combined male/female point of view. Moving beyond sexism, beyond even the sexes, this view emphasizes shifting away from male-oriented cultures toward a world where the aesthetics and feelings of both female and male are fused. The cultural enrichment possible through an androgynous point of view, feminists assert, will be the fruition of decades of struggle.

What an androgynous society and thus an androgynous literature might be like is indicative of feminist idealism and feminist goals. In androgynous literature, characters do not have prescribed, stereotypical roles simply because of their sex. The most fundamental feminist belief, the right of each individual to have free, open, and unpredetermined choices, is emphasized. The themes move beyond the rigidity of sexism to deal with all characters' unique humanness without regard to a character's gender. For example, characters' occupations—farmers, doctors, lawyers, mechanics, truckdrivers, firefighters, ministers, presidents, nurses, secretaries, or grammar school teachers—do not determine their gender. Furthermore, unlike the current fashion of certain performers who simply cross-dress like the other gender, the androgynous point of view emphasizes each person's bisexual nature as emphasized in Jung's theory about the anima/animus. (See page 160.) Each individual, in this view, has the natural or cultural characteristics of both sexes: creativity, logic, independence, tenderness, intuition, and emotion. As a movement and as an ideal, feminists believe that one of the best ways to illustrate that for which they have so long fought is through realistic androgynous literature like the works of Doris Lessing (*Briefing for a Descent into Hell*) and Dorothy Bryant (*The Kin of Ata are Waiting for You, Prisoners*) and through androgynous analysis.

Read Charlotte Perkins Gilman's short story "The Yellow Wallpaper" (page 253) then read the essay "The Pitfalls of Womanhood" by Dan Salter to see feminist analysis in practice.

Dan Salter

English 1B   8 TTH

Dr. Guches

17 April 1989

(Feminist Analysis)

The Pitfalls of Womanhood

Charlotte Perkins Gilman's short story, "The Yellow Wallpaper," is a story about the traps a society sets for women. The story concerns the attitudes held by the dominant male society towards women and the attitudes women have towards themselves. The unnamed protagonist who narrates the story and her husband, John, are both one dimensional characters symbolizing different aspects of society. These characters are purposely never fully developed because to do so would diminish their symbolic effect. Gilman's extensive use of symbolism illustrates some of the many pitfalls that a woman must face in a society dominated by men.

John symbolizes the stifling attitudes held by many men. He continually forces demeaning roles on women. He "absolutely forbids" his wife to work at anything except entertaining and ordering. He repeatedly states that his wife is just being a "silly girl" and is not really sick, but he allows her to be sick because "she'll be as sick as she pleases." He will not allow her to see her baby, a particularly demoralizing and humiliating situation for a person to endure. "It is fortunate Mary is good with the baby. Such a dear baby! And yet I <u>cannot</u> be with him, it makes me so nervous." He also suggests that his wife should have more self-control, implying that she cannot control herself. ". . . John says if I feel so, I shall neglect proper self-control, so I take pains to control myself before him . . . . He says . . . that I must use my will and self-control and not let any silly fancies run away with me." He also forbids his wife to write, believing that the writing will lead to "flights of fancy." "There comes John, and I must put this away--he hates to have me write a word." Attempting to stifle his wife's creativity is particularly repressive for writing is her sole mental release.

John also epitomzies the repressive attitudes of science. "He is practical to the extreme. He has no patience with faith, an intense horror of superstition, and he scoffs openly at things that cannot be felt and seen and put down in figures." The scientific attitude is important because science is impersonal and that is how John, treats his wife. He takes her out to the country and leaves her alone all day. "John is away all day, and even some nights when his cases are serious." He never listens to his wife's complaints, just hears them. He will not listen to her when she asks to leave, just tells her that she is better. "You know the place is doing you good." He also threatens to send her to another doctor, an act so impersonal that it frightens his wife.

The protagonist symbolizes the repressive roles some women accept for themselves. Never named in the story, referred to only as "John's wife," she does whatever her husband tells her to do, even if those things are against her wishes. She does not care to live in the old house but continues to do so because her husband demands it. She wants to visit her cousin but does not make the trip because her husband says it would not be good for her. The only thing she does for which her husband did not give her permission is to write. She never informs John about the writing for if she were to do so, she would be in deep trouble. She also accepts the degrading roles her husband forces upon her. She doesn't work, and she allows herself to become separated from her baby. Her acceptance of this dependent position leads eventually to madness.

The room with the yellow wallpaper where the narrator is confined is a symbolic reference to the position of women in society. The room is isolated from the rest of the house, epitomizing the isolation many women feel. Upstairs and away from the rest of the house, it symbolizes the false pedestal upon which men put women. The windows in the room are varied, isolating the woman from society. The steadfastness of the bed hints of John's unchangeably repressive attitudes, "I lie here on this great immovable bed." It typifies the traditional male view of womens' primary function.

The major symbol in the story is the wallpaper. The wallpaper exemplifies the different attitudes and traps that society has set for women. It acts as a cage for the main character, holding her in, not allowing her to move. She sees herself trapped by its perplexing pattern, "a woman stooping down and creeping behind the pattern." The wallpaper's intricate turns and somersaults mirror the unbreakable holds society has for women. "You think you have mastered it, but just as you get underway in following it turns a back somersault and there you are. It slaps you in the face, knocks you down, and tramples upon you. It is like a bad dream." The wallpaper has a foul odor, one from which the main character cannot escape. "It creeps all over the house. It gets into my hair." This odor exemplifies how there is no escape, for wherever she goes she finds the stench. The fact that there are two patterns, one inside the other, indicates that women must break two traps to be free: the pattern or trap men have set for them and the one they have set for themselves.

"The Yellow Wallpaper" is a story symbolizing a woman's desperate thirst for freedom. When denied this freedom she retreats into madness. Her insanity is caused by her surroundings and her repression. Gilman employs powerful symbols to effectively highlight the stumbling-blocks a woman must overcome to achieve freedom. Furthermore, she suggests that yellow wallpaper traps remain set to ensnare the unwary.

EXERCISE 8.1

List the ideas that would be emphasized in a feminist analysis of the poem "Equity" by Charlene Nichols. (page 218)

_____

_____

_____

_____

_____

_____

_____

_____

EXERCISE 8.2

Write a one-page feminist analysis of Kate Chopin's short story "The Story of an Hour." (page 227)

Eclectic Analysis

Students sometimes ask which one, of all the different analytical approaches, is the best. The desire for one "right" way is readily understandable; it would require far less effort to examine all literature from the same perspective. The wish to pursue the easiest path does not consider, however, the multiple varieties of literature: its many forms—drama, poetry, prose; its diversity of elements—plot, character, setting; its assortment of figurative language—metaphor, symbol, hyperbole, irony; its various techniques—imagery, connotation, allusion, tone; its significant themes—conflict, love, death; its quality—compelling, truthful, trite; its reception—popular, "withstood the test of time," flop. The vast assortment of literary forms and styles enhances the richness and the universality of literature's appeal. While those new to the study of literature may find the many choices disquieting, once critical points of view are mastered, the variety of approaches becomes an invitation to a much greater understanding and a much deeper appreciation of all literature.

Objectives:

After completing this chapter, you will be able to:
1. Define eclecticism.
2. Distinguish among analytical points of view to assess the ones with the most value to a particular literary selection.
3. Evaluate a literary selection's multiple appeal.
4. Write an eclectic analysis.
5. Express more critical judgment in evaluating what you choose to read and view.

_____ 1. The main characteristic of eclecticism as an analytic approach is (A) rigidity (B) selectivity (C) esoterica (D) bias (E) difficulty.

_____ 2. Eclectic critics may NOT (A) simply choose whatever they wish (B) choose more than two perspectives (C) delve into the biography of an author (D) rely on the psychology of Carl Jung (E) analyze movies.

_____ 3. Eclecticism gives the analyst more (A) insight (B) choice (C) responsibility (D) freedom (E) all of the above.

_____ 4. In eclectic analysis, the boundaries of different perspectives may be crossed when they lead to greater (A) prestige (B) GPA (C) understanding (D) sympathy (E) diversity.

_____ 5. In any one analysis, the eclectic critic is NOT obligated to (A) be honest (B) be truthful (C) include all perspectives (D) be fair (E) choose different points of view.

ECLECTIC ANALYSIS

Some scholars have become dissatisfied with the seemingly arbitrary and often rigid restrictions that are imposed by the purists of several of the analytical approaches. These restrictions have led many modern readers to the view that literary analysis should be **eclectic**, that is, they believe that they should be free to select perspectives from more than one approach. Those who adhere to this view begin by reading (or viewing) a literary work and then deciding what combination of analytic points of view will contribute the most insight and understanding. Rather than simply choosing whatever they wish, however, eclectic critics may employ only those approaches, or parts of approaches, that allow greater insight into the literature. For example, the boundaries between contextual analysis, the psychology, the archetypes, and the feminist perspective may be crossed when they lead to a greater understanding that can enhance appreciation.

Neither a new nor an original idea, eclecticism is gaining in acceptance. One reason for its growing popularity is that the freedom to choose among approaches leads to a more thoughtful intermingling of ideas which, rather than complicating, actually tends to simplify and make analysis more comprehensible.

The main characteristic of eclecticism as an analytical approach is selectivity. In any one analysis, critics are not obligated to include all analytical perspectives or even more than one. The chief virtue of eclecticism is in the choice it offers; many literary works seem almost to demand a particular analytical view. Often choosing one predominant analytical point of view, and one or more insightful sections from others, gives a more perceptive analysis than would otherwise be possible. This kind of selectivity gives the analyst more freedom as well as more responsibility. Because its insights are so much more rewarding, because the choices are the analysts to make, and because different literary selections require different points of view, eclecticism may well combine the best of all analytical perspectives.

Read the following eclectic analysis of the short story "Circe" by Eudora Welty (page 293). You should notice that Carmichael's paper includes elements from formalistic, archetypal, and feminist points-of-view.

BeBe Carmichael

English 1B MWF 9

Dr. Guches

8 January 1989

(Eclectic Analysis)

Immortal Attraction

Homer's <u>Odyssey</u> is an epic tale in the mode of the Hero's Journey --
a story of a man's adventure told from the male perspective. As in all
true Hero's Journey tales, the protagonist, Odysseus, encounters several
entities who initiate his transformation into a more complex human being.
Circe is one of these, an archetypal enchantress who, from the masculine
point-of-view, seduces Odysseus and his men, holding them captive
presumably to do her bidding. In her short story "Circe," Eudora Welty
offers this portion of the saga from a female perspective, thus creating
a Heroine's Journey. This dramatic shift in character point-of-view
alters the narrative emphasis away from seduction and conquest. By
relying upon literary technique, Welty pursues a theme of attraction and
frustration in the male/female relationship. In "Circe," Welty employs
nature as a metaphor for the masculine and mortality and the gods as a
metaphor for the feminine and immortality.

Circe's attraction to Odysseus results from her immortal yearning
and his mortality. Mortals ". . . live by frailty! By the moment!" and
this furnishes them with a vitality that Circe envies. She is not
certain what sparks that acuteness, yet she longs for it. The magic
world of immortality holds no surprises, no challenges. Circe hungers
for the excitement her virile, mortal visitor exudes. "There exists a
mortal mystery . . . I swear that only to possess that one, trifling
secret, I would willingly turn myself into a harmless dove for the rest
of eternity!" When she is with Odysseus, she catches a glimmering of
that secret. "His short life and my long one have their ground in
common. Passion is our ground, our island . . . ." Without his
mortality to stimulate her, she is bereft of emotions; she cannot find
even grief at his departure. ". . . grief that cannot be round or plain
or solid-bright or running on its track, . . . it has no heavenly course;
it is like mystery, and knows where to hide itself."

As Circe describes the nuances of the mens' mortality, she calls upon the transitory aspects of the natural world. Men with their changing and shallow nature are animals. "In the end, it takes phenomenal neatness of housekeeping to put it through the heads of men that they are swine." Circe turns them into pigs and later back into men. As animals they were more content. "They were not so forlorn when they could eat acorns and trot quickly where they would go." Because of their shallowness, mortals seem unable to appreciate subtlty. "That moment of transformation -- only the gods really like it!" Odysseus ". . . care[d] nothing for beauty that was not of the world, he did not want the first taste of anything new." Circe laments the men's headlong flight toward death. "Ever since the morning Time came and sat on the world, men have been on the run as fast as they can go, with beauty flung over their shoulders." Finally, Odysseus leaves her, again alone on her island. "We are a . . . ring on the sea. His ship was a moment's gleam on a wave."

Circe despairs within the structure of her immortality by expressing her relationship with the gods. She laments her lack of freedom, ". . . tied to my island, as Cassiopia must be to the sticks and stars of her chair." The Sun is Circe's father, yet Odysseus will not dine from the sun's golden bowl, preferring instead the company of his crew. Offered a "god's breakfast," Circe is appalled that even the sausages, made from the crew's swine brothers, are eaten thoughtlessly. Venus leans at Circe's window as she attempts to seduce Odysseus. But in the end Circe's immortality keeps her separate. "Though I could shriek at the rising Moon, and she, so near, would wax or wane, there was still grief that couldn't hear me . . . ."

Eudora Welty's "Circe" explores mortality and immortality using nature and the gods as metaphors. Told from the point of view of the Heroine's Journey, mortality becomes a transitory aspect of the natural world. Immortality is bland and to live as a god is to live without mystery. Circe, because of her encounter with Odysseus, achieves a glimmering of the excitement of mortality. Yet because she is immortal, she cannot even mourn the passing of that vitality when it leaves her.

EXERCISE 9.1

List at least one analytical point for each of the following approaches for a short story of your choice (and approved by your instructor).

1. contextual: _____

_____

_____

_____

2. formalistic: _____

_____

_____

_____

1. archetypal: _____

_____

_____

_____

1. feminist: _____

_____

_____

_____

EXERCISE 9.2

On the selection chosen for Exercise 9.1, write an analysis that combines at least two analytical approaches.

APPENDIX

I

Reference Sources

HOW TO FIND INFORMATION ABOUT AN AUTHOR

To locate the background and other details of an author, it is helpful to know some basic facts about the person's life. One way to find some clues is to look at the listings of the author's books in the library computer catalog.

1. The listing giving the author's name often shows **birth and death dates** also.
2. The title of the book or the subject headings often reveals the author's **profession or interests.**
3. The place of publication may be a clue to the **nationality** of the author.

Clues are also given on the book jacket, in the foreword, or in the text of the book itself. Further information may be obtained in the library Reference Room, in biographical dictionaries, or from online databases.

For Living Authors

BIOGRAPHY INDEX (Ref Z 5301 B5)
CONTEMPORARY AUTHORS (Ref Z 1224 C6)
WHO'S WHO (Ref DA 28 W6) British Only
WHO'S WHO IN AMERICA (Ref E 176 W642) U.S. Only
WHO'S WHO OF AMERICAN WOMEN (Ref CT 3260 W5)
CURRENT BIOGRAPHY (Ref CT 100 C8)

For Authors No Longer Living

DICTIONARY OF AMERICAN BIOGRAPHY (Ref E 176 D563)
DICTIONARY OF NATIONAL BIOGRAPHY (Ref DA 28 D4) British Only
BIOGRAPHY INDEX (Ref Z 5301 B5)
WHO WAS WHO IN AMERICA (Ref E 663 W54)

NOTE:

Use the older issues of CURRENT BIOGRAPHY, WHO'S WHO, and WHO'S WHO IN AMERICA for information about recently deceased.

For Authors of Literature

AMERICAN AUTHORS, 1600-1900 (Ref PS 21 K8)
BRITISH AUTHORS OF THE NINETEENTH CENTURY (Ref PR 451 K8 1936)
BRITISH AUTHORS BEFORE 1800 (Ref PR 105 K9)
CONTEMPORARY DRAMATISTS (Ref PR 106 V5)
CONTEMPORARY NOVELISTS (Ref PR 737 V5)
COMTEMPORARY POETS (Ref PS 324 C63)
EUROPEAN AUTHORS 1000-1900 (Ref PN 451 K8)
JUNIOR BOOK OF AUTHORS (Ref PN 1009 A1 K8 1951)
LIVING BLACK AMERICAN AUTHORS (Ref PS 153 N5 S5)
TWENTIETH CENTURY AUTHORS (Ref PN 771 K86)
WORLD AUTHORS 1950-1970 (Ref PN 451 W3)

For Authors With Other Occupations

AMERICAN MEN AND WOMEN OF SCIENCE (Ref Q 141 A47)
DICTIONARY OF SCIENTIFIC BIOGRAPHY (Ref Q 141 D5)
DICTIONARY OF AMERICAN SCHOLARS (Ref LA 2311 C32)
WHO'S WHO IN AMERICAN POLITICS (Ref E 176 W6424)
WHO'S WHO IN FINANCE AND INDUSTRY (Ref 3023 A2 W5)

DICTIONARY OF NATIONAL BIOGRAPHY (Ref DA 28 D4) British Only

INTERNATIONAL WHO'S WHO (Ref CT 120 I 5)

WEBSTER'S BIOGRAPHICAL DICTIONARY (Ref CT 103 W4)

WHO'S WHO (Ref DA 28 W6) British Only

WORLD BIOGRAPHY (Ref CT 120 W65)

SUGGESTIONS:

1. Longer biographies of an author may be found in the library listing under the name. Books *about* a person are filed after books written *by* that person. The person's name is entered in capital letters to differentiate the person as the subject of a book from the person as the author.

2. For additional material, look under such headings as:

ARTISTS, AMERICAN   SCIENTISTS

AUTHORS   THEATER-U.S.

GREAT BRITAIN-BIOGRAPHY   WOMAN-BIOGRAPHY

3. For magazine articles about an author, consult the READERS' GUIDE TO PERIODICAL LITERATURE, THE HUMANITIES INDEX, or other indexes.

4. Information about authors who have written little or whose published work is especially recent may be difficult to find. For these authors, try book reviews. These sometimes contain information about authors.

HOW TO FIND BOOK REVIEWS

A **review** is a notice, published in a periodical, of a current book. A review announces a book, describes its subject, discusses its method and technical qualities, and examines its merit when compared with other similar works.

A **critique**, on the other hand, is an essay or article which is more serious than a review. It is a critical examination of a literary work and attempts to explain and interpret. (See page 194.)

Some special publications in the Reference Room index book review published in magazines. To use these books the following information is needed:

1. The full name of the **author**.

2. The exact **title** of the book.

3. The **year** the book was published. (Reviews usually appear soon after a book is published)

Note: Look for the date of publication or the copyright date on the front or back of the title page on the book. When more than one date is given, use the earliest date cited.

This information may be found in the library listing or in *Books In Print*.

Special Book Review Indexes

REF Z 1219 C95	BOOK REVIEW DIGEST, 1905 to date. Locates reviews in more than 70 magazines and is kept up-to-date by monthly supplements. Entries are under author's name. Look first in the volume for the year the book was published. If the book is not listed, try the next annual volume. A short description of the book, references to magazines containing reviews, and quotations from some of those reviews will be found under the citation.

REF Z 1035 A1 I 63	INDEX TO BOOK REVIEWS IN THE HUMANITIES, 1961 to date. Publishes annually, listing reviews in the humanities. Includes history, biography, personal narratives, travel, and adventure. No quotations given.
REF Z 1035 A1 B6	BOOK REVIEW INDEX, 1965 to date. An index to reviews in about 200 periodicals. Important for the number of scholarly journals in the humanities and social sciences represented. Specialized scientific and technical periodicals are excluded. No quotations given.

Reviews of Books in General

SER or REF AI 3 R48	READER'S GUIDE TO PERIODICAL LITERATURE, 1932 to date, lists book reviews under name of author. A policy from 1976 issues is to group all book reviews at end of the main body of the text in a separate section headed "Book Review." It also lists movie reviews under "Moving Picture Plays--Criticisms--Single Works." Play reviews are listed under "Dramas--Criticisms" and full entries are under name of author.
SER AI 3 P76	POPULAR PERIODICALS INDEX, 1973 to date. This indexes magazines not covered by *Readers' Guide to Periodical Literature*. Reviews are listed under "Book Reviews."

Reviews of Books on Special Subjects

APPLIED SCIENCE AND TECHNOLOGY (Ser Z 7913 I 7)
ART INDEX (Ser Z 5937 A78)
BIOLOGICAL AND AGRICULTURAL INDEX (Ser Z 5073 A46)
BUSINESS PERIODICALS INDEX (Ser Z 7164 C81 B983)
EDUCATION INDEX (Ser Z 5813 E23)
HUMANITIES INDEX (Ser AI 3 H85)
SOCIAL SCIENCE INDEX (Ser AI 3 S62)

Note: Book Review section since 1976 edition of each of these titles is in a separate section at the back of the issue. Older issues list them in the "Bs" under "Book Reviews."

Newspaper Indexes

SER AI 21 N44	NEW YORK TIMES INDEX, 1964 to date. Lists citations under "Book Reviews."

Reviews of Very New Books

If the book is so new that reviews have not yet been listed in any of the general book reviewing indexes, you may find it reviewed in the latest numbers of current magazines regularly having book review sections, for example:

ATLANTIC MONTHLY	NEW YORK TIMES
HARPER'S	BOOK REVIEW
NEW YORK REVIEW OF BOOKS	SATURDAY REVIEW
	TIMES LITERARY SUPPLEMENT

HOW TO FIND LITERARY CRITICISM

A critical essay usually is written several years after the original publication, and it attempts to assess the importance of the work. Information needed for a search for criticism includes:

1. writer's name
2. title of literature
3. country of its origin
4. literary form (poem, novel, etc.)

A. SPECIAL INDEXES

1. POETRY

Poetry Explication (Ref Z 2014 P7 K8) Covers British & American poetry. Indexes criticism written between 1925 and 1977.

Index to Criticisms of British and American Poetry (Ref Z 2014 P7 C6) Indexes criticism written between 1960 and 1971.

American and British Poetry: 1925-1978.

2. SHORT STORY

Short Fiction Criticism (Ref Z 5917 S5 T5) Indexes criticism written from 1800 to 1958. Covers American, British & Continental.

American Short Fiction Criticism and Scholarship, 1959-1977 (Ref Z 1231 F4 W3) Updates the American portion of the above book.

Twentieth Century Short Story Explication (Ref z 5917 S5 W33) (1977 volume plus two supplements) Indexes criticism printed between 1900 and 1981. Covers stories of all countries published after 1800.

3. DRAMA

European Drama Criticism (Ref Z 5781 P2) Covers classical to modern drama. Criticism written between 1900 to 1975.

Modern Drama (Ref Z 5781 A35) covers drama & criticism from 1900 to 1967.

American Drama Criticism (Ref Z 5781 P36) covers only American plays. Indexes criticism written from 1890 to 1977.

Guide to Critical Reviews (Ref Z 5782 S342)
 Part I: American Drama (1900-1969)
 Part II: Foreign Drama (1909-1977)

Dramatic Criticism Index (Ref Z 5781 B8) Covers English, American and foreign, from Ibsen to avant-garde. Criticism to 1971.

Drama Criticism (Ref Z 5781 C66)
 Vol. 1: English & American drama. Essays written between 1940 & 1966.
 Vol. 2: Classical & Continental. Essays written between 1940 & 1970.

4. NOVEL

English Novel (Ref Z 2014 F4 B4) Includes novels written between 1578 & 1956. Criticism from 1900 to 1957.

English Novel Explication (Ref Z 2014 F5 P26) (plus two supplemental volumes) Criticism written between 1958 and 1979.

English 20th Century Criticism 2 vol. (on order) Novels from Defoe through 1980.

American Novel (Ref Z 1231 F4 G4) (in 2 volumes) Novels written between 1789 and 1968. Criticism written between 1900 and 1968.

Contemporary Novel (Ref Z 1231 F4 A34) British & American novels written between 1945 to 1969.

Continental Novel (Ref Z 5916 K4) Criticism written between 1900 and 1966. Includes French, Spanish, Portuguese, Italian, German, Scandinavian, Russian and East European novels.

Continental Novel, 1983 edition (Ref Z 5916 F57 1983) Extends criticism from 1967 to 1980.

B. OTHER SOURCES

1. LIBRARY LISTING

Look up the author's name in the library listing to see if the library has entire books devoted to the author's life or work. Sometimes a particular literary piece will be discussed in a book of this kind. Check the index at the back of the book for your title.

Criticism of short works such as poetry and short stories usually cannot be located by looking under titles in the library listing. However, there may be entries in the library listing under the author's name along with the title; these books deal with only one play or one novel, if it is a classic. For example:

MELVILLE, HERMAN. MOBY DICK.

In addition a search under certain subject headings in the card catalog can lead you to more books which might contain useful information. Check the indexes of the books. Many of these books have been included in sources already consulted, but you might find a few not covered elsewhere. Some subjects to check are:

DRAMA—HISTORY AND CRITICISM (or AMERICAN, ENGLISH,
FICTION—HISTORY AND CRITICISM etc. as appropriate to
LITERATURE—HISTORY AND CRITICISM the author's nationality)
POETRY—HISTORY AND CRITICISM

2. *Essay and General Literature Index* (Ref AI 3 E752) Index Area.

This indexes essays within books and provides exact page references to criticism of an author's particular work. Look under author's name, then the subdivision: "About individual works." Titles will then be listed alphabetically.

3. *Reader's Index to "Twentieth Century Views" Literary Criticism Series* (Ref Z 6511 T86) Index Area

This is an index to the contents of the volumes in the Literary Criticism Series.

SPECIAL COLLECTION

Moulton's Library of Literary Criticism (Ref PR 83 M73 1966).
Covers English and American authors. 19th century criticism.

The Critical Temper (Ref PR 83 C764).
Covers English and American literature up to 20th century.

Contemporary Literary Criticism (Ref PN 771 C59).
Covers writers now living or who have died since 1960. Criticism written during the past thirty-five years approximately.

A Library of Literary Criticism: Modern British Literature (Ref PR 473 T4).

A Library of Literary Criticism: Modern American Literature (Ref PS 221 C8).

American Writers (Ref PS 129 A55).
A collection of literary biographies. Gives lengthy discussion of lives, careers and works of major American writers, and includes lists of additional critical studies in books and periodicals.

LIBRARY OF CONGRESS CLASSIFICATION SYSTEM
(a basic outline)

Class Letter	Major Subjects and Divisions

A   GENERAL WORKS (collected works, encyclopedias, general reference works)

B   PHILOSOPHY - RELIGION
- B - BJ .... Philosophy
- BF .... Psychology
- BL - BX .... Religion

C   HISTORY - AUXILIARY SCIENCES
- CC.................... Archaeology
- CT.................... Biography (general and collective)
  (Single biographies are in their various subject areas.)

D   HISTORY: GENERAL AND OLD WORLD
- DA .... Great Britain
- DC .... France
- DD .... Germany
- DK .... Russia
- DP.................... Spain and Portugal
- DS.................... Asia
- DT .... Africa

E   HISTORY: AMERICA (general) and UNITED STATES (general) by period
- E 77 - 99 .... Indians
- E 184 .... Blacks and other minorities

F   HISTORY: UNITED STATES (local) and AMERICA (other than the United States)
- F 856 - 870 .... California

G   GEOGRAPHY
- GN .... Anthropology
- GR - GT .... Folk-Lore, Customs, Costumes
- GV .... Sports and Recreation

H   SOCIAL SCIENCES
- HB - HJ .... Economics and Business
- HM - HX............. Sociology

J   POLITICAL SCIENCE
- JK .... U.S. Politics (federal and state)

K   LAW

L   EDUCATION

M   MUSIC
- M.................... Scores (instrumental and vocal)
- ML .... Literature of Music (history and criticism)
- MT .... Instruction and Technique

N	FINE ARTS (in West Wing)	
	NA	Architecture
	NB...................	Sculpture
	NC - NE	Drawing, Painting, Prints
	NK	Interior Design, Ceramics, Textiles, etc.
P	LANGUAGE AND LITERATURE	
	PE	English Language, Grammar, Composition
	PN...................	Literary History, Drama Collections
	PQ...................	French, Italian, Spanish Literature
	PR...................	English Literature
	PS	American Literature
	PZ...................	Fiction (modern and childrens)
Q	SCIENCE	
	QA	Mathematics
	QB...................	Astronomy
	QC	Physics
	QD	Chemistry
	QE	Geology
	QF	Biology
	QK	Botany
	QL...................	Zoology
	QM - QP	Anatomy and Physiology
	QR	Bacteriology
R	MEDICINE	
	RB - RC	Diseases
	RJ	Pediatrics
	RS	Drugs
	RT...................	Nursing
S	AGRICULTURE: PLANT AND ANIMAL	
	SB	Horticulture
	SD...................	Forestry
	SF	Pets
	SH - SK	Fishing and Hunting
T	TECHNOLOGY	
	TA - TH..............	Civil Engineering
	TJ	Mechanical Engineering
	TK...................	Electrical Engineering
	TL...................	Motor Vehicles, Aeronautics
	TX	Nutrition, Cookery
U	MILITARY SCIENCE	
V		
Z	NAVAL SCIENCE	
	LIBRARY SCIENCE, PRINTING, PUBLISHING	

APPENDIX

II

Literature for Analysis

FOUR POEMS FOR COMPARISON

WHEN I HEARD THE LEARN'D ASTRONOMER

When I heard the learn'd astronomer,
When the proofs, the figures, were ranged in columns before me,
When I was shown the charts and diagrams, to add, divide,
   and measure them,
When I sitting heard the astronomer where he lectured with much
    applause in the lecture-room,
How soon unaccountable I became tired and sick,
Till rising and gliding out I wandered off by myself,
In the mystical moist night-air, and from time to time,
Looked up in perfect silence at the stars.

                  Walt Whitman (1819-1892)

THE WORLD IS TOO MUCH WITH US

The world is too much with us; late and soon,
Getting and spending, we lay waste our powers:
Little we see in Nature that is ours;
We have given our hearts away, a sordid boon!
This sea that bares her bosom to the moon;   5
The winds that will be howling at all hours,
And are up-gathered now like sleeping flowers;
For this, for everything, we are out of tune;
It moves us not.—Great God! I'd rather be
A Pagan suckled in a creed outworn;   10
So might I, standing on this pleasant lea,
Have glimpses that would make me less forlorn;
Have sight of Proteus rising from the sea;
Or hear old Triton blow his wreathed horn.

        —*William Wordsworth (1770-1850)*

pity this busy monster,manunkind

pity this busy monster,manunkind,

not. Progress is a comfortable disease:
your victim (death and life safely beyond)

plays with the bigness of his littleness
—electrons deify one razorblade
into a mountainrange; lenses extend

unwish through curving wherewhen till unwish
returns on its unself.
           A world of made
is not a world of born—pity poor flesh   10

and trees, poor stars and stones, but never this
fine specimen of hypermagical

ultraomnipotence. We doctors know

a hopeless case if—listen: there's a hell
of a good universe next door; let's go

         —*e. e. cummings (1894-1962)*

MOON, SON OF HEAVEN

When I was a child
in all sorts of magazines and newspapers
— how many — photographs of the moon:
face scarred by jagged craters
I clearly saw that the sun light strikes it.
later I learned it's terribly cold
                            and no air.
maybe three times I saw it eclipsed —
the earth's shadow
slipped over it, clearly
next, that it probably broke off from earth.
and last, a fellow I met during rice planting
    from the Morioka meteorological observatory
    once showed me that heavenly body through
    a something-mm little telescope
    and explained how its orbit and motions
accord with a simple formula.

However. ah,
for me in the end there's no obstacle
to reverently titling that heavenly body
Emperor Moon.
if someone says
    man is his body
    that's a mistake.
    and if someone says
    man is body and mind
    that too is an error
    and if one says man is mind,
    still it's wrong.

so — I —
hail the moon as Emperor Moon.
this is not mere personification.

—*Gary Snyder (1930-   )*

BARBARA ALLEN (Child 84)
Traditional Scottish Version

1 It was in and about the Martinmas[1] time,
       When the green leaves were a-falling,
   That Sir John Graeme in the west country
       Fell in love with Barbara Allan.

2 He sent his man down through the town,
       To the place where she was dwelling,
   "O haste and come to my master dear,
       Gin* ye be Barbara Allan.   *gin,* if

3 O hooly, hooly* rose she up,   *hooly,* slowly, softly
       To the place where he was lying,
   And when she drew the curtain by—
       "Young man, I think you're dying."

202

4 "O it's I'm sick, and very, very sick,
    And 'tis a' for Barbara Allan."
  "O the better for me ye's never be,
    Tho' your heart's blood were a-spilling.

5 "O dinna ye mind*, young man," said she, *dinna ye mind,
    "When ye was in the tavern a-drinking,   don't you
  That ye made the healths gae round and round, remember
    and slighted Barbara Allan."

6 He turn'd his face unto the wall,
    And death was with him dealing:
  "Adieu, adieu, my dear friends all,
    And be kind to Barbara Allan."

7 And slowly, slowly raise she up,
    And slowly, slowly left him;
  And sighing, said she cou'd not stay,
    Since death of life had reft him.

8 She had not gane a mile but twa,
    When she heard a dead-bell ringing,
  And every jow* that the dead-bell geid,   *jow, stroke
    It cry'd, Woe to Barbara Allan.

9 "O mother, mother, make my bed,
    O make it saft and narrow,
  Since my love died for me today,
    I'll die for him tomorrow."

1. Martinmas: St. Martin's Day,
November 11.

BARBARA ALLEN
American Version—from West Virginia

1   In Scarlet town, where I was born,
    There was a fair maid dwelling,
    Made every youth cry "Well away!"
    Her name was Barbara Allen.

2   All in the merry month of May,
    When green buds they are swelling,
    Young Jimmy Green on his death bed lay
    For the love of Barbara Allen.

3   He sent his man unto her there,
    To the town where she was dwelling;
    "O you must come to my master dear,
    If your name be Barbara Allen.

4   "For death is printed on his face
    And o'er his heart is stealing;
    O haste away to comfort him,
    O lovely Barbara Allen!"

5   "If death is printed on his face
    And o'er his heart is stealing,

Yet little better shall he be
For the love of Barbara Allen."

6   So, slowly, slowly, she came up,
And slowly she came nigh him;
And all she said when there she came,
"Young man, I think you're dying."

7   He turned his face unto her straight,
With deadly sorrow sighing:
"O lovely maid, come pity me!
I'm on my death bed lying."

8   "If on your death bed you do lie,
What need the tale you're telling?
I cannot keep you from your death:
Farewell," said Barbara Allen.

9   He turned his face unto the wall,
And deadly pains he fell in:
"Adieu, adieu, adieu to all,
Adieu to Barbara Allen."

10   As she was walking o'er the fields,
She heard the bell a-knelling;
And every stroke it seemed to say,
"Unworthy Barbara Allen."

11   She turned herself around about
And spied the corpse a-coming:
"Lay down, lay down the corpse," said she,
"That I may look upon him."

12   With scornful eyes she did look down,
Her cheeks with laughter swelling;
While all her friends cried out amen [*for* amain],
"Unworthy Barbara Allen!"

13   When he was dead and laid in grave,
Her heart was struck with sorrow:
"O mother, mother, make my bed,
For I shall die to-morrow.

14   "Hard-hearted creature him to slight,
He who loved me so dearly!
O had I been more kind to him,
When he was alive and near me!"

15   On her death bed as she did lay,
She begged to be buried by him,
And sorely repented of that day
That she e'er did deny him.

16   "Farewell, ye virgins all," she said,
"And shun the fault I've fell in;
Henceforward take warning by the fall
Of cruel Barbara Allen."

16* [One was buried in the high churchyard,
     The other in the choir;
     On one there grew a rose bush,
     On the other there grew a brier.

17* They grew and they grew to the high steeple top,
     Till they could grow no higher;
     And there they locked in a true-lover's knot,
     For true lovers to admire.]

* Floating stanzas - they "float" from one ballad to another.

THE TWA CORBIES* (Child 26)   *ravens*

     As I was walking all alane,
     I heard twa corbies making a mane;*   *moan*
     The tane* unto the t'other say,   *one*
     "Where sall* we gang* and dine to-day?"   *shall / go*

5   "In behint you auld fail* dike,   *turf*
     I wot there lies a new slain knight;
     And naebody kens* that he lies there,   *knows*
     But his hawk, his hound, and lady fair.

     "His hound is to the hunting gane,
10   His hawk to fetch a wild-fowl hame,
     His lady's ta'en another mate,
     So we may mak our dinner sweet.

     "Ye'll sit on his white hause-bane,*   *neck-bone*
     And I'll pike* out his bonny blue een;*   *pick / eyes*
15   Wi' ai* lock o'his gowden* hair   *one / golden*
     We'll theek* our nest when it grows bare.   *thatch*

     "Mony a one for him makes mane,
     But nane sall ken where he is gane;
     O'er his white banes, when they are bare,
20   The wind sall blaw for evermair."

205

OEDIPUS AND US

. . . for jh & cc

If Oedipus had been a woman this would perhaps have been Antigone's
song.

Oh Mother,
I am in reverence of your beauty.
Your power shines like a prism
Of wonderous light
Filling your children
With a magnificent vision
Of a world emergent
Whole and true and awake.

They tell me
I look like you
A smaller, younger version
A smaller, younger vision
We will draw that vision large.

Mother,
I call you so because
I am the Being you created
From that bright point.
Conceived with Nous,
I am what you have birthed.

But I am fathered
By the same source
By the same energy
By the same essence
That birthed you.
That movement too
Flows thick and strong
Through the veins of my spirit.

And so,
We too are sisters.
The power of my Being
Originates from your source
And from you.

Sister,
Place your hand upon my back.
Together, we walk
Lightfully
Through
The heartland.

Oh Sister,
Oh Demeter,
Rejoice!
For in the growing
Of this closeness of spirit
Comes the energy
To propel the vision
To reality.

—Candace Cave (1951-   )

KUBLA KHAN
A Vision in a Dream

In Xanadu did Kubla Khan
A stately pleasure-dome decree:
Where Alph, the sacred river, ran
Through caverns measureless to man
    Down to a sunless sea.
So twice five miles of fertile ground
With walls and towers were girdled round:
And here were gardens bright with sinuous rills,
Where blossomed many an incense-bearing tree;
And here were forests ancient as the hills,   10
Enfolding sunny spots of greenery.

But oh! that deep romantic chasm which slanted
Down the green hill athwart a cedarn cover!
A savage place! as holy and enchanted
As e'er beneath a waning moon was haunted
By woman wailing for her demon-lover!
And from this chasm, with ceaseless turmoil seething,
As if this earth in fast thick pants were breathing,
A mighty fountain momently was forced:
Amid whose swift half-intermitted burst   20
Huge fragments vaulted like rebounding hail,
Or chaffy grain beneath the thresher's flail:
And 'mid these dancing rocks at once and ever
It flung up momently the sacred river.
Five miles meandering with a mazy motion
Through wood and dale the sacred river ran,
Then reached the caverns measureless to man,
And sank in tumult to a lifeless ocean:
And 'mid this tumult Kubla heard from far
Ancestral voices prophesying war!   30
    The shadow of the dome of pleasure
    Floated midway on the waves;
    Where was heard the mingled measure
    From the fountain and the caves.
It was a miracle of rare device,
A sunny pleasure-dome with caves of ice!

    A damsel with a dulcimer
    In a vision once I saw:
    It was an Abyssinian maid,
    And on her dulcimer she played,   40
    Singing of Mount Abora.
    Could I revive within me,
    Her symphony and song,
    To such a deep delight 'twould win me,
That with music loud and long,
I would build that dome in air,
That sunny dome! those caves of ice!
And all who heard should see them there,
And all should cry, Beware! Beware!
His flashing eyes, his floating hair!   50

Weave a circle round him thrice,
And close your eyes with holy dread,
For he on honey-dew hath fed,
And drunk the milk of Paradise.

                Samuel Taylor Coleridge (1772-1834)

MY LIFE HAD STOOD, A LOADED GUN

My life had stood, a loaded gun,
In corners, till a day
The owner passed, identified,
And carried me away.

And now we roam in sovereign woods,
And now we hunt the doe,
And every time I speak for him,
The mountains straight reply.

And do I smile, such cordial light
Upon the valley glow,   10
It is as a Vesuvian face
Had let its pleasure through.

And when at night, our good day done,
I guard my master's head,
'Tis better than the eider-duck's
Deep pillow, to have shared.

To foe of his I'm deadly foe:
None stir the second time
On whom I lay a yellow eye
Or an emphatic thumb.   20

Though I than he may longer live,
He longer must than I,
For I have but the power to kill,
Without the power to die.

                —Emily Dickinson (1830-1886)

APPARENTLY WITH NO SURPRISE

Apparently with no surprise
To any happy flower,
The frost beheads it at its play
In accidental power.
The blond assassin passes on,
The sun proceeds unmoved
To measure off another day
For an approving God.

                Emily Dickinson (1830-1886)

THE LOVE SONG OF J. ALFRED PRUFROCK

S'io credessi che mia risposta fosse
a persona che mai tornasse al mondo,
questa fiamma staria senza più scosse.
Ma per ciò che giammai di questo fondo
non tornò vivo alcun, s'i'odo il vero,
senza tema d'infamia ti rispondo. *

Let us go then, you and I,
When the evening is spread out against the sky
Like a patient etherised upon a table;
Let us go, through certain half-deserted streets,
The muttering retreats
Of restless nights in one-night cheap hotels
And sawdust restaurants with oyster-shells:
Streets that follow like a tedious argument
Of insidious intent
To lead you to an overwhelming question . . .   10
Oh, do not ask, "What is it?"
Let us go and make our visit.

In the room the women come and go
Talking of Michelangelo.

The yellow fog that rubs its back upon the window-panes,
The yellow smoke that rubs its muzzle on the window-panes,
Licked its tongue into the corners of the evening,
Lingered upon the pools that stand in drains,
Let fall upon its back the soot that falls from chimneys,
Slipped by the terrace, made a sudden leap,   20
And seeing that it was a soft October night,
Curled once about the house, and fell asleep.

And indeed there will be time
For the yellow smoke that slides along the street
Rubbing its back upon the window-panes;
There will be time, there will be time
To prepare a face to meet the faces that you meet;
There will be time to murder and create,
And time for all the works and days of hands
That lift and drop a question on your plate;   30
Time for you and time for me,
And time yet for a hundred indecisions,
And for a hundred visions and revisions,
Before the taking of a toast and tea.

In the room the women come and go
Talking of Michelangelo.

And indeed there will be time
To wonder, "Do I dare?" and, "Do I dare?"
Time to turn back and descend the stair,
With a bald spot in the middle of my hair—   40
(They will say: "How his hair is growing thin!")
My morning coat, my collar mounting firmly to the chin,
My necktie rich and modest, but asserted by a simple pin—
(They will say: "But how his arms and legs are thin!")
Do I dare

Disturb the universe?
In a minute there is time
For decisions and revisions which a minute will reverse.

For I have known them all already, known them all—
Have known the evenings, mornings, afternoons,   50
I have measured out my life with coffee spoons;
I know the voices dying with a dying fall
Beneath the music from a farther room.
    So how should I presume?

And I have known the eyes already, known them all—
The eyes that fix you in a formulated phrase,
And when I am formulated, sprawling on a pin,
When I am pinned and wriggling on the wall,
Then how should I begin
To spit out all the butt-ends of my days and ways?   60
    And how should I presume?

And I have known the arms already, known them all—
Arms that are braceleted and white and bare
(But in the lamplight, downed with light brown hair!)
Is it perfume from a dress
That makes me so digress?
Arms that lie along a table, or wrap about a shawl.
    And should I then presume?
    And how should I begin?
            . . . . .

Shall I say, I have gone at dusk through narrow streets   70
And watched the smoke that rises from the pipes
Of lonely men in shirt-sleeves, leaning out of windows? . . .

I should have been a pair of ragged claws
Scuttling across the floors of silent seas.
            . . . . .
And the afternoon, the evening, sleeps so peacefully!
Smoothed by long fingers,
Asleep . . . tired . . . or it malingers,
Stretched on the floor, here beside you and me.
Should I, after tea and cakes and ices,
Have the strength to force the moment to its crisis?   80
But though I have wept and fasted, wept and prayed,
Though I have seen my head (grown slightly bald) brought in
        upon a platter,
I am no prophet—and here's no great matter;
I have seen the moment of my greatness flicker,
And I have seen the eternal Footman hold my coat, and snicker,
And in short, I was afraid.

And would it have been worth it, after all,
After the cups, the marmalade, the tea,
Among the porcelain, among some talk of you and me,
Would it have been worth while,   90
To have bitten off the matter with a smile,
To have squeezed the universe into a ball
To roll it towards some overwhelming question,

To say: "I am Lazarus, come from the dead,
Come back to tell you all, I shall tell you all"—
If one, settling a pillow by her head,
     Should say: 'That is not what I meant at all.
     That is not it, at all.'

And would it have been worth it, after all,
Would it have been worth while,   100
After the sunsets and the dooryards and the sprinkled streets,
After the novels, after the teacups, after the skirts that trail along
          the floor—
And this, and so much more?—
It is impossible to say just what I mean!
But as if a magic lantern threw the nerves in patterns on a
          screen:
Would it have been worth while
If one, settling a pillow or throwing off a shawl,
And turning toward the window, should say:
     "That is not it at all,
     That is not what I meant, at all."   110
          . . . . .

No! I am not Prince Hamlet, nor was meant to be;
Am an attendant lord, one that will do
To swell a progress, start a scene or two,
Advise the prince; no doubt, an easy tool,
Deferential, glad to be of use,
Politic, cautious, and meticulous;
Full of high sentence, but a bit obtuse;
At times, indeed, almost ridiculous—
Almost, at times, the Fool.

I grow old . . . I grow old . . .   120
I shall wear the bottoms of my trousers rolled.

Shall I part my hair behind? Do I dare to eat a peach?
I shall wear white flannel trousers, and walk upon the beach.
I have heard the mermaids singing, each to each.

I do not think that they will sing to me.

I have seen them riding seaward on the waves
Combing the white hair of the waves blown back
When the wind blows the water white and black.

We have lingered in the chambers of the sea
By sea-girls wreathed with seaweed red and brown   130
'Till human voices wake us, and we drown.

                                        —*T. S. Eliot (1888-1965)*

*"If I thought that my response would be addressed to one
  who might go back alive, this flame would shake no more;
  but since no one ever goes back alive out of these deeps (if
  what I hear be true), without fear of infamy I answer you."
                                        —*Dante's Inferno*

STOPPING BY WOODS ON A SNOWY EVENING

Whose woods these are I think I know.
His house is in the village though;
He will not see me stopping here
To watch his woods fill up with snow.

My little horse must think it queer
To stop without a farmhouse near
Between the woods and frozen lake
The darkest evening of the year.

He gives his harness bells a shake
To ask if there is some mistake.   10
The only other sound's the sweep
Of easy wind and downy flake.

The woods are lovely, dark and deep,
But I have promises to keep,
And miles to go before I sleep,
And miles to go before I sleep.

— Robert Frost (1874-1963)

HE STANDS UPON HIS TOWER GAZING

He stands upon his tower gazing
    into the pool,
        dreaming
            of dancing and
                fire.

She sits absorbed
    by her ring,
        fantasizing the high
            flying serpent,
                beginning to
                    tire.   10

Together they are apart,
    apart together; opposed in flesh,
        combined in spirit.
Apart is dependence but no freedom;
    together fleshly — one,
        but feeling
            separate.

Union is tough,
    single is lonely and
        rough.   20

The id, super-ego battle is endless;
    ego,
        caught between pleasure and
            morality.
The only success is reality.

—Richard C. Guches (1938-   )

"AN APPROVING GOD"

Life, what there was of it,
    had gone
      before I ever saw the wet
    bodies.

She struggled, wounded and confused,
    to deliver
      her first litter—
    alive.

Her foot, thorn swollen,
    made her groggy   10
      with stumbling
    pain.

Exhausted, lying beside two hairless lumps,
    I found her
      beyond help;
    numb.

More came, before the hour was out.
    I put all four
      into a bread
    sack.   20

Abandoned, she sank into a corner,
    her great paw
      throbbing without
    mercy.

Despondent, she waited alone,
    for the peace of death
      to grant its
    release.

          —Richard C. Guches (1938-   )

TO THE STONE-CUTTERS

Stone-cutters fighting time with marble, you foredefeated
Challengers of oblivion
Eat cynical earnings, knowing rock splits, records fall down,
The square limbed Roman letters
Scale in the thaws, wear in the rain. The poet as well
Builds his monument mockingly;
For man will be blotted out, the blithe earth die, the brave sun
Die blind and blacken to the heart.
Yet stones have stood for a thousand years, and pained
    thoughts found
The honey of peace in old poems.

          —Robinson Jeffers (1887-1962)

PATTERNS

I walk down the garden-paths,
And all the daffodils
Are blowing, and the bright blue squills*   *Bell-shaped flowers*
I walk down the patterned garden-paths
In my stiff, brocaded gown.   5
With my powdered hair and jeweled fan,
I too am a rare
Pattern. As I wander down
The garden-paths.

My dress is richly figured,   10
And the train
Makes a pink and silver stain
On the gravel, and the thrift
Of the borders.
Just a plate of current fashion,   15
Tripping by in high-heeled, ribboned shoes.
Not a softness anywhere about me,
Only whalebone and brocade.
And I sink on a seat in the shade
Of a lime tree. For my passion   20
Wars against the stiff brocade.
The daffodils and squills
Flutter in the breeze
As they please.
And I weep;   25
For the lime-tree is in blossom
And one small flower has dropped upon my bosom.

And the splashing waterdrops
In the marble fountain
Comes down the garden-paths.   30
The dripping never stops.
Underneath my stiffened gown
Is the softness of a woman bathing in a marble basin,
A basin in the midst of hedges grown
So thick, she cannot see her lover hiding,   35
But she guesses he is near,
And the sliding of the water
Seems the stroking of a dear
Hand upon her.
What is Summer in a fine brocaded gown!   40
I should like to see it lying in a heap upon the ground.
All the pink and silver crumpled up on the ground.

I would be the pink and silver as I ran along the paths,
And he would stumble after,
Bewildered by my laughter.   45
I should see the sun flashing from his sword-hilt and the buckles on his
    shoes.
I would choose
To lead him in a maze along the patterned paths,
A bright and laughing maze for my heavy-booted lover.
Till he caught me in the shade,   50

214

And the buttons of his waiscot bruised my body as he clasped me,
Aching, meltin, unafraid.
With the shadows of the leaves and the sundrops
And the plopping of the waterdrops,
All about us in the open afternoon—   55
I am very like to swoon
With the weight of his brocade,
For the sun sifts through the shade.

Underneath the fallen blossom
In my bosom,   60
Is a letter I have hid.
It was brought to me this morning by a rider from the Duke.
"Madam, we regret to inform you that Lord Hartwell
Died in action Thursday se'nnight*."   *A week ago Thursday
As I read it in the white, morning sunlight,   65
The letters squirmed like snakes.
"Any answer, Madam?" said my footman.
"No," I told him.
"See that the messenger takes some refreshment.
No, no answer."   70
And I walked into the garden,
Up and down the patterned paths,
In my stiff, correct brocade.
The blue and yellow flowers stood up proudly in the sun,
Each one.   75
I stood upright too,
Held rigid to the pattern
By the stiffness of my gown.
Up and down I walked,
Up and down   80

In a month he would have been my husband.
In a month, here, underneath this lime,
We would have broke the pattern;
He for me, and I for him,
He as colonel, I as Lady,   85
On this shady seat,
He had a whim
That sunlight carried blessing.
And I answered, "It shall be as you have said."
Now he is dead.   90

In Summer and in Winter I shall walk
Up and down
The patterned garden-paths
In my stiff, brocaded gown.
The squills and daffodils   95
Will give place to pillared roses, and to asters, and to snow.
I shall go
Up and down,
In my gown.
Gorgeously arrayed,   100
Boned and stayed.
And the softness of my body will be guarded from embrace
By each button, hook, and lace.

For the man who should loos me is dead,
Fighting with the Duke in Flanders,   105
In a pattern called a war.
Christ! What are patterns for?

—Amy Lowell (1874-1925)

WAS THIS THE FACE THAT LAUNCHED
A THOUSAND SHIPS*

Was this the face that launched a thousand ships,
And burnt the topless towers of Ilium?
Sweet Helen, make me immortal with a kiss!
Her lips suck forth my soul; see where it flies.
Come, Helen, come, give me my soul again.   5
Here will I dwell, for heaven is in these lips,
And all is dross that is not Helena.
I will be Paris, and for love of thee
Instead of Troy shall Wittenberg be sacked,
And I will combat with weak Menelaus,   10
And wear thy colors on my plumed crest.
Yea, I will wound Achilles in the heel,
And then return to Helen for a kiss.
O, thou art fairer than the evening's air,
Clad in the beauty of a thousand stars.   15
Brighter art thou than flaming Jupiter,
When he appeared to hapless Semele;
More lovely than the monarch of the sky,
In wanton Arethusa's azured arms,
And none but thou shalt be my paramour.   20

—Christopher Marlowe (1564-1593)

* from *Doctor Faustus*

TO HIS COY MISTRESS

Had we but world enough, and time,
This coyness*, lady, were no crime.   *modesty, reluctance
We would sit down, and think which way
To walk, and pass our long love's day.
Thou by the Indian Ganges' side
Shouldst rubies find; I by the tide
Of Humber would complain*. I would   *sing sad songs
Love you ten years before the Flood;
and you should, if you please, refuse
Till the conversion of the Jews.   10
My vegetable love should grow
Vaster than empires, and more slow.
A hundred years should go to praise
Thine eyes, and on thy forehead gaze;
Two hundred to adore each breast:
But thirty thousand to the rest;
An age at least to every part,
And the last age should show your heart.

For, lady, you deserve this state,
Nor would I love at lower rate.   20

    But at my back I always hear
Time's wingèd chariot hurrying near;
And yonder all before us lie
Deserts of vast eternity.
Thy beauty shall no more be found,
Nor in thy marble vault should sound
My echoing song; then worms shall try
That long preserved virginity,
And your quaint honor turn to dust,
And into ashes all my lust.   30
The grave's a fine and private place,
But none, I think, do there embrace.

    Now therefore, while the youthful hue
Sits on thy skin like morning dew*,   *glow, warmth
And while thy willing soul transpires
At every pore with instant* fires,   *urgent, eager
Now let us sport us while we may;
And now, like am'rous birds of prey,
Rather at once our time devour,
Than languish in his slow-chapped power.   40
Let us roll all our strength, and all
Our sweetness, up into one ball;
And tear our pleasure with rough strife
Thorough* the iron gate of life.   *through
Thus, though we cannot make our sun
Stand still, yet we will make him run.

                Andrew Marvell (1621-1678)

BIRTHING A GREAT RIVER

    High
    Higher in the Rockies,
Water trickling over granite,
    cutting thin ribbons
    through fine moss, velvet
    clusters nurtured by the
    rills that slice them.
Summer verdure shelters
    this primal
    crib, half-hidden   10
    in fern fronds and wild strawberries
    and scant straying white daisies
    amid prayer-shaped
        pines.

Our breathing blends with pulsing
            quiet

        hush
    broken only by
    natal whispers of rippling water
            joining rippling waters.

            —Charlyne Nichols (1937-   )

EQUITY

I (generic female of the species
    whose name is not even my own)

Did lawfully take that man
    (assertive, macho-proud)

To be my wedded husband,

To love, honor, and cherish . . .

    But later he insisted
        I'd promised to obey:
            "Clean the house,
                Do the laundry.   10
                Mow the lawn and
                Fix the faucet.
                Gas the car,
                Pay the bills
    And get this kid outa here, he's buggin' me.
                *

    And go get a job—
            You're in a rut and we need the money.
            *

    And by the way,   20
            bring me a beer, I'm
            right in the middle
            of a ballgame—jeez
            looka that sonofabitch Go!"
                    *
                    *
                    *
                    *

I do solemnly swear:
            "I'm tired, Judge,   30
            Just tell him, please,
            Marrying means sharing—
            It goes both ways."

The gavel sounded: Divorce Granted.
            —Charlyne Nichols (1937-   )

THE APPLICANT

First, are you our sort of person?
Do you wear
A glass eye, false teeth or a crutch,
A brace or a hook,
Rubber breasts or a rubber crotch,

Stitches to show something's missing? No, no? Then
How can we give you a thing?
Stop crying.
Open your hand.
Empty? Empty. Here is a hand   10

To fill it and willing
To bring teacups and roll away headaches
And do whatever you tell it.
Will you marry it?
It is guaranteed

To thumb shut your eyes at the end
And dissolve of **sorrow**.
We make new stock from the salt.
I notice you are stark naked.
How about this suit—   20

Black and stiff, but not a bad fit.
Will you marry it?
It is waterproof, shatterproof, proof
Against fire and bombs through the roof.
Believe me, they'll bury you in it.

Now your head, excuse me, is empty.
I have the ticket for that.
Come here, sweetie, out of the closet.
Well, what do you think of *that*?
Naked as paper to start   30

But in twenty-five years she'll be silver,
In fifty, gold.
A living doll, everywhere you look.
It can sew, it can cook,
It can talk, talk, talk.

It works, there is nothing wrong with it.
You have a hole, it's a poultice.
You have an eye, it's an image.
My boy, it's your last resort.
Will you marry it, marry it, marry it.

   —Sylvia Plath (1932-1963)

MIRROR

I am silver and exact. I have no preconceptions.
Whatever I see I swallow immediately
Just as it is, unmisted by love or dislike.
I am not cruel, only truthful—
The eye of a little god, four-cornered.
Most of the time I meditate on the opposite wall.
It is pink, with speckles. I have looked at it so long
I think it is a part of my heart. But it flickers.
Faces and darkness separate us over and over.

Now I am a lake. A woman bends over me,   10
Searching my reaches for what she really is.
Then she turns to those liars, the candles or the moon.
I see her back, and reflect it faithfully.
She rewards me with tears and an agitation of hands.
I am important to her. She comes and goes.
Each morning it is her face that replaces the darkness.
In me she has drowned a young girl, and in me an old woman
Rises toward her day after day, like a terrible fish.

—Sylvia Plath (1932-1963)

I AM A COWBOY IN THE BOAT OF RA

I am a cowboy in the boat of Ra,
sidewinders in the saloons of fools
bit my forehead   like   0
the untrustworthiness of Egyptologists
Who do not know their trips. Who was that
dog-faced man? they asked, the day I rode
from town.

School marms with halitosis cannot see
the Nefertiti fake chipped on the run by slick
germans, the hawk behind Sonny Rollins' head or   10
the ritual beard of his axe; a longhorn winding
its bells thru the Field of Reeds.

I am a cowboy in the boat of Ra. I bedded
down with Isis, Lady of the Boogaloo, dove
down deep in her horny, stuck up her Wells-Far-ago
in daring midday get away. "Start grabbing the
blue," i said from top of my double crown.

I am a cowboy in the boat of Ra. Ezzard Charles
of the Chisholm Trail. Took up the bass but they
blew off my thumb. Alchemist in ringmanship but a   20
sucker for the right cross.

I am a cowboy in the boat of Ra. Vamoosed from
the temple i bide my time. The price on the wanted
poster was a-going down, outlaw alias copped my stance
and moody greenhorns were making me dance; while my mouth's
shooting iron got its chambers jammed.

I am a cowboy in the boat of Ra. Boning-up in
the ol West i bide my time. You should see
me pick off these tin cans whippersnappers. I
write the motown longplays for the comeback of   30
Osiris. Make them up when stars stare at sleeping
steer out here near the campfire. Women arrive
on the backs of goats and throw themselves on
my Bowie.

I am a cowboy in the boat of Ra. Lord of the lash,
the Loup Garou Kid. Half breed son of Pisces and
Aquarius. I hold the souls of men in my pot. I do
the dirty boogie with scorpions. I make the bulls
keep still and was the first swinger to grape the taste

I am a cowboy in his boat. Pope Joan of the   40
Ptah Ra. C/mere a minute willya doll?
Be a good girl and
Bring me my Buffalo Horn of black powder
Bring me my headdress of black feathers
Bring me my bones of Ju-Ju snake
Go get my eyelids of red paint.
Hand me my shadow
I'm going into town after Set

I am a cowboy in the boat of Ra
Look out Set   here i come Set
to get Set   to sunset Set
to unseat Set   to Set down Set
                    usurper of the Royal couch
                    imposter RAdio of Moses' bush
                    party pooper O hater of dance
                    vampire outlaw of the milky way

                    —Ishmael Reed (1938-   )

WHAT HAPPENED HERE BEFORE

—300,000,000—

First a sea: soft sands, muds, and marls
     —loading, compressing, heating, crumpling,
      crushing, recrystallizing, infiltrating,
several times lifted and submerged.
intruding molten granite magma
     deep-cooled and speckling,
       gold quartz fills the cracks—

—80,000,000—

sea-bed strata raised and folded,
     granite far below.
warm quiet centuries of rains
     (make dark red tropic soils)
     wear down two miles of surface,
lay bare the veins and tumble heavy gold
     in steambeds
       slate and schist rock-riffles catch it—
volcanic ash floats down and dams the streams,
     piles up the gold and gravel—

—3,000,000

flowing north, two rivers joined,
     to make a wide long lake.
and then it tilted and the rivers fell apart
     all running west
     to cut the gorges of the Feather,
      Bear, and Yuba.
Ponderosa pine, manzanita, black oak, mountain yew.
     deer, coyote, bluejay, gray squirrel,
     ground squirrel, fox, blacktail hare,
      ringtail, bobcat, bear,
       all came to live here.

—40,000—

And human people came with basket hats and nets
     winter-houses underground
     yew bows painted green,
     feasts and dances for the boys and girls
      songs and stories in the smoky dark.

—125—

Then came the white man: tossed up trees and
     boulders with big hoses,
     going after that old gravel and the gold.
horses, apple-orchards, card-games,
     pistol-shooting, churches, county jail.

We asked, who the land belongs to.
        and where one pays tax.
(two gents who never used it twenty years,
and before them the widow
        of the son of the man
        who got him a patented deed
        on a worked-out mining claim,)
laid hasty on land that was deer and acorn
        grounds of the Nisenan?
        branch of the Maidu?
(they never had a chance to speak, even,
        their name.)
(and who remembers the Treaty of Guadalupe Hidalgo.)

        the land belongs to itself.
        "no self in self; no self in things"

        Turtle Island swims
        in the ocean-sky swirl-void
        biting its tail while the worlds go
            on-and-off
                winking

& Mr. Tobiassen, a Cousin Jack,
        assesses the county tax.
(the tax is our body-mind, guest at the banquet
        Memorial and Annual, in honor
        of sunlight grown heavy and tasty
        while moving up food-chains
in search of a body with eyes and a fairly large
        brain—
        to look back at itself
        on high.)

        now,

we sit here near the diggings
in the forest, by our fire, and watch
the moon and planets and the shooting stars—

my sons ask, who are we?
drying apples picked from homestead trees
drying berries, curing meat,
shooting arrows at a bale of straw.

military jets head northeast, roaring, every dawn.
my sons ask, who are they?

        WE SHALL SEE
        WHO KNOWS
        HOW TO BE

Bluejay screeches from a pine.
                —Gary Snyder (1930-   )

ULYSSES

It little profits that an idle king,
By this still hearth, among these barren crags,
Matched with an agèd wife, I mete and dole
Unequal laws unto a savage race,
That hoard, and sleep, and feed, and know not me.
I cannot rest from travel; I will drink
Life to the lees. All times I have enjoyed
Greatly, have suffered greatly, both with those
That loved me, and alone; on shore, and when
Through scudding drifts the rainy Hyades   10
Vext the dim sea. I am become a name;
For always roaming with a hungry heart
Much have I seen and known,—cities of men
And manners, climates, councils, governments,
Myself not least, but honored of them all;
And drunk delight of battle with my peers,
Far on the ringing plains of windy Troy.
I am a part of all that I have met;
Yet all experience is an arch wherethrough
Gleams that untraveled world, whose margin fades   20
For ever and for ever when I move.
How dull it is to pause, to make an end,
To rust unburnished, not to shine in use!
As though to breathe were life! Life piled on life
Were all too little, and of one to me
Little remains; but every hour is saved
From that eternal silence, something more,
A bringer of new things; and vile it were
For some three suns to store and hoard myself,
And this grey spirit yearning in desire   30
To follow knowledge like a sinking star,
Beyond the utmost bound of human thought.

This is my son, mine own Telemachus,
To whom I leave the scepter and the isle—
Well-loved of me, discerning to fulfil
This labor, by slow prudence to make mild
A rugged people, and through soft degrees
Subdue them to the useful and the good.
Most blameless is he, centered in the sphere
Of common duties, decent not to fail   40
In offices of tenderness, and pay
Meet adoration to my household gods,
When I am gone. He works his work, I mine.

There lies the port; the vessel puffs her sail:
There gloom the dark, broad seas. My mariners,
Souls that have toiled, and wrought, and thought with me—
That ever with a frolic welcome took
The thunder and the sunshine, and opposed
Free hearts, free foreheads—you and I are old;
Old age hath yet his honor and his toil.   50
Death closes all; but something ere the end,

Some work of noble note, may yet be done,
Not unbecoming men that strove with Gods.
The lights begin to twinkle from the rocks;
The long day wanes; the slow moon climbs; the deep
Moans round with many voices. Come, my friends,
'Tis not too late to seek a newer world.
Push off, and sitting well in order smite
The sounding furrows; for my purpose holds
To sail beyond the sunset, and the baths 60
Of all the western stars, until I die.
It may be that the gulfs will wash us down;
It may be we shall touch the Happy Isles,
And see the great Achilles, whom we knew.
Though much is taken, much abides; and though
We are not now that strength which in old days
Moved earth and heaven, that which we are, we are:
One equal temper of heroic hearts,
Made weak by time and fate, but strong in will
To strive, to seek, to find, and not to yield. 70

Alfred, Lord Tennyson (1809-1892)

THE RED WHEELBARROW

so much depends
upon

a red wheel
barrow

glazed with rain
water

beside the white
chickens.
—William Carlos Williams (1883-1963)

BIRTHDAY PARTY

They were a couple in their late thirties, and they looked unmistakably married. They sat on the banquette opposite us in a little narrow restaurant, having dinner. The man had a round, self-satisfied face, with glasses on it; the woman was fadingly pretty, in a big hat. There was nothing conspicuous about them, nothing particularly noticeable, until the end of their meal, when it suddenly became obvious that this was an Occasion—in fact, the husband's birthday, and the wife had planned a little surprise for him.

It arrived, in the form of a small but glossy birthday cake, with one pink candle burning in the center. The headwaiter brought it in and placed it before the husband, and meanwhile the violin-and-piano orchestra played "Happy Birthday to You" and the wife beamed with shy pride over her little surprise, and such few people as there were in the restaurant tried to help out with a pattering of applause. It became clear at once that help was needed, because the husband was not pleased. Instead he was hotly embarrassed, and indignant at his wife for embarrassing him.

You looked at him and you saw this and you thought, "Oh, now, don't be like that!" But he was like that, and as soon as the little cake had been deposited on the table, and the orchestra had finished the birthday piece, and the general attention had shifted from the man and woman, I saw him say something to her under his breath—some punishing thing, quick and curt and unkind. I couldn't bear to look at the woman then, so I stared at my plate and waited for quite a long time. Not long enough, though. She was still crying when I finally glanced over there again. Crying quietly and heartbrokenly and hopelessly, all to herself, under the gay big brim of her best hat.

—*Katharine Brush* (*1902-1952*)

Knowing that Mrs. Mallard was afflicted with a heart trouble, great care was taken to break to her as gently as possible the news of her husband's death.

It was her sister Josephine who told her, in broken sentences; veiled hints that revealed in half concealing. Her husband's friend Richards was there, too, near her. It was he who had been in the newspaper office when intelligence of the railroad disaster was received, with Brently Mallard's name leading the list of "killed." He had only taken the time to assure himself of its truth by a second telegram, and had hastened to forestall any less careful, less tender friend in bearing the sad message.

She did not hear the story as many women have heard the same, with a paralyzed inability to accept its significance. She wept at once, with sudden, wild abandonment, in her sister's arms. When the storm of grief had spent itself she went away to her room alone. She would have no one follow her.

There stood, facing the open window, a comfortable, roomy armchair. Into this she sank, pressed down by a physical exhaustion that haunted her body and seemed to reach into her soul.

She could see in the open square before her house the tops of trees that were all aquiver with the new spring life. The delicious breath of rain was in the air. In the street below a peddler was crying his wares. The notes of a distant song which someone was singing reached her faintly, and countless sparrows were twittering in the eaves.

There were patches of blue sky showing here and there through the clouds that had met and piled one above the other in the west facing her window.

She sat with her head thrown back upon the cushion of the chair, quite motionless, except when a sob came up into her throat and shook her, as a child who has cried itself to sleep continues to sob in its dreams.

She was young, with a fair, calm face, whose lines bespoke repression and even a certain strength. But now there was a dull stare in her eyes, whose gaze was fixed away off yonder on one of those patches of blue sky. It was not a glance of reflection, but rather indicated a suspension of intelligent thought.

There was something coming to her and she was waiting for it, fearfully. What was it? She did not know; it was too subtle and elusive to name. But she felt it, creeping out of the sky, reaching toward her through the sounds, the scents, the color that filled the air.

Now her bosom rose and fell tumultuously. She was beginning to recognize this thing that was approaching to possess her, and she was striving to beat it back with her will—as powerless as her two white slender hands would have been.

When she abandoned herself a little whispered word escaped her slightly parted lips. She said it over and over under her breath: "free, free, free!" The vacant stare and the look of terror that had followed it went from her eyes. They stayed keen and bright. Her pulses beat fast, and the coursing blood warmed and relaxed every inch of her body.

She did not stop to ask if it were or were not a monstrous joy that held her. A clear and exalted perception enabled her to dismiss the suggestion as trivial.

She knew that she would weep again when she saw the kind, tender hands folded in death; the face that had never looked save with love upon her, fixed and gray and dead. But she saw beyond that bitter moment a long procession of years to come that would belong to her absolutely. And she opened and spread her arms out to them in welcome.

There would be no one to live for her during those coming years; she would live for herself. There would be no powerful will bending hers in that blind persistence with which men and women believe they have a right to impose a private will upon a fellow creature. A kind intention or a cruel intention made the act seem no less a crime as she looked upon it in that brief moment of illumination.

And yet she had loved him—sometimes. Often she had not. What did it matter! What could love, the unsolved mystery, count for in face of this possession of self-assertion which she suddenly recognized as the strongest impulse of her being!

"Free! Body and soul free!" she kept whispering.

Josephine was kneeling before the closed door with her lips to the keyhole, imploring for admission. "Louise, open the door! I beg; open the door—you will make yourself ill. What are you doing, Louise? For heaven's sake open the door."

"Go away. I am not making myself ill." No; she was drinking in a very elixir of life through that open window.

Her fancy was running riot along those days ahead of her. Spring days, summer days, and all sorts of days that would be her own. She breathed a quick prayer that life might be long. It was only yesterday she had thought with a shudder that life might be long.

She arose at length and opened the door to her sister's importunities. There was a feverish triumph in her eyes, and she carried herself unwittingly like a goddess of Victory. She clasped her sister's waist, and together they descended the stairs. Richards stood waiting for them at the bottom.

Someone was opening the front door with a latchkey. It was Brently Mallard who entered, a little travel-stained, composedly carrying his grip-sack and umbrella. He had been far from the scene of accident, and did not even know there had been one. He stood amazed at Josephine's piercing cry; at Richards's quick motion to screen him from the view of his wife.

But Richards was too late.

When the doctors came they said she had died of heart disease—of joy that kills.

—*Kate Chopin* (*1851-1904*)

THE OPEN BOAT

A TALE INTENDED TO BE AFTER THE FACT:
BEING THE EXPERIENCE OF FOUR MEN FROM THE SUNK STEAMER *Commodore*

I

None of them knew the colour of the sky. Their eyes glanced level, and were fastened upon the waves that swept toward them. These waves were of the hue of slate, save for the tops, which were of foaming white, and all of the men knew the colours of the sea. The horizon narrowed and widened, and dipped and rose, and at all times its edge was jagged with waves that seemed thrust up in points like rocks.

Many a man ought to have a bathtub larger than the boat which here rode upon the sea. These waves were most wrongfully and barbarously abrupt and tall, and each froth-top was a problem in small-boat navigation.

The cook squatted in the bottom, and looked with both eyes at the six inches of gunwale which separated him from the ocean. His sleeves were rolled over his fat forearms, and the two flaps of his unbuttoned vest dangled as he bent to bail out the boat. Often he said, "Gawd! that was a narrow clip." As he remarked it he invariably gazed eastward over the broken sea.

The oiler, steering with one of the two oars in the boat, sometimes raised himself suddenly to keep clear of water that swirled in over the stern. It was a thin little oar, and it seemed often ready to snap.

The correspondent, pulling at the other oar, watched the waves and wondered why he was there.

The injured captain, lying in the bow, was at the time buried in that profound dejection and indifference which comes, temporarily at least, to even the bravest and most enduring when, willy-nilly, the firm fails, the army loses, the ship goes down. The mind of the master of a vessel is rooted deep in the timbers of her, though he command for a day or a decade; and this captain had on him the stern impression of a scene in the greys of dawn of seven turned faces, and later a stump of a topmast with a white ball on it, that slashed to and fro at the waves, went low and lower, and down. Thereafter there was something strange in his voice. Although steady, it was deep with mourning, and of a quality beyond oration or tears.

"Keep 'er a little more south, Billie," said he.

"A little more south sir," said the oiler in the stern.

A seat in his boat was not unlike a seat upon a bucking broncho, and by the same token a broncho is not much smaller. The craft pranced and reared and plunged like an animal. As each wave came, and she rose for it, she seemed like a horse making at a fence outrageously high. The manner of her scramble over these walls of water is a mystic thing, and, moreover, at the top of them were ordinarily these problems in white water, the foam racing down from the summit of each wave requiring a new leap, and a leap from the air. Then, after scornfully bumping a crest, she would slide and race and splash down a long incline, and arrive bobbing and nodding in front of the next menace.

A singular disadvantage of the sea lies in the fact that after successfully surmounting one wave you discover that there is another behind it just as important and just as nervously anxious to do something effective in the way of swamping boats. In a ten-foot dinghy one can get an idea of the resources of the sea in the line of waves that is not probable to the average experience which is never at sea in a dinghy. As each slaty wall of water approached, it shut all else from view of the men in the boat, and it was not difficult to imagine that this particular wave was the final outburst of the ocean, the last effort of the grim water. There was a terrible grace in the move of the waves, and they came in silence, save for the snarling of the crests.

In the wan light the faces of the men must have been grey. Their eyes must have glinted in strange ways as they gazed steadily astern. Viewed from a balcony, the whole thing would doubtless have been weirdly picturesque. But the men in the boat had no time to see it, and if they had had leisure, there were other things to occupy their minds. The sun swung steadily up the sky, and they knew it was broad day because the colour of the sea changed from slate to emerald green streaked with amber lights, and the foam was like tumbling snow. The process of the breaking day was unknown to them. They were aware only of this effect upon the colour of the waves that rolled toward them.

In disjointed sentences the cook and the correspondent argued as to the difference between a life-saving station and a house of refuge. The cook had said: "There's a house of refuge just north of the Mosquito Inlet Light, and as soon as they see us they'll come off in their boat and pick us up."

"As soon as who see us?" said the correspondent.

"The crew," said the cook.

"Houses of refuge don't have crews," said the correspondent. "As I understand them, they are only places where clothes and grub are stored for the benefit of shipwrecked people. They don't carry crews."

"Oh, yes they do," said the cook.

"No, they don't," said the correspondent.

"Well, we're not there yet, anyhow," said the oiler, in the stern.

"Well," said the cook, "perhaps it's not a house of refuge that I'm thinking of as being near Mosquito Inlet Light; perhaps it's a life-saving station."

"We're not there yet," said the oiler in the stern.

II

As the boat bounced from the top of each wave the wind tore through the hair of the hatless men, and as the craft plopped her stern down again the spray slashed past them. The crest of each of these waves was a hill, from the top of which the men surveyed for a moment a broad tumultuous expanse, shining and wind-riven. It was probably splendid, it was probably glorious, this play of the free sea, wild with lights of emerald and white and amber.

"Bully good thing it's an on-shore wind," said the cook. "If not, where would we be? Wouldn't have a show."

"That's right," said the correspondent.

The busy oiler nodded his assent.

Then the captain, in the bow, chuckled in a way that expressed humour, contempt, tragedy, all in one. "Do you think we've got much of a show now, boys?" said he.

Whereupon the three were silent, save for a trifle of hemming and hawing. To express any particular optimism at this time they felt to be childish and stupid, but they all doubtless possessed this sense of the situation in their minds. A young man thinks doggedly at such times. On the other hand, the ethics of their condition was decidedly against any open suggestion of hopelessness. So they were silent.

"Oh, well," said the captain, soothing his children, "we'll get ashore all right."

But there was that in his tone which made them think; so the oiler quoth, "Yes! if this wind holds."

The cook was bailing. "Yes! if we don't catch hell in the surf."

Canton-flannel gulls flew near and far. Sometimes they sat down on the sea, near patches of brown seaweed that rolled over the waves with a movement like carpets on a line in a gale. The birds sat comfortably in groups, and they were envied by some in the dinghy, for the wrath of the sea was no more to them than it was to a covey of prairie chickens a thousand miles inland. Often they came very close and stared at the men with black bead-like eyes. At these times they were uncanny and sinister in their unblinking scrutiny, and the men hooted angrily at them, telling them to be gone. One came, and evidently decided to alight on the top of the captain's head. The bird flew parallel to the boat and did not circle, but made short sidelong jumps in the air in chicken-fashion. His black eyes were wistfully fixed upon the captain's head. "Ugly brute," said the oiler to the bird. "You look as if you were made with a jack-knife." The cook and the correspondent swore darkly at the creature. The captain naturally wished to knock it away with the end of the heavy painter, but he did not dare do it, because anything resembling an emphatic gesture would have capsized this freighted boat;

230

and so, with his open hand, the captain gently and carefully waved the gull away. After it had been discouraged from the pursuit the captain breathed easier on account of his hair, and others breathed easier because the bird struck their minds at this time as being somehow gruesome and ominous.

In the meantime the oiler and the correspondent rowed. And also they rowed. They sat together in the same seat, and each rowed an oar. Then the oiler took both oars; then the correspondent took both oars; then the oiler; then the correspondent. They rowed and they rowed. The very ticklish part of the business was when the time came for the reclining one in the stern to take his turn at the oars. By the very last star of truth, it is easier to steal eggs from under a hen than it was to change seats in the dinghy. First the man in the stern slid his hand along the thwart and moved with care, as if he were of Sevres. Then the man in the rowing-seat slid his hand along the other thwart. It was all done with the most extraordinary care. As the two sidled past each other, the whole party kept watchful eyes on the coming wave, and the captain cried: "Look out, now! Steady, there!"

The brown mats of seaweed that appeared from time to time were like islands, bits of earth. They were travelling, apparently, neither one way nor the other. They were, to all intents, stationary. They informed the men in the boat that it was making progress slowly toward the land.

The captain, rearing cautiously in the bow after the dinghy soared on a great swell, said that he had seen the lighthouse at Mosquito Inlet. Presently the cook remarked that he had seen it. The correspondent was at the oars then, and for some reason he too wished to look at the lighthouse; but his back was toward the far shore, and the waves were important, and for some time he could not seize an opportunity to turn his head. But at last there came a wave more gentle than the others, and when at the crest of it he swiftly scoured the western horizon.

"See it?" said the captain.

"No," said the correspondent, slowly; "I didn't see anything."

"Look again," said the captain. He pointed. "It's exactly in that direction."

At the top of another wave the correspondent did as he was bid, and this time his eyes chanced on a small, still thing on the edge of the swaying horizon. It was precisely like the point of a pin. It took an anxious eye to find a lighthouse so tiny.

"Think we'll make it, Captain?"

"If this wind holds and the boat don't swamp, we can't do much else," said the captain.

The little boat, lifted by each towering sea and splashed viciously by the crests, made progress that in the absence of seaweed was not apparent to those in her. She seemed just a wee thing wallowing, miraculously top up, at the mercy of five oceans. Occasionally a great spread of water, like white flames, swarmed into her.

"Bail her, cook," said the captain, serenely.

"All right, Captain," said the cheerful cook.

III

It would be difficult to describe the subtle brotherhood of men that was here established on the seas. No one said that it was so. No one mentioned it. But it dwelt in the boat, and each man felt it warm him. They were a captain, an oiler, a cook, and a correspondent, and they were friends—friends in a more curiously iron-bound degree than may be common. The hurt captain, lying against the water-jar in the bow, spoke always in a low voice and calmly; but he could never command a more ready and swiftly obedient crew than the motley three of the dinghy. It was more than a mere recognition of what was best for the common safety. There was surely in it a quality that was personal and heart-felt. And after this devotion to the commander of the boat, there was this comradeship, that the corespondent, for instance, who had been taught to be cynical of men, knew even at the time was the best experience of his life. But no one said that it was so. No one mentioned it.

"I wish we had a sail," remarked the captain. "We might try my overcoat on the end of an oar, and give you two boys a chance to rest." So the cook and the correspondent held the mast and spread wide the overcoat; the oiler steered; and the little boat made good way with her new rig. Sometimes the oiler had to scull sharply to keep a sea from breaking into the boat, but otherwise sailing was a success.

Meanwhile the lighthouse had been growing slowly larger. It had now almost assumed colour, and appeared like a little grey shadow on the sky. The man at the oars could not be prevented from turning his head rather often to try for a glimpse of this little grey shadow.

At last, from the top of each wave, the men in the tossing boat could see land. Even as the lighthouse was an upright shadow on the sky, this land seemed but a long black shadow on the sea. It certainly was thinner than paper. "We must be about opposite New Smyrna," said the cook, who had coasted this shore often in schooners. "Captain, by the way, I believe they abandoned that life-saving station there about a year ago."

"Did they?" said the captain.

The wind slowly died away. The cook and the correspondent were not now obliged to slave in order to hold high the oar. But the waves continued their old impetuous swooping at the dinghy, and the little craft, no longer underway, struggled woundily over them. The oiler or the correspondent took the oars again.

Shipwrecks are apropos of nothing. If men could only train for them and have them occur when the men had reached pink condition, there would be less drowning at sea. Of the four in the dinghy none had slept any time worth mentioning for two days and two nights previous to embarking in the dinghy, and in the excitement of clambering about the deck of a foundering ship they had also forgotten to eat heartily.

For these reasons, and for others, neither the oiler nor the correspondent was fond of rowing at this time. The correspondent wondered ingenuously how in the name of all that was sane could there be people who thought it amusing to row a boat. It was not an amusement; it was a diabolical punishment, and even a genius of mental aberrations could never conclude that it was anything but a horror to the muscles and a crime against the back. He mentioned to the boat in general how the amusement of rowing struck him, and the weary-faced oiler smiled in full sympathy. Previously to the foundering, by the way, the oiler had worked a double watch in the engine-room of the ship.

"Take her easy now, boys," said the captain. "Don't spend yourselves. If we have to run a surf you'll need all your strength, because we'll sure have to swim for it. Take your time."

Slowly the land arose from the sea. From a black line it became a line of black and a line of white—trees and sand. Finally the captain said that he could make out a house on the shore. "That's the house of refuge, sure," said the cook. "They'll see us before long, and come out after us."

The distant lighthouse reared high. "The keeper ought to be able to make us out now, if he's looking through a glass," said the captain. "He'll notify the life-saving people."

"None of those other boats could have got ashore to give word of this wreck," said the oiler, in a low voice, "else the life-boat would be out hunting us."

Slowly and beautifully the land loomed out of the sea. The wind came again. It had veered from the north-east to the south-east. Finally a new sound struck the ears of the men in the boat. It was the low thunder of the surf on the shore. "We'll never be able to make the lighthouse now," said the captain. "Swing her head a little more north, Billie."

"A little more north, sir," said the oiler.

Whereupon the little boat turned her nose once more down the wind, and all but the oarsman watched the shore grow. Under the influence of this expansion doubt and direful apprehension were leaving the minds of the men. The management of the boat was still most absorbing, but it could not prevent a quiet cheerfulness. In an hour, perhaps, they would be ashore.

Their backbones had become thoroughly used to balancing in the boat, and they now rode this wild colt of a dinghy like circus men. The correspondent thought that he had been drenched to the skin, but happening to feel in the top pocket of his coat, he found therein eight cigars. Four of them were soaked with sea-water; four were perfectly scatheless. After a search, somebody produced three dry matches; and thereupon the four waifs rode impudently in their little boat and, with an assurance of an impending rescue shining in their eyes, puffed at the big cigars, and judged well and ill of all men. Everybody took a drink of water.

IV

"Cook," remarked the captain, "there don't seem to be any signs of life about your house of refuge."

"No," replied the cook. "Funny they don't see us!"

A broad stretch of lowly coast lay before the eyes of the men. It was of low dunes topped with dark vegetation. The roar of the surf was plain, and sometimes they could see the white lip of a wave as it spun up the beach. A tiny house was blocked out black upon the sky. Southward, the slim lighthouse lifted its little grey length.

Tide, wind, and waves were swinging the dinghy northward. "Funny they don't see us," said the men.

The surf's roar was here dulled, but its tone was nevertheless thunderous and mighty. As the boat swam over the great rollers the men sat listening to this roar. "We'll swamp sure," said everybody.

It is fair to say here that there was not a life-saving station within twenty miles in either direction; but the men did not know this fact, and in consequence they made dark and opprobrious remarks concerning the eyesight of the nation's life-savers. Four scowling men sat in the dinghy and surpassed records in the invention of epithets.

"Funny they don't see us."

The light-heartedness of a former time had completely faded. To their sharpened minds it was easy to conjure pictures of all kinds of incompetency and blindness and, indeed, cowardice. There was the shore of the populous land, and it was bitter and bitter to them that from it came no sign.

"Well," said the captain, ultimately, "I suppose we'll have to make a try for ourselves. If we stay out here too long, we'll none of us have strength left to swim after the boat swamps."

And so the oiler, who was at the oars, turned the boat straight for the shore. There was a sudden tightening of muscles. There was some thinking.

"If we don't all get ashore," said the captain—"if we don't all get ashore, I suppose you fellows know where to send news of my finish?"

They then briefly exchanged some addresses and admonitions. As for the reflections of the men, there was a great deal of rage in them. Perchance they might be formulated thus: "If I am going to be drowned—if I am going to be drowned—if I am going to be drowned, why, in the name of the seven mad gods who rule the sea, was I allowed to come this far and contemplate sand and trees? Was I brought here merely to have my nose dragged away as I was about to nibble the sacred cheese of life? It is preposterous. If this old ninny-woman, Fate, cannot do better than this, she should be deprived of the management of men's fortunes. She is an old hen who knows not her intention. If she has decided to drown me, why did she not do it in the beginning and save me all this trouble? The whole affair is absurd.—But no; she cannot mean to drown me. She dare not drown me. She cannot drown me. Not after all this work." Afterward the man might have had an impulse to shake his fist at the clouds. "Just you drown me, now, and then hear what I call you!"

The billows that came at this time were more formidable. They seemed always just about to break and roll over the little boat in a turmoil of foam. There was a preparatory and long growl in the speech of them. No mind unused to the sea would have concluded that the dinghy could ascend these sheer heights in time. The shore was still afar. The oiler was a wily surfman. "Boys," he said swiftly, "she won't live three minutes more, and we're too far out to swim. Shall I take her to sea again, Captain?"

"Yes; go ahead!" said the captain.

This oiler, by a series of quick miracles and fast and steady oarsmanship, turned the boat in the middle of the surf and took her safely to sea again.

There was a considerable silence as the boat bumped over the furowed sea to deeper water. Then somebody in gloom spoke: "Well, anyhow, they must have seen us from the shore by now."

The gulls went in slanting flight up the wind toward the grey, desolate east. A squall, marked by dingy clouds and clouds brick-red like smoke from a burning building, appeared from the south-east.

"What do you think of those life-saving people? Ain't they peaches?"

"Funny they haven't seen us."

"Maybe they think we're out here for sport! Maybe they think we're fishin'. Maybe they think we're damned fools."

It was a long afternoon. A changed tide tried to force them southward, but wind and wave said northward. Far ahead, where coast-line, sea, and sky formed their mighty angle, there were little dots which seemed to indicate a city on the shore.

"St. Augustine?"

The captain shook his head. "Too near Mosquito Inlet."

And the oiler rowed, and then the correspondent rowed; then the oiler rowed. It was a weary business. The human back can become the seat of more aches and pains than are registered in books for the composite anatomy of a regiment. It is a limited area, but it can become the theatre of innumerable muscular conflicts, tangles, wrenches, knots, and other comforts.

"Did you ever like to row, Billie?" asked the correspondent.

"No," said the oiler; "hang it!"

When one exchanged the rowing-seat for a place in the bottom of the boat, he suffered a bodily depression that caused him to be careless of everything save an obligation to wiggle one finger. There was cold sea-water swashing to and fro in the boat, and he sat in it. His head, pillowed on a thwart, was within an inch of the swirl of a wave-crest, and sometimes a particularly obstreperous sea came inboard and drenched him once more. But these matters did not annoy him. It is almost certain that if the boat had capsized he would have tumbled comfortably out upon the ocean as if he felt sure that it was a great soft mattress.

"Look! There's a man on the shore!"

"Where?"

"There! See 'im? See 'im?"

"Yes, sure! He's walking along."

"Now he's stopped. Look! He's facing us!"

"He's waving at us!"

"So, he is! By thunder!"

"Ah, now we're all right! Now we're all right! There'll be a boat out here for us in half an hour."

"He's going on. He's running. He's going up to that house there."

The remote beach seemed lower than the sea, and it required a searching glance to discern the little black figure. The captain saw a floating stick, and they rowed to it. A bath towel was by some weird chance in the boat, and, tying this on the stick, the captain waved it. The oarsman did not dare turn his head, so he was obliged to ask questions.

"What's he doing now?"

"He's standing still again. He's looking, I think.—There he goes again—toward the house.—Now he's stopped again."

"Is he waving at us?"

"No, not now; he was, though."

"Look! There comes another man!"

"He's running."

"Look at him go, would you!"

"Why, he's on a bicycle. Now he's met the other man. They're both waving at us. Look!"

"There comes something up the beach."

"What the devil is that thing?"

"Why, it looks like a boat."

"Why, certainly, it's a boat."

"No; it's on wheels."

"Yes, so it is. Well, that must be the life-boat. They drag them along shore on a wagon."

"That's the life boat, sure."

"No, by God, it's—it's an omnibus."

"I tell you it's a life-boat."

"It is not! It's an omnibus. I can see it plain. See? One of these big hotel omnibuses."

"By thunder, you're right. It's an omnibus, sure as fate. What do you suppose they are doing with an omnibus? Maybe they are going around collecting the life-crew, hey?"

"That's it, likely. Look! There's a fellow waving a little black flag. He's standing on the steps of the omnibus. There come those other two fellows. Now they're all talking together. Look at the fellow with the flag. Maybe he ain't waving it!"

"That ain't a flag, is it? That's his coat. Why, certainly, that's his coat."

"So it is; it's his coat. He's taken it off and is waving it around his head. But would you look at him swing it!"

"Oh, say, there isn't any life-saving station there. That's just a winter-resort hotel omnibus that has brought over some of the boarders to see us drown."

"What's that idiot with the coat mean? What's he signalling, anyhow?"

"It looks as if he were trying to tell us to go north. There must be a life-saving station up there."

"No; he thinks we're fishing. Just giving us a merry hand. See? Ah, there, Willie!"

"Well, I wish I could make something out of those signals. What do you suppose he means?"

"He don't mean anything; he's just playing."

"Well, if he'd just signal us to try the surf again, or to go to sea and wait, or go north, or go south, or go to hell, there would be some reason in it. But look at him! He just stands there and keeps his coat revolving like a wheel. The ass!"

"There come more people."

"Now there's quite a mob. Look! Isn't that a boat?"

"Where? Oh, I see where you mean. No, that's no boat."

"He must think we like to see him do that. Why don't he quit it? It don't mean anything."

"I don't know. I think he is trying to make us go north. It must be that there's a life-saving station there somewhere."

"Say, he ain't tired yet. Look at 'im wave!"

"Wonder how long he can keep that up. He's been revolving his coat ever since he caught sight of us. He's an idiot. Why aren't they getting men to bring a boat out? A fishing boat—on of those big yawls—could come out here all right. Why don't he do something?"

"Oh, it's all right now."

"They'll have a boat out here for us in less than no time, now that they've seen us."

A faint yellow tone came into the sky over the low land. The shadows on the sea slowly deepened. The wind bore coldness with it, and the men began to shiver.

"Holy smoke!" said one, allowing his voice to express his impious mood, "if we keep on monkeying out here! If we've got to flounder out here all night!"

"Oh, we'll never have to stay here all night! Don't worry. They've seen us now, and it won't be long before they'll come chasing out after us."

The shore grew dusky. The man waving a coat blended gradually into this gloom, and it swallowed in the same manner the omnibus and the group of people. The spray, when it dashed uproariously over the side, made the voyagers shrink and swear like men who were being branded.

"I'd like to catch the chump who waved the coat. I feel like socking him one, just for luck."

"Why? What did he do?"

"Oh, nothing, but then he seemed so damned cheerful."

In the meantime the oiler rowed, and then the correspondent rowed, and then the oiler rowed. Grey-faced and bowed forward, they mechanically, turn by turn, plied the leaden oars. The form of the lighthouse had vanished from the southern horizon, but finally a pale star appeared, just lifting from the sea. The streaked saffron in the west passed before the all-merging darkness, and the sea to the east was black. The land had vanished, and was expressed only by the low and drear thunder of the surf.

"If I am going to be drowned—if I am going to be drowned—if I am going to be drowned, why, in the name of the seven mad gods who rule the sea, was I allowed to come thus far and contemplate sand and trees? Was I brought here merely to have my nose dragged away as I was about to nibble the sacred cheese of life?"

The patient captain, drooped over the water-jar, was sometimes obliged to speak to the oarsman.

"Keep her head up! Keep her head up!"

"Keep her head up, sir." The voices were weary and low.

This was surely a quiet evening. All save the oarsman lay heavily and listlessly in the boat's bottom. As for him, his eyes were just capable of noting the tall black waves that swept forward in the most sinister silence, save for an occasional subdued growl of a crest.

The cook's head was on a thwart, and he looked without interest at the water under his nose. He was deep in other scenes. Finally he spoke. "Billie," he murmured, dreamfully, "what kind of pie do you like best?"

V

"Pie!" said the oiler and the correspondent, agitatedly. "Don't talk about those things, blast you!"

"Well," said the cook, "I was just thinking about ham sandwiches and—"

A night on the sea in an open boat is a long night. As darkness settled finally, the shine of the light, lifting from the sea in the south, changed to full gold. On the northern horizon a new light appeared, a small bluish gleam on the edge of the waters. These two lights were the furniture of the world. Otherwise there was nothing but waves.

Two men huddled in the stern and distances were so magnificent in the dinghy that the rower was enabled to keep his feet partly warm by thrusting them under his companions. Their legs indeed extended far under the rowing-seat until they touched the feet of the captain forward. Sometimes, despite the efforts of the tired oarsman, a wave came piling into the boat, an icy wave of the night, and the chilling water soaked them anew. They would twist their bodies for a moment and groan, and sleep the dead sleep once more, while the water in the boat gurgled about them as the craft rocked.

The plan of the oiler and the correspondent was for one to row until he lost the ability, and then arouse the other from his sea-water couch in the bottom of the boat.

The oiler plied the oars until his head drooped forward and overpowering sleep blinded him; and he rowed yet afterward. Then he touched a man in the bottom of the boat, and called his name. "Will you spell me for a little while?" he said, meekly.

"Sure, Billie," said the correspondent, awaking and dragging himself to a sitting position. They exchanged places carefully and the oiler, cuddling down in the seawater at the cook's side, seemed to go to sleep instantly.

The particular violence of the sea had ceased. The waves came without snarling. The obligation of the man at the oars was to keep the boat headed so that the tilt of the rolers would not capsize her, and to preserve her from filling when the crests rushed past. The black waves were silent and hard to be seen in the darkness. Often one was almost upon the boat before the oarsman was aware.

In a low voice the correspondent addressed the captain. He was not sure that the captain was awake, although this iron man seemed to be always awake. "Captain, shall I keep her making for that light north, sir?"

The same steady voice answered him. "Yes. Keep it about two points off the port bow."

The cook had tied a life-belt around himself in order to get even the warmth which this clumsy cork contrivance could donate, and he seemed almost stove-like when a rower, whose teeth invariably chattered wildly as soon as he ceased his labour, dropped down to sleep.

The correspondent, as he rowed, looked down at the two men sleeping underfoot. The cook's arm was around the oiler's shoulders, and, with their fragmentary clothing and haggard faces, they were the babes of the sea—a grotesque rendering of the old babes in the wood.

Later he must have grown stupid at his work, for suddenly there was a growling of water, and a crest came with a roar and a swash into the boat, and it was a wonder that it did not set the cook afloat in his life-belt. The cook continued to sleep, but the oiler sat up, blinking his eyes and shaking with the new cold.

"Oh, I'm awful sorry, Billie," said the correspondent, contritely.

"That's all right, old boy," said the oiler, and lay down again and was asleep.

Presently it seemed that even the captain dozed, and the correspondent thought that he was the one man afloat on all the oceans. The wind had a voice as it came over the waves, and it was sadder than the end.

There was a long, loud swishing astern of the boat, and a gleaming trail of phosphorescence, like blue flame, was furrowed on the black waters. It might have been made by a monstrous knife.

Then there came a stillness, while the correspondent breathed with open mouth and looked at the sea.

Suddenly there was another swish and another long flash of bluish light, and this time it was alongside the boat, and might almost been reached with an oar. The correspondent saw an enormous fin speed like a shadow through the water, hurling the crystalline spray and leaving the long glowing trail.

The correspondent looked over his shoulder at the captain. His face was hidden, and he seemed to be asleep. He looked at the babes of the sea. They certainly were asleep. So, being bereft of sympathy, he leaned a little way to one side and swore softly into the sea.

But the thing did not then leave the vicinity of the boat. Ahead or astern, on one side or the other, at intervals long or short, fled the long sparkling streak, and there was to be heard the whirroo of the dark fin. The speed and power of the thing was greatly to be admired. It cut the water like a gigantic and keen projectile.

The presence of this biding thing did not affect the man with the same horror that it would if he had been a picnicker. He simply looked at the sea dully and swore in an undertone.

Nevertheless, it is true that he did not wish to be alone with the thing. He wished one of his companions to awake by chance and keep him company with it. But the captain hung motionless over the water-jar, and the oiler and the cook in the bottom of the boat were plunged in slumber.

VI

"If I am going to be drowned—if I am going to be drowned—if I am going to be drowned, why, in he name of the seven mad gods who rule the sea, was I allowed to come thus far and comtemplate sand and trees?"

During this dismal night, it may be remarked that a man would conclude that it was really the intention of the seven mad gods to drown him, despite the abominable injustice of it. For it was certainly an abominable injustice to drown a man who had worked so hard, so hard. The man felt it would be a crime most unnatural. Other people had drowned at sea since galleys swarmed with painted sails, but still—

When it occurs to a man that nature does not regard him as important, and that she feels she would not maim the universe by disposing of him, he at first wishes to throw bricks at the temple, and he hates deeply the fact that there are no bricks and no temples. Any visible expression of nature would surely be pelleted with his jeers.

Then, if there be no tangible thing to hoot, he feels, perhaps, the desire to confront a personification and indulge in pleas, bowed to one knee, and with hands supplicant, saying, "Yes, but I love myself."

A high cold star on a winter's night is the word he feels that she says to him. Thereafter he knows the pathos of his situation.

The men in the dinghy had not discussed these matters, but each had, no doubt, reflected upon them in silence and according to his mind. There was seldom any expression upon their faces save the general one of complete weariness. Speech was devoted to the business of the boat.

To chime the notes of his emotion, a verse mysteriously entered the correspondent's head. He had even forgotten that he had forgotten this verse, but it suddenly was in his mind.

> *A soldier of the Legion lay dying in Algiers;*
> *There was lack of woman's nursing, there was*
> *dearth of woman's tears;*
> *But a comrade stood beside him, and he took*
> *that comrade's hand,*
> *And he said, "I never more shall see my own,*
> *my native land."*

In his childhood the correspondent had been made acquainted with the fact that a soldier of the Legion lay dying in Algiers, but he had never regarded the fact as important. Myriads of his school-fellows had informed him of the soldier's plight, but the dinning had naturally ended by making him perfectly indifferent. He had never considered it his affair that a soldier of the Legion lay dying in Algiers, nor had it appeared to him as a matter for sorrow. It was less to him than the breaking of a pencil's point.

Now however, it quaintly came to him as a human, living thing. It was no longer merely a picture of a few throes in the breast of a poet, meanwhile drinking tea and warming his feet at the grate; it was an actuality—stern, mournful, and fine.

The correspondent plainly saw the soldier. He lay on the sand with he feet out straight and still. While his pale left hand was upon his chest in an attempt to thwart the going of his life, the blood came between his fingers. In the far Algerian distance, a city of low square forms was set against a sky that was faint with the last sunset hues. The correspondent, plying the oars and dreaming of the slow and slower movements of the lips of the soldier, was moved by a profound and perfectly impersonal comprehension. He was sorry for the soldier of the Legion who lay dying in Algiers.

The thing which had followed the boat and waited had evidently grown bored at the delay. There was no longer to be heard the slash of the cutwater, and there was no longer the flame of the long trail. The light in the north still glimmered, but it was apparently no nearer to the boat. Sometimes the boom of the surf rang in the correspondent's ears, and he turned the craft seaward then and rowed harder. Southward, some one had evidently built a watch-fire on the beach. It was too low and too far to be seen, but it made a shimmering, roseate reflection upon the bluff in back of it, and this ocult be discerned from the boat. The wind came stronger, and sometimes a wave suddenly raged out like a mountain cat, and there was to be seen the sheen and sparkle of a broken crest.

The captain, in the bow, moved on his water-jar and sat erect. "Pretty long night," he observed to the correspondent. He looked at the shore. "Those life-saving people take their time."

"Did you see that shark playing around?"

"Yes, I saw him. He was a big fellow, all right."

"Wish I had known you were awake."

Later the correspondent spoke into the bottom of the boat. "Billie!" There was a slow and gradual disentanglement. "Billie, will you spell me?"

"Sure," said the oiler.

As soon as the correspondent touched the cold, comfortable sea-water in the bottom of the boat and had huddled close to the cook's life-belt he was deep in sleep, despite the fact that his teeth played all the popular airs. This sleep was so good to him that it was but a moment before he heard a voice call his name in a tone that demonstrated the last stages of exhaustion. "Will you spell me?"

"Sure, Billie."

The light in the north had mysteriously vanished, but the correspondent took his course from the wide-awake captain.

Later in the night they took the boat farther out to sea, and the captain directed the cook to take one oar at the stern and keep the boat facing the seas. He was to call out if he should hear the thunder of the surf. This plan enabled the oiler and the correspondent to get respite together. "We'll give those boys a chance to get into shape again," said the captain. They curled down and, after a few preliminary chatterings and trembles, slept once more the dead sleep. Neither knew they had bequeathed to the cook the company of another shark, or perhaps the same shark.

As the boat caroused on the waves, spray occasionally bumped over the side and gave them a fresh soaking, but this had no power to break their repose. The ominous slash of the wind and the water affected them as it would have affected mummies.

"Boys," said the cook, with the notes of every reluctance in his voice, "she's drifted in pretty close. I guess one of you had better take her to sea again." The correspondent, aroused, heard the crash of the toppled crests.

As he was rowing, the captain gave him some whisky-and-water, and this steadied the chills out of him. "If I ever get ashore and anybody shows me even a photograph of an oar—"

At last there was a short conversation.

"Billie!—Billie, will you spell me?"

"Sure," said the oiler.

VII

When the correspondent again opened his eyes, the sea and the sky were each of the grey hue of the dawning. Later, carmine and gold was painted upon the waters. The morning appeared finally, in its splendour, with a sky of pure blue, and the sunlight flame on the tips of the waves.

On the distant dunes were set many little black cottages, and a tall white windmill reared above them. No man, nor dog, nor bicycle appeared on the beach. The cottages might have formed a deserted village.

The voyagers scanned the shore. A conference was held in the boat. "Well," said the captain, "if no help is coming, we might better try a run through the surf right away. If we stay out here much longer we will be too weak to do anything for ourselves at all." The others silently acquiesced in this reasoning. The boat was headed for the beach. The correspondent wondered if none ever ascended the tall wind-tower, and if then they never looked seaward. This tower was a giant, standing with its back to the plight of the ants. It represented in a degree, to the correspondent, the serenity of nature amid the struggles of the individual— nature in the wind, and nature in the vision of men. She did not seem cruel to him then, nor beneficent, nor treacherous, nor wise. But she was indifferent, flatly indifferent. It is, per- haps, plausible that a man in this situation, impressed with the unconcern of the universe, should see the innumerable flaws of his life, and have them taste wickedly in his mind, and wish for another chance. A distinction between right and wrong seems absurdly clear to him, then, in this new ignorance of the grave-edge, and he understands that if he were given another opportunity he would mend his conduct and his words, and be better and brighter during an introduction or at a tea.

"Now, boys," said the captain, "she is going to swamp sure. All we can do is to work her in as far as possible, and then when she swamps, pile out and scramble for the beach. Keep cool now, and don't jump until she swamps sure."

The oiler took the oars. Over his shoulders he scanned the surf. "Captain," he said, "I think I'd better bring her about and keep her head-on to the seas and back her in."

"All right, Billie," said the captain. "Back her in." The oiler swung the boat then, and, seated in the stern, the cook and the correspondent were obliged to look over their shoulders to contemplate the lonely and indifferent shore.

The monstrous inshore rollers heaved the boat high until the men were again enabled to see the white sheets of water scudding up the slanted beach. "We won't get in very close," said the captain. Each time a man could wrest his attention from the rollers, he turned his glance toward the shore, and in the expression of the eyes during this contemplation there was a singular quality. The correspondent, observing the others, knew that they were not afraid, but the full meaning of their glances was shrouded.

As for himself, he was too tired to grapple fundamentally with the fact. He tried to coerce his mind into thinking of it, but the mind was dominated at this time by the muscles, and the muscles said they did not care. It merely occurred to him that if he should drown it would be a shame.

There were no hurried words, no pallor, no plain agitation. The men simply looked at the shore. "Now, remember to get well clear of the boat when you jump," said the captain.

Seaward the crest of a roller suddenly fell with a thunderous crash, and the long white comber came roaring down upon the boat.

"Steady now," said the captain. The men were silent. They turned their eyes from the shore to the comber and waited. The boat slid up the incline, leaped at the furious top, bounced over it, and swung down the long back of the wave. Some water had been shipped, and the cook bailed it out.

But the next crest crashed also. The tumbling, boiling flood of white water caught the boat and whirled it almost perpendicular. Water swarmed in from all sides. The correspondent had his hands on the gunwale at this time, and when the water entered at that place he swiftly withdrew his fingers, as if he objected to wetting them.

The little boat, drunken with this weight of water, reeled and snuggled deeper into the sea.

"Bail her out, cook! Bail her out!" said the captain.

"All right, Captain," said the cook.

"Now boys, the next one will do for us sure," said the oiler. "Mind to jump clear of the boat."

The third wave moved forward, huge, furious, implacable. It fairly swallowed the dinghy, and almost simultaneously the men tumbled into the sea. A piece of life-belt had lain in the bottom of the boat, and as the correspondent went overboard he held this to his chest with his left hand.

The January water was icy, and he reflected immediately that it was colder than he had expected to find it off the coast of Florida. This appeared to his dazed mind as a fact important enough to be noted at the time. The coldness of the water was sad; it was tragic. This fact was somehow mixed and confused with his opinion of his own situation, so that it seemed almost a proper reason for tears. The water was cold.

When he came to the surface he was conscious of little but the noisy water. Afterward he saw his companions in the sea. The oiler was ahead in the race. He was swimming strongly and rapidly. Off to the correspondent's left, the cook's great white and corked back bulged out of the water; and in the rear the captain was hanging with his one good hand to the keel of the overturned dinghy.

There is a certain immovable quality to a shore, and the correspondent wondered at it amid the confusion of the sea.

It seemed also very attractive; but the correspondent knew that it was a long journey, and he paddled leisurely. The piece of life-preserver lay under him, and sometimes he whirled down the incline of a wave as if he were on a hand-sled.

But finally he arrived at a place in the sea where travel was beset with difficulty. He did not pause swimming to inquire what manner of current had caught him, but there his progress ceased. The shore was set before him like a bit of scenery on a stage, and he looked at it and understood with his eyes each detail of it.

As the cook passed, much farther to the left, the captain was calling to him, "Turn over on your back, cook! Turn over on your back and use the oar."

"All right sir." The cook turned on his back, and, paddling with an oar, went ahead as if he were a canoe.

Presently the boat also passed to the left of the correspondent, with the captain clinging with one hand to the keel. He would have appeared like a man raising himself to look over a board fence if it were not for the extraordinary gymnastics of the boat. The correspondent marvelled that the captain could still hold to it.

They passed on nearer to shore—the oiler, the cook, the captain—and following them went the water-jar, bouncing gaily over the seas.

The correspondent remained in the grip of this strange new enemy—a current. The shore, with its white slope of sand and its green bluff topped with little silent cottages, was spread like a picture before him. It was very near to him then, but he was impressed as one who, in a gallery, looks at a scene from Brittany or Algiers.

He thought: "I am going to drown? Can it be possible? Can it be possible? Can it be possible? Perhaps an individual must consider his own death to be the final phenomenon of nature.

But later a wave perhaps whirled him out of this small deadly current, for he found suddenly that he could again make progress toward the shore. Later still he was aware that the captain, clinging with one hand to the keel of the dinghy, had his face turned away from the shore and toward him, and was calling his name. "Come to the boat! Come to the boat!"

In his struggle to reach the captain and the boat, he reflected that when one gets properly wearied drowning must really be a comfortable arrangement—a cessation of hostilities accompanied by a large degree of relief; and he was glad of it, for the main thing in his mind for some moments had been horror of the temporary agony. He did not wish to be hurt.

Presently he saw a man running along the shore. He was undressing with most re-markable speed. Coat, trousers, shirt, everything flew magically off him.

"Come to the boat!" called the captain.

"All right, Captain." As the correspondent paddled, he saw the captain let himself down to the bottom and leave the boat. Then the correspondent performed his one little marvel of the voyage. A large wave caught him and flung him with ease and supreme speed completely over the boat and far beyond it. It struck him even then as an event in gymnastics and a true miracle of the sea. An overturned boat in the surf is not a plaything to a swimming man.

The correspondent arrived in water that reached only to his waist, but his condition did not enable him to stand for more than a moment. Each wave knocked him into a heap, and the undertow pulled at him.

Then he saw the man who had been running and undressing, and undressing and run-ning, come bounding into the water. He dragged ashore the cook, and then waded toward the captain; but the captain waved him away and sent him to the correspondent. He was naked—naked as a tree in winter; but a halo was about his head, and he shone like a saint. He gave a strong pull, and a long drag, and a bully heave at the correspondent's hand. The corre-spondent, schooled in the minor formulae, said, "Thanks, old man." But suddenly the man cried, "What's that?" He pointed a swift finger. The correspondent said, "Go."

In the shallows, face downward, lay the oiler. His forehead touched sand that was periodically, between each wave, clear of the sea.

The correspondent did not know all that transpired afterward. When he achieved safe ground he fell, striking the sand with each particular part of his body. It was as if he had dropped from a roof, but the thud was grateful to him.

It seemed that instantly the beach was populated with men with blankets, clothes, and flasks, and women with coffee-pots and all the remedies sacred to their minds. The welcome of the land to the men from the sea was warm and generous; but a still and dripping shape was carried slowly up the beach, and the land's welcome for it could only be the different and sinister hospitality of the grave.

When it came night, the white waves paced to and fro in the moonlight, and the wind brought the sound of the great sea's voice to the men on the shore, and they felt that they could then be interpreters.

—Stephen Crane (1871-1900)

THE OLD PEOPLE

At first there was nothing. There was the faint, cold, steady rain, the gray and constant light of the late November dawn, with the voices of the hounds converging somewhere in it and toward them. Then Sam Fathers, standing just behind the boy as he had been standing when the boy shot his first running rabbit with his first gun and almost with the first load it ever carried, touched his shoulder and he began to shake, not with any cold. Then the buck was there. He did not come into sight; he was just there, looking not like a ghost but as if all of light were condensed in him and he were the source of it, not only moving in it but disseminating it, already running, seen first as you always see the deer, in that split second after he has already seen you, already slanting away in that first soaring bound, the antlers even in that dim light looking like a small rocking-chair balanced on his head.

"Now," Sam Fathers said, "shoot quick, and slow."

The boy did not remember that shot at all. He would live to be eighty, as his father and his father's twin brother and their father in his turn had lived to be, but he would never hear that shot nor remember even the shock of the gun-butt. He didn't even remember what he did with the gun afterward. He was running. Then he was standing over the buck where it lay on the wet earth still in the attitude of speed and not looking at all dead, standing over it shaking and jerking, with Sam Fathers beside him again, extending the knife. "Dont walk up to him in front," Sam said. "If he aint dead, he will cut you all to pieces with his feet. Walk up to him from behind and take him by the horn first, so you can hold his head down until you can jump away. Then slip your other hand down and hook your fingers in his nostrils."

The boy did that—drew the head back and the throat taut and drew Sam Fathers' knife across the throat and Sam stooped and dipped his hands in the hot smoking blood and wiped them back and forth across the boy's face. Then Sam's horn rang in the wet gray woods and again and again; there was a boiling wave of dogs about them, with Tennie's Jim and Boon Hogganbeck whipping them back after each had had a taste of the blood, then the men, the true hunters—Walter Ewell whose rifle never missed, and Major de Spain and old General Compson and the boy's cousin, McCaslin Edmonds, grandson of his father's sister, sixteen years his senior and, since both he and McCaslin were only children and the boy's father had been nearing seventy when he was born, more his brother than his cousin and more his father than either—sitting their horses and looking down at them: at the old man of seventy who had been a negro for two generations now but whose face and bearing were still those of the Chickasaw chief who had been his father; and the white boy of twelve with the prints of the bloody hands on his face, who had nothing to do now but stand straight and not let the trembling show.

"Did he do all right, Sam?" his cousin McCaslin said.

"He done all right," Sam Fathers said.

They were the white boy, marked forever, and the old dark man sired on both sides by savage kings, who had marked him, whose bloody hands had merely formally consecrated him to that which, under the man's tutelage, he had already accepted, humbly and joyfully, with abnegation and with pride too; the hands, the touch, the first worthy blood which he had been found at last worthy to draw, joining him and the man forever, so that the man would continue to live past the boy's seventy years and then eighty years, long after the man himself had entered the earth as chiefs and kings entered it;—the child, not yet a man, whose grandfather had lived in the same country and in almost the same manner as the boy himself would grow up to live, leaving his descendants in the land in his turn as his grandfather had done, and the old man past seventy whose grandfathers had owned the land long before the white men ever saw it and who had vanished from it now with all their kind, what of blood they left behind them running now in another race and for a while even in bondage and now drawing toward the end of its alien and irrevocable course, barren, since Sam Fathers had no children.

His father was Ikkemotubbe himself, who had named himself Doom. Sam told the boy about that—how Ikkemotubbe, old Issetibbcha's sister's son, had run away to New Orleans in his youth and returned seven years later with a French companion calling himself the Chevalier Soeur-Blonde de Vitry, who must have been the Ikkemotubbe of his family too and who was already addressing Ikkemotubbe as *Du Homme*;—returned, came home again, with his foreign Aramis and the quadroon slave woman who was to be Sam's mother, and a gold-laced hat and coat and a wicker wine-hamper containing a litter of month-old puppies and a gold snuff-box filled with a white powder resembling fine sugar. And how he was met at the River landing by three or four companions of his bachelor youth, and while the light of a smoking torch gleamed on the glittering braid of the hat and coat Doom squatted in the mud of the land and took one of the puppies from the hamper and put a pinch of the white powder on its tongue and the puppy died before the one who was holding it could cast it away. And how they returned to the Plantation where Issetibbeha, dead now, had been succeeded by his son, Doom's fat cousin Moketubbe, and the next day Moketubbe's eight-year-old son died suddenly and that afternoon, in the presence of Moketubbe and most of the others (the People, Sam Fathers called them) Doom produced another puppy from the wine-hamper and put a pinch of the white powder on its tongue and Moketubbe abdicated and Doom became in fact The Man which his French friend already called him. And how on the day after that, during the ceremony of accession, Doom pronounced a marriage between the pregnant quadroon and one of the slave men which he had just inherited (that was how Sam Fathers got his name, which in Chickasaw had been Had-Two-Fathers) and two years later sold the man and woman and the child who was his own son to his white neighbor, Carothers McCaslin.

That was seventy years ago. The Sam Fathers whom the boy knew was already sixty—a man not tall, squat rather, almost sedentary, flabby-looking though he actually was not, with hair like a horse's mane which even at seventy showed no trace of white and a face which showed no age until he smiled, whose only visible trace of negro blood was a slight dullness of the hair and the fingernails, and something else which you did notice about the eyes, which you noticed because it was not always there, only in repose and not always then—something not in their shape nor pigment but in their expression, and the boy's cousin McCaslin told him what that was: not the heritage of Ham, not the mark of servitude but of bondage; the knowledge that for a while that part of his blood had been the blood of slaves. "Like an old lion or a bear in a cage," McCaslin said. "He was born in the cage and has been in it all his life; he knows nothing else. Then he smells something. It might be anything, any breeze blowing past anything and then into his nostrils. But there for a second was the hot sand or the cane-brake that he never even saw himself, might not even know if he did see it and probably does know he couldn't hold his own with it if he got back to it. But that's not what he smells then. It was the cage he smelled. He hadn't smelled the cage until that minute. Then the hot sand or the brake blew into his nostrils and blew away, and all he could smell was the cage. That's what makes his eyes look like that."

"Then let him go!" the boy cried. "Let him go!"

His cousin laughed shortly. Then he stopped laughing, making the sound that is. It had never been laughing. "His cage aint McCaslins," he said. "He was a wild man. When he was born, all his blood on both sides, except the little white part, knew things that had been tamed out of our blood so long ago that we have not only forgotten them, we have to live together in herds to protect ourselves from our own sources. He was the direct son not only of a warrior but of a chief. Then he grew up and began to learn things, and all of a sudden one day he found out that he had been betrayed, the blood of the warriors and chiefs had been betrayed. Not by his father," he added quickly. "He probably never held it against old Doom for selling him and his mother into slavery, because he probably believed the damage was already done before then and it was the same warriors' and chiefs' blood in him and Doom both that was betrayed through the black blood which his mother gave him. Not betrayed by the black blood and not wilfully betrayed by his mother, but betrayed by her all the same, who had bequeathed him not only the blood of slaves but even a little of the very blood which had enslaved it; himself his own battleground, the scene of his own vanquishment and the mausoleum of his defeat. His cage aint us," McCaslin said. "Did you ever know anybody yet, even your father and Uncle Buddy, that ever told him to do or not do anything that he ever paid any attention to?"

That was true. The boy first remembered him as sitting in the door of the plantation blacksmith-shop, where he sharpened plow-points and mended tools and even did rough carpenter-work when he was not in the woods. And sometimes, even when the woods had not drawn him, even with the shop cluttered with work which the farm waited on, Sam would sit there, doing nothing at all for half a day or a whole one, and no man, neither the boy's father and twin uncle in their day nor his cousin McCaslin after he became practical though not yet titular master, ever to say to him, "I want this finished by sundown" or "why wasn't this done yesterday?" And once each year, in the late fall, in November, the boy would watch the wagon, the hooped canvas top erected now, being loaded—the food, hams and sausage from the smokehouse, coffee and flour and molasses from the commissary, a whole beef killed just last night for the dogs until there would be meat in camp, the crate containing the dogs themselves, then the bedding, the guns, the horns and lanterns and axes, and his cousin McCaslin and Sam Fathers in their hunting clothes would mount to the seat and with Tennie's Jim sitting on the dog-crate they would drive away to Jefferson, to join Major de Spain and General Compson and Boon Hogganbeck and Walter Ewell and go on into the big bottom of the Tallahatchie where the deer and bear were, to be gone two weeks. But before the wagon was even loaded the boy would find that he could watch no longer. He would go away, running almost, to stand behind the corner where he could not see the wagon and nobody could see him, not crying, holding himself rigid except for the trembling, whispering to himself: "Soon now. Soon now. Just three more years" (or two more or one more) "and I will be ten. Then Cass said I can go."

White man's work, when Sam did work. Because he did nothing else: farmed no allotted acres of his own, as the other ex-slaves of old Carothers McCaslin did, performed no field-work for daily wages as the younger and newer negroes did—and the boy never knew just how that had been settled between Sam and old Carothers, or perhaps with old Carothers' twin sons after him. For, although Sam lived among the negroes, in a cabin among the other cabins in the quarters, and consorted with negroes (what of consorting with anyone Sam did after the boy got big enough to walk alone from the house to the blacksmith-shop and then to carry a gun) and dressed like them and talked like them and even went with them to the negro church now and then, he was still the son of that Chickasaw chief and the negroes knew it. And, it seemed to the boy, not only negroes. Boon Hogganbeck's grandmother had been a Chickasaw woman too, and although the blood had run white since and Boon was a white man, it was not chief's blood. To the boy at least, the difference was apparent immediately you saw Boon and Sam together, and even Boon seemed to know it was there—even Boon, to whom in his tradition it had never occurred that anyone might be better born than himself. A man might be smarter, he admitted that, or richer (luckier, he called it) but not better born. Boon was a mastiff, absolutely faithful, dividing his fidelity equally between Major de Spain and the boy's cousin McCaslin, absolutely dependent for his very bread and dividing that impartially too between Major de Spain and McCaslin, hardy, generous, courageous enough, a slave to all the appetites and almost unratiocinative. In the boy's eyes at least it was Sam Fathers, the negro, who bore himself not only toward his cousin McCaslin and Major de Spain but toward all white men, with gravity and dignity and without servility or recourse to that impenetrable wall of ready and easy mirth which negroes sustain between themselves and white men, bearing himself toward his cousin McCaslin not only as one man to another but as an older man to a younger.

He taught the boy the woods, to hunt, when to shoot and when not to shoot, when to kill and when not to kill, and better, what to do with it afterward. Then he would talk to the boy, the two of them sitting beneath the close fierce stars on a summer hilltop while they waited for the hounds to bring the fox back within hearing, or beside a fire in the November or December woods while the dogs worked out a coon's trail along the creek, or fireless in the pitch dark and heavy dew of April mornings while they squatted beneath a turkey-roost. The boy would never question him; Sam did not react to questions. The boy would just wait and then listen and Sam would begin, talking about the old days and the People whom he had not had time ever to know and so could not remember (he did not remember ever having seen his father's face), and in place of whom the other race into which his blood had run supplied him with no substitute.

And as he talked about those old times and those dead and vanished men of another race from either that the boy knew, gradually to the boy those old times would cease to be old times and would become a part of the boy's present, not only as if they had happened yesterday but as if they were still happening, the men who walked through them actually walking in breath and air and casting an actual shadow on the earth they had not quitted. And more: as if some of them had not happened yet but would occur tomorrow, until at last it would seem to the boy that he himself had not come into existence yet, that none of his race nor the other subject race which his people had brought with them into the land had come here yet; that although it had been his grandfather's and then his father's and uncle's and was now his cousin's and someday would be his own land which he and Sam hunted over, their hold upon it actually was as trivial and without reality as the now faded and archaic script in the chancery book in Jefferson which allocated it to them and that it was he, the boy, who was the guest here and Sam Father's voice was the mouthpiece of the host.

Until three years ago there had been two of them, the other a full-blood Chickasaw, in a sense even more incredibly lost than Sam Fathers. He called himself Jobaker, as if it were one word. Nobody knew his history at all. He was a hermit, living in a foul little shack at the forks of the creek five miles from the plantation and about that far from any other habitation. He was a market hunter and fisherman and he consorted with nobody, black or white; no negro would even cross his path and no man dared approach his hut except Sam. And perhaps once a month the boy would find them in Sam's shop—two old men squatting on their heels on the dirt floor, talking in a mixture of negroid English and flat hill dialect and now and then a phrase of that old tongue which as time went on and the boy squatted there too listening, he began to learn. Then Jobaker died. That is, nobody had seen him in some time. Then one morning Sam was missing, nobody, not even the boy, knew when nor where, until that night when some negroes hunting in the creek bottom saw the sudden burst of flame and approached. It was Jobaker's hut, but before they got anywhere near it, someone shot at them from the shadows beyond it. It was Sam who fired, but nobody ever found Jobaker's grave.

The next morning, sitting at breakfast with his cousin, the boy saw Sam pass the dining-room window and he remembered then that never in his life before had he seen Sam nearer the house than the blacksmith-shop. He stopped eating even; he sat there and he and his cousin both heard the voices from beyond the pantry door, then the door opened and Sam entered, carrying his hat in his hand but without knocking as anyone else on the place except a house servant would have done, entered just far enough for the door to close behind him and stood looking at neither of them—the

Indian face above the nigger clothes, looking at something over their heads or at something not even in the room.

"I want to go," he said. "I want to go to the Big Bottom to live."

"To live?" the boy's cousin said.

"At Major de Spain's and your camp, where you go to hunt," Sam said. "I could take care of it for you all while you aint there. I will build me a little house in the woods, if you rather I didn't stay in the big one."

"What about Isaac here?" his cousin said. "How will you get away from him? Are you going to take him with you?" But still Sam looked at neither of them, standing just inside the room with that face which showed nothing, which showed that he was an old man only when it smiled.

"I want to go," he said. "Let me go."

"Yes," the cousin said quietly. "Of course. I'll fix it with Major de Spain. You want to go soon?"

"I'm going now," Sam said. He went out. And that was all. The boy was nine then; it seemed perfectly natural that nobody, not even his cousin McCaslin, should argue with Sam. Also, since he was nine now, he could understand that Sam could leave him and their days and nights in the woods together without any wrench. He believed that he and Sam both knew that this was not only temporary but that the exigencies of his maturing, of that for which Sam had been training him all his life some day to dedicate himself, required it. They had settled that one night last summer while they listened to the hounds bringing a fox back up the creek valley; now the boy discerned in that very talk under the high, fierce August stars a presage, a warning, of this moment today. "I done taught you all there is of this settled country," Sam said. "You can hunt it good as I can now. You are ready for the Big Bottom now, for bear and deer. Hunter's meat," he said. "Next year you will be ten. You will write your age in two numbers and you will be ready to become a man. Your pa" (Sam always referred to the boy's cousin as his father, establishing even before the boy's orphanhood did that relation between them not of the ward to his guardian and kinsman and chief and head of his blood, but of the child to the man who sired his flesh and his thinking too.) "promised you can go with us then." So the boy could understand Sam's going. But he couldn't understand why now, in March, six months before the moon for hunting.

"If Jobaker's dead like they say," he said, "and Sam hasn't got anybody but us at all kin to him, why does he want to go to the Big Bottom now, when it will be six months before we get there?"

"Maybe that's what he wants," McCaslin said. "Maybe he wants to get away from you a little while."

But that was all right. McCaslin and other grown people often said things like that and he paid no attention to them, just as he paid no attention to Sam saying he wanted to go to the Big Bottom to live. After all, he would have to live there for six months, because there would be no use in going at all if he was going to turn right around and come back. And, as Sam himself had told him, he already knew all about hunting in this settled country that Sam or anybody else could teach him. So it would be all right. Summer, then the bright days after the first frost, then the cold and himself on the wagon with McCaslin this time and the moment would come and he would draw the blood, the big blood which would make him a man, a hunter, and Sam would come back home with them and he too would have outgrown the child's pursuit of rabbits and possums. Then he too would make one before the winter fire, talking of the old hunts and the hunts to come as hunters talked.

So Sam departed. He owned so little that he could carry it. He walked. He would neither let McCaslin send him in the wagon, nor take a mule to ride. No one saw him go even. He was just gone one morning, the cabin which had never had very much in it, vacant and empty, the shop in which there never had been very much done, standing idle.Then November came at last, and now the boy made one—himself and his cousin McCaslin and Tennie's Jim, and Major de Spain and General Compson and Walter Ewell and Boon and old Uncle Ash to do the cooking, waiting for them in Jefferson with the other wagon, and the surrey in which he and McCaslin and General Compson and Major de Spain would ride.

Sam was waiting at the camp to meet them. If he was glad to see them, he did not show it. And if, when they broke camp two weeks later to return home, he was sorry to see them go, he did not show that either. Because he did not come back with them. It was only the boy who returned, returning solitary and alone to the settled familiar land, to follow for eleven months the childish business of rabbits and such while he waited to go back, having brought with him, even from his brief first sojourn, an unforgettable sense of the big woods—not a quality dangerous or particularly inimical, but profound, sentient, gigantic and brooding amid which he had been permitted to go to and fro at will, unscathed, why he knew not, but dwarfed and, until he had drawn honorably blood worthy of being drawn, alien.

Then November, and they would come back. Each morning Sam would take the boy out to the stand allotted him. It would be one of the poorer stands of course, since he was only ten and eleven and twelve and he had never even seen a deer running yet. But they would stand there, Sam a little behind him and without a gun himself, as he had been standing when the boy shot the running rabbit when he was eight years old. They would stand there in the November dawns, and after a while they would hear the dogs. Sometimes the chase would sweep up and past quite close, belling and invisible; once they heard the two heavy reports of Boon Hogganbeck's old gun with which he had never killed anything larger than a squirrel and that sitting, and twice they heard the flat unreverberant clap of Walter Ewell's rifle, following which you did not even wait to hear his horn.

"I'll never get a shot," the boy said. "I'll never kill one."

"Yes you will," Sam said. "You wait. You'll be a hunter. You'll be a man."

But Sam wouldn't come out. They would leave him there. He would come as far as the road where the surrey waited, to take the riding horses back, and that was all. The men would ride the horses and Uncle Ash and Tennie's Jim and the boy would follow in the wagon with Sam, with the camp equipment and the trophies, the meat, the heads, the antlers, the good ones, the wagon winding on among the tremendous gums and cypresses and oaks where no axe save that of the hunter had ever sounded, between the impenetrable walls of cane and brier—the two changing yet constant walls just beyond which the wilderness whose mark he had brought away forever on his spirit even from that first two weeks seemed to lean, stooping a little, watching them and listening, not quite inimical because they were too small, even those such as Walter and Major de Spain and old General Compson who had killed many deer and bear, their sojourn too brief and too harmless to excite to that, but just brooding, secret, tremendous, almost inattentive.

Then they would emerge, they would be out of it, the line as sharp as the demarcation of a doored wall. Suddenly skeleton cotton- and corn-fields would flow away on either hand, gaunt and motionless beneath the gray rain; there would be a house, barns, fences, where the hand of man had clawed for an instant, holding, the wall of the wilderness behind them now, tremendous and still and seemingly impenetrable in the gray and fading light, the very tiny orifice through which they had emerged apparently swallowed up. The surrey would be waiting, his cousin McCaslin and Major de Spain and General Compson and Walter and Boon dismounted beside it. Then Sam would get down from the wagon and mount one of the horses and, with the others on a rope behind him, he would turn back. The boy would watch him for a while against that tall and secret wall, growing smaller and smaller against it, never looking back. Then he would enter it, returning to what the boy believed, and thought that his cousin McCaslin believed, was his loneliness and solitude.

So the instant came. He pulled the trigger and Sam Fathers marked his face with the hot blood which he had spilled and he ceased to be a child and became a hunter and a man. It was the last day. They broke camp that afternoon and went out, his cousin and Major de Spain and General Compson and Boon on the horses, Walter Ewell and the negroes in the wagon with him and Sam and his hide and antlers. There could have been (and were) other trophies in the wagon. But for him they did not exist, just as for all practical purposes he and Sam Fathers were still alone together as they had been that morning. The wagon wound and jolted between the slow and shifting yet constant walls from beyond and above which the wilderness watched them pass, less than inimical now and never to be inimical again since the buck still and forever leaped, the shaking gun-barrels coming constantly and forever steady at last, crashing, and still out of his instant of immortality the buck sprang, forever immortal; —the wagon jolting and bouncing on, the moment of the buck, the shot, Sam Fathers and himself and the blood with which Sam had marked him forever one with the wilderness which had accepted him since Sam said that he had done all right, when suddenly Sam reined back and stopped the wagon and they all heard the unmistakable and unforgettable sound of a deer breaking cover.

Then Boon shouted from beyond the bend of the trail and while they sat motionless in the halted wagon, Walter and the boy already reaching for their guns, Boon came galloping back, flogging his mule with his hat, his face wild and amazed as he shouted down at them. Then the other riders came around the bend, also spurring.

"Get the dogs!" Boon cried. "Get the dogs! If he had a nub on his head, he had fourteen points! Laying right there by the road in the pawpaw thicket! If I'd a knowed he was there, I could have cut his throat with my pocket knife!"

"Maybe that's why he run," Walter said. "He saw you never had your gun." He was already out of the wagon with his rifle. Then the boy was out too with his gun, and the other riders came up and Boon got off his mule somehow and was scrabbling and clawing among the duffel in the wagon, still shouting, "Get the dogs! Get the dogs!" And it seemed to the boy too that it would take them forever to decide what to do—the old men in whom the blood ran cold and slow, in whom during the intervening years between them and himself the blood had become a different and colder substance from that which ran in him and even in Boon and Walter.

"What about it, Sam?" Major de Spain said. "Could the dogs bring him back?"

"We wont need the dogs," Sam said. "If he dont hear the dogs behind him, he will circle back in here about sundown to bed."

"All right," Major de Spain said. "You boys take the horses. We'll go out to the road in the wagon and wait there." He and General Compson and McCaslin got into the wagon and Boon and Walter and Sam and the boy mounted the horses and turned back and out of the trail. Sam led them for an hour through the gray and unmarked afternoon whose light was little different from what it had been at dawn and which would become darkness without any graduation between. Then Sam stopped them.

"This is far enough," he said. "He'll be coming upwind, and he dont want to smell the mules." They tied the mounts in a thicket. Sam led them on foot now, unpathed through the markless afternoon, the boy pressing close behind him, the two others, or so it seemed to the boy, on his heels. But they were not. Twice Sam turned his head slightly and spoke back to him across his shoulder, still walking: "You got time. We'll get there fore he does."

So he tried to go slower. He tried deliberately to decelerate the dizzy rushing of time in which the buck which he had not even seen was moving, which it seemed to him must be carrying the buck farther and farther and more and more irretrievably away from them even though there were no dogs behind him now to make him run, even though, according to Sam, he must have completed his circle now and was heading back toward them. They went on; it could have been another hour or twice that or less than half, the boy could not have said. Then they were on a ridge. He had never been in here before and he could not see that it was a ridge. He just knew that the earth had risen slightly because the underbrush had thinned a little, the ground sloping invisibly away toward a dense wall of cane. Sam stopped. "This is it," he said. He spoke to Walter and Boon: "Follow this ridge and you will come to two crossings. You will see the tracks. If he crosses, it will be at one of these three."

Walter looked about for a moment. "I know it," he said. "I've even seen your deer. I was in here last Monday. He aint nothing but a yearling."

"A yearling?" Boon said. He was panting from the walking. His face still looked a little wild. "If the one I saw was any yearling, I'm still in kindergarten."

"Then I must have seen a rabbit," Walter said. "I always heard you quit school altogether two years before the first grade."

Boon glared at Walter. "If you dont want to shoot him, get out of the way," he said. "Set down somewhere. By God, I—"

"Aint nobody going to shoot him standing here," Sam said quietly.

"Sam's right," Walter said. He moved, slanting the worn, silver-colored barrel of his rifle downward to walk with it again. "A little more moving and a little more quiet too. Five miles is still Hogganbeck range, even if we wasn't downwind." They went on. The boy could still hear Boon talking, though presently that ceased too. Then once more he and and Sam stood motionless together against a tremendous pin oak in a little thicket, and again there was nothing. There was only the soaring and sombre solitude in the dim light, there was the thin murmur of the faint cold rain which had not ceased all day. Then, as if it had waited for them to find their positions and become still, the wilderness breathed again. It seemed to lean inward above them, above himself and Sam and Walter and Boon in their separate lurking-places, tremendous, attentive, impartial and omniscient, the buck moving in it somewhere, not running yet since he had not been pursued, not frightened yet and never fearsome but just alert also as they were alert, perhaps already circling back, perhaps quite near, perhaps conscious also of the eye of the ancient immortal Umpire. Because he was just twelve then, and that morning something had happened to him: in less than a second he had ceased forever to be the child he was yesterday. Or perhaps that made no difference, perhaps even a city-bred man, let alone a child, could not have understood it; perhaps only a country-bred one could comprehend loving the life he spills. He began to shake again.

"I'm glad it's started now," he whispered. He did not move to speak; only his lips shaped the expiring words: "Then it will be gone when I raise the gun—"

Nor did Sam. "Hush," he said.

"Is he that near?" the boy whispered. "Do you think—"

"Hush," Sam said. So he hushed. But he could not stop the shaking. He did not try, because he knew it would go away when he needed the steadiness—had not Sam Fathers already consecrated and absolved him from weakness and regret too?—not from love and pity for all which lived and ran and then ceased to live in a second in the very midst of splendor and speed, but from weakness and regret. So they stood motionless, breathing deep and quiet and steady. If there had been any sun, it would be near to setting now; there was a condensing, a densifying, of what he had thought was the gray and unchanging light until he realized suddenly that it was his own breathing, his heart, his blood—something, all things, and that Sam Fathers had marked him indeed, not as a mere hunter, but with something Sam had had in his turn of his vanished and forgotten people. He stopped breathing then; there was only his heart, his blood, and in the following silence the wilderness ceased to breathe also, leaning, stooping overhead with its breath held, tremendous and impartial and waiting. Then the shaking stopped too, as he had known it would, and he drew back the two heavy hammers of the gun.

Then it had passed. It was over. The solitude did not breathe again yet; it had merely stopped watching him and was looking somewhere else, even turning its back on him, looking on away up the ridge at another point, and the boy knew as well as if he had seen him that the buck had come to the edge of the cane and had either seen or scented them and faded back into it. But the solitude did not breathe again. It should have suspired again then but it did not. It was still facing, watching, what it had been watching and it was not here, not where he and Sam stood; rigid, not breathing himself, he thought, cried *No! No!*, knowing already that it was too late, thinking with the old despair of two and three years ago: *I'll never get a shot.* Then he heard it—the flat single clap of Walter Ewell's rifle which never missed. Then the mellow sound of the horn came down the ridge and something went out of him and he knew then he had never expected to get the shot at all.

"I reckon that's it," he said. "Walter got him." He had raised the gun slightly without knowing it. He lowered it again and had lowered one of the hammers and was already moving out of the thicket when Sam spoke.

"Wait."

"Wait?" the boy cried. And he would remember that—how he turned upon Sam in the truculence of a boy's grief over the missed opportunity, the missed luck. "What for? Dont you hear that horn?"

And he would remember how Sam was standing. Sam had not moved. He was not tall, squat rather and broad, and the boy had been growing fast for the past year or so and there was not much difference between them in height, yet Sam was looking over the boy's head and up the ridge toward the sound of the horn and the boy knew that Sam did not even see him; that Sam knew he was still there beside him but he did not see the boy. Then the boy saw the buck. It was coming down the ridge, as if it were walking out of the very sound of the horn which related its death. It was not running, it was walking, tremendous, unhurried, slanting and tilting its head to pass the antlers through the undergrowth, and the boy standing with Sam beside him now instead of behind him as Sam always stood, and the gun still partly aimed and one of the hammers still cocked.

Then it saw them. And still it did not begin to run. It just stopped for an instant, taller than any man, looking at them; then its muscles suppled, gathered. It did not even alter its course, not fleeing, not even running, just moving with that winged and effortless ease with which deer move, passing within twenty feet of them, its head high and the eye not proud and not haughty but just full and wild and unafraid, and Sam standing beside the boy now, his right arm raised at full length, palm-outward, speaking in that tongue which the boy had learned from listening to him and Joe Baker in the blacksmith shop, while up the ridge Walter Ewell's horn was still blowing them in to a dead buck.

"Oleh, Chief," Sam said. "Grandfather."

When they reached Walter, he was standing with his back toward them, quite still, bemused almost, looking down at his feet. He didn't look up at all.

"Come here, Sam," he said quietly. When they reached him he still did not look up, standing above a little spike buck which had still been a fawn last spring. "He was so little I pretty near let him go," Walter said. "But just look at the track he was making. It's pretty near big as a cow's. If there were any more tracks here besides the ones he is laying in, I would swear there was another buck here that I never even saw."

3.

It was dark when they reached the road where the surrey waited. It was turning cold, the rain had stopped, and the sky was beginning to blow clear. His cousin and

Major de Spain and General Compson had a fire going. "Did you get him?" Major de Spain said.

"Got a good-sized swamp-rabbit with spike horns," Walter said. He slid the little buck down from his mule. The boy's cousin McCaslin looked at it.

"Nobody saw the big one?" he said.

"I dont even believe Boon saw it," Walter said. "He probably jumped somebody's straw cow in that thicket." Boon started cursing, swearing at Walter and at Sam for not getting the dogs in the first place and at the buck and all.

"Never mind," Major de Spain said. "He'll be here for us next fall. Let's get started home."

It was after midnight when they let Walter out at his gate two miles from Jefferson and later still when they took General Compson to his house and then returned to Major de Spain's, where he and McCaslin would spend the rest of the night, since it was still seventeen miles home. It was cold, the sky was clear now; there would be a heavy frost by sunup and the ground was already frozen beneath the horses' feet and the wheels and beneath their own feet as they crossed Major de Spain's yard and entered the house, the warm dark house, feeling their way up the dark stairs until Major de Spain found a candle and lit it, and into the strange room and the big deep bed, the still cold sheets until they began to warm to their bodies and at last the shaking stopped and suddenly he was telling McCaslin about it while McCaslin listened, quietly until he had finished. "You dont believe it," the boy said. "I know you dont—"

"Why not?" McCaslin said. "Think of all that has happened here, on this earth. All the blood hot and strong for living, pleasuring, that has soaked back into it. For grieving and suffering too, of course, but still getting something out of it for all that, getting a lot out of it, because after all you dont have to continue to bear what you believe is suffering; you can always choose to stop that, put an end to that. And even suffering and grieving is better than nothing; there is only one thing worse than not being alive, and that's shame. But you cant be alive forever, and you always wear out life long before you have exhausted the possibilities of living. And all that must be somewhere; all that could not have been invented and created just to be thrown away. And the earth is shallow; there is not a great deal of it before you come to the rock. And the earth dont want to just keep things, hoard them; it wants to use them again. Look at the seed, the acorns, at what happens even to carrion when you try to bury it: it refuses too, seethes and struggles too until it reaches light and air again, hunting the sun still. And they—" the boy saw his hand in silhouette for a moment against the window beyond which, accustomed to the darkness now, he could see sky where the scoured and icy stars glittered "—they dont want it, need it. Besides, what would it want, itself, knocking around out there, when it never had enough time about the earth as it was, when there is plenty of room about the earth, plenty of places still unchanged from what they were when the blood used and pleasured in them while it was still blood?"

"But we want them," the boy said. "We want them too. There is plenty of room for us and them too."

"That's right," McCaslin said. "Suppose they dont have substance, cant cast a shadow—"

"But I saw it!" the boy cried. "I saw him!"

"Steady," McCaslin said. For an instant his hand touched the boy's flank beneath the covers. "Steady. I know you did. So did I. Sam took me in there once after I killed my first deer."

—*William Faulkner (1897-1962)*

It is very seldom that mere ordinary people like John and myself secure ancestral halls for the summer.

A colonial mansion, a hereditary estate, I would say a haunted house, and reach the height of much of fate!

Still I will proudly declare that there is something queer about it.

Else, why should it be let so cheaply? And why have stood so long untenanted?

John laughs at me, of course, but one expects that in marriage.

John is practical in the extreme. He has no patience with faith, an intense horror of superstition, and he scoffs openly at any talk of things not to be felt and seen and put down in figures.

John is a physician, and *perhaps*—(I would not say it to a living soul, of course, but this is dead paper and a great relief to my mind)—*perhaps* that is one reason I do not get well faster.

You see he does not believe I am sick!

And what can one do?

If a physician of high standing, and one's own husband, assures friends and relatives that there is really nothing the matter with one but temporary nervous depression—a slight hysterical tendency—what is one to do?

My brother is also a physician, and also of high standing, and he says the same thing.

So I take phosphates or phosphites—whichever it is, and tonics, and journeys, and air, and exercise, and am absolutely forbidden to "work" until I am well again.

Personally, I disagree with their ideas.

Personally, I believe that congenial work, with excitement and change, would do me good.

But what is one to do?

I did write for a while in spite of them; but it does exhaust me a good deal—having to be so sly about it, or else meet with heavy opposition.

I sometimes fancy that in my condition if I had less opposition and more society and stimulus—but John says the very worst thing I can do is to think about my condition, And I confess it always makes me feel bad.

So I will let it alone and talk about the house.

The most beautiful place! It is quite alone, standing well back from the road, quite three miles from the village. It makes me think of English places that you read about, for there are hedges and walls and gates that lock, and lots of separate little houses for the gardeners and people.

There is a *delicious* garden! I never saw such a garden—large and shady, full of box-bordered paths, and lined with long grape-covered arbors with seats under them.

There were greenhouses, too, but they are all broken now.

There was some legal trouble, I believe, something about the heirs and coheirs; anyhow, the place has been empty for years.

That spoils my ghostliness, I am afraid, but I don't care—there is something strange about the house—I can feel it.

I even said so to John one moonlight evening, but he said what I felt was a *draught*, and shut the window.

I get unreasonably angry with John sometimes. I'm sure I never used to be so sensitive. I think it is due to this nervous condition.

But John says if I feel so, I shall neglect proper self-control; so I take pains to control myself—before him, at least, and that makes me very tired.

I don't like our room a bit. I wanted one downstairs that opened on the piazza and had roses all over the window, and such pretty old-fashioned chintz hangings! but John would not hear of it.

He said there was only one window and not room for two beds, and no near room for him if he took another.

He is very careful and loving, and hardly lets me stir without special direction.

I have a schedule prescription for each hour in the day; he takes all care from me, and so I feel basely ungrateful not to value it more.

He said we came here solely on my account, that I was to have perfect rest and all the air I could get. "Your exercise depends on your strength, my dear," said he, "and your food somewhat on your appetite; but air you can absorb all the time." So we took the nursery at the top of the house.

It is a big, airy room, the whole floor nearly, with windows that look all ways, and air and sunshine galore. It was nursery first and then playroom and gymnasium, I should judge; for the windows are barred for little children, and there are rings and things in the walls.

The paint and paper look as if a boys' school had used it. It is stripped off—the paper—in great patches all around the head of my bed, about as far as I can reach, and in a great place on the other side of the room low down. I never saw a worse paper in my life.

One of those sprawling flamboyant patterns committing every artistic sin.

It is dull enough to confuse the eye in following, pronounced enough to constantly irritate and provoke study, and when you follow the lame uncertain curves for a little distance they suddenly commit suicide—plunge off at our outrageous angles, destroy themselves in unheard of contradictions.

The color is repellent, almost revolting; a smouldering unclean yellow, strangely faded by the slow-turning sunlight.

It is a dull yet lurid orange in some places, a sickly sulphur tint in others.

No wonder the children hated it! I should hate it myself if I had to live in this room long.

There comes John, and I must put this away,—he hates to have me write a word.

We have been here two weeks, and I haven't felt like writing before, since that first day.

I am sitting by the window now, up in this atrocious nursery, and there is nothing to hinder my writing as much as I please, save lack of strength.

John is away all day, and even some nights when his cases are serious.

I am glad my case is not serious!

But these nervous troubles are dreadfully depressing.

John does not know how much I really suffer. He knows there is no *reason* to suffer, and that satisfies him.

Of course it is only nervousness. It does weigh on me so not to do my duty in any way!

I meant to be such a help to John, such a real rest and comfort, and here I am a comparative burden already!

Nobody would believe what an effort it is to do what little I am able,—to dress and entertain, and order things.

It is fortunate Mary is so good with the baby. Such a dear baby!

And yet I *cannot* be with him, it makes me so nervous.

I suppose John never was nervous in his life. He laughs at me so about this wallpaper!

At first he meant to repaper the room, but afterwards he said that I was letting it get the better of me, and that nothing was worse for a nervous patient than to give way to such fancies.

He said that after the wallpaper was changed it would be the heavy bedstead, and then the barred windows, and then that gate at the head of the stairs, and so on.

254

"You know the place is doing you good," he said, "and really, dear, I don't care to renovate the house just for a three-months' rental."

"Then do let us go downstairs," I said, "there are such pretty rooms there."

Then he took me in his arms and called me a blessed little goose, and said he would go down to the cellar, if I wished, and have it whitewashed into the bargain.

But he is right enough about the beds and windows and things.

It is an airy and comfortable room as any one need wish, and, of course, I would not be so silly as to make him uncomfortable just for a whim.

I'm really getting quite fond of the big room, all but that horrid paper.

Out of one window I can see the garden, those mysterious deepshaded arbors, the riotous old-fashioned flowers, and bushes and gnarly trees.

Out of another I get a lovely view of the bay and a little private wharf belonging to the estate. There is a beautiful shaded lane that runs down there from the house. I always fancy I see people walking in these numerous paths and arbors, but John has cautioned me not to give way to fancy in the least. He says that with my imaginative power and habit of story-making, a nervous weakness like mine is sure to lead to all manner of excited fancies, and that I ought to use my will and good sense to check the tendency. So I try.

I think sometimes that if I were only well enough to write a little it would relieve the press of ideas and rest me.

But I find I get pretty tired when I try.

It is so discouraging not to have any advice and companionship about my work. When I get really well, John says we will ask Cousin Henry and Julia down for a long visit; but he says he would as soon put fireworks in my pillow-case as to let me have those stimulating people about now.

I wish I could get well faster.

But I must not think about that. This paper looks to me as if it *knew* what a vicious influence it had!

There is a recurrent spot where the pattern lolls like a broken neck and two bulbous eyes stare at you upside down.

I get positively angry with the impertinence of it and the everlastingness. Up and down and sideways they crawl, and those absurd, unblinking eyes are everywhere. There is one place where two breadths didn't match, and the eyes go all up and down the line, one a little higher than the other.

I never saw so much expression in an inanimate thing before, and we all know how much expression they have! I used to lie awake as a child and get more entertainment and terror out of blank walls and plain furniture than most children could find in a toy-store.

I remember what a kindly wink the knobs of our big, old bureau used to have, and there was one chair that always seemed like a strong friend.

I used to feel that if any of the other things looked too fierce I could always hop into that chair and be safe.

The furniture in this room is no worse than inharmonious, however, for we had to bring it all from downstairs. I suppose when this was used as a playroom they had to take the nursery things out, and no wonder! I never saw such ravages as the children have made here.

The wallpaper, as I said before, is torn off in spots, and it sticketh closer than a brother—they must have had perseverance as well as hatred.

Then the floor is scratched and gouged and splintered, the plaster itself is dug out here and there, and this great heavy bed which is all we found in the room, looks as if it had been through the wars.

But I don't mind it a bit—only the paper.

There comes John's sister. Such a dear girl as she is, and so careful of me! I must not let her find me writing.

She is a perfect and enthusiastic housekeeper, and hopes for no better professions. I verily believe she thinks it is the writing which made me sick!

But I can write when she is out, and see her a long way off from these windows.

There is one that commands the road, a lovely shaded winding road, and one that just looks off over the country. A lovely country, too, full of great elms and velvet meadows.

This wallpaper has a kind of subpattern in a different shade, a particularly irritating one, for you can only see it in certain lights, and not clearly then.

But in the places where it isn't faded and where the sun is just so—I can see a strange, provoking, formless sort of figure, that seems to skulk about behind that silly and conspicuous front design.

There's sister on the stairs!

Well, the Fourth of July is over! The people are all gone and I am tired out. John thought it might do me good to see a little company, so we just had mother and Nellie and the children down for a week.

Of course I didn't do a thing. Jennie sees to everything now.

But it tired me all the same.

John says if I don't pick up faster he shall send me to Weir Mitchell in the fall.

But I don't want to go there at all. I had a friend who was in his hands once, and she says he is just like John and my brother, only more so!

Besides, it is such an undertaking to go so far.

I don't feel as if it was worthwhile to turn my hand over for anything, and I'm getting dreadfully fretful and querulous.

I cry at nothing, and cry most of the time.

Of course I don't when John is here, or anybody else, but when I am alone.

And I am alone a good deal just now. John is kept in town very often by serious cases, and Jennie is good and lets me alone when I want her to.

So I walk a little in the garden or down that lovely lane, sit on the porch under the roses, and lie down up here a good deal.

I'm getting really fond of the room in spite of the wallpaper. Perhaps *because* of the wallpaper.

It dwells in my mind so!

I lie here on this great immovable bed—it is nailed down, I believe—and follow that pattern about by the hour. It is as good as gymnastics, I assure you. I start, we'll say, at the bottom, down in the corner over there where it has not been touched, and I determine for the thousandth time that I *will* follow that pointless pattern to some sort of a conclusion.

I know a little of the principle of design, and I know this thing was not arranged on any laws of radiation, or alternation, or repetition, or symmetry, or anything else that I ever heard of.

It is repeated, of course, by the breadths, but not otherwise.

Looked at in one way each breadth stands alone, the bloated curves and flourishes—a kind of "debased Romanesque" with *delirium tremens*—go waddling up and down in isolated columns of fatuity.

But, on the other hand, they connect diagonally, and the sprawling outlines run off in great slanting waves of optic horror, like a lot of wallowing seaweeds in full chase.

The whole thing goes horizontally, too, at least it seems so, and I exhaust myself in trying to distinguish the order of its going in that direction.

They have used a horizontal breadth for a frieze, and that adds wonderfully to the confusion.

There is one end of the room where it is almost intact, and there, when the cross-lights fade and the low sun shines directly upon it, I can almost fancy radiation after all,—the interminable grotesques seem to form around a common center and rush off in headlong plunges of equal distraction.

It makes me tired to follow it. I will take a nap I guess.

I don't know why I should write this.

I don't want to.

I don't feel able.

And I know John would think it absurd. But I *must* say what I feel and think in some way—it is such a relief!

But the effort is getting to be greater than the relief.

Half the time now I am awfully lazy, and lie down ever so much.

John says I mustn't lose my strength, and has me take cod liver oil and lots of tonics and things, to say nothing of ale and wine and rare meat.

Dear John! He loves me very dearly, and hates to have me sick. I tried to have a real earnest reasonable talk with him the other day, and tell him how I wish he would let me go and make a visit to Cousin Henry and Julia.

But he said I wasn't able to go, nor able to stand it after I got there; and I did not make out a very good case for myself, for I was crying before I had finished.

It is getting to be a great effort for me to think straight. Just this nervous weakness I suppose.

And dear John gathered me up in his arms, and just carried me upstairs and laid me on the bed, and sat by me and read to me till it tired my head.

He said I was his darling and his comfort and all he had, and that I must take care of myself for his sake, and keep well.

He says no one but myself can help me out of it, that I must use my will and self-control and not let any silly fancies run away with me.

There's one comfort, the baby is well and happy, and does not have to occupy this nursery with the horrid wallpaper.

If we had not used it, that blessed child would have! What a fortunate escape! Why, I wouldn't have a child of mine, an impressionable little thing, live in such a room for worlds.

I never thought of it before, but it is lucky that John kept me here after all, I can stand it so much easier than a baby, you see.

Of course I never mention it to them any more—I am too wise,—but I keep watch of it all the same.

There are things in that paper that nobody knows but me, or ever will.

Behind that outside pattern the dim shapes get clearer every day.

It is always the same shape, only very numerous.

And it is like a woman stooping down and creeping about behind that pattern. I don't like it a bit. I wonder—I begin to think—I wish John would take me away from here!

It is so hard to talk with John about my case, because he is so wise, and because he loves me so.

But I tried it last night.

It was moonlight. The moon shines in all around just as the sun does.

I hate to see it sometimes, it creeps so slowly, and always comes in by one window or another.

John was asleep and I hated to waken him, so I kept still and watched the moonlight on that undulating wallpaper till I felt creepy.

The faint figure behind seemed to shake the pattern, just as if she wanted to get out.

I got up softly and went to feel and see if the paper *did* move, and when I came back John was awake.

"What is it, little girl?" he said. "Don't go walking about like that—you'll get cold."

I thought it was a good time to talk, so I told him that I really was not gaining here, and that I wished he would take me away.

"Why darling!" said he, "our lease will be up in three weeks, and I can't see how to leave before.

"The repairs are not done at home, and I cannot possibly leave town just now. Of course if you were in any danger, I could and would, but you really are better, dear, whether you can see it or not. I am a doctor, dear, and I know. You are gaining flesh and color, your appetite is better, I feel really much easier about you."

"I don't weigh a bit more," said I, "nor as much; and my appetite may be better in the evening when you are here, but it is worse in the morning when you are away!"

"Bless her little heart!" said he with a big hug, "she shall be as sick as she pleases! But now let's improve the shining hours by going to sleep, and talk about it in the morning!"

"And you won't go away?" I asked gloomily.

"Why, how can I, dear? It is only three weeks more and then we'll take a nice little trip of a few days while Jennie is getting the house ready. Really, dear, you are better!"

"Better in body perhaps—" I began, and stopped short, for he sat up straight and looked at me with such a stern, reproachful look that I could not say another word.

"My darling," said he, "I beg of you, for my sake and for our child's sake, as well as for your own, that you will never for one instant let that idea enter your mind! There is nothing so dangerous, so fascinating, to a temperament like yours. It is a false and foolish fancy. Can you not trust me as a physician when I tell you so?"

So of course I said no more on that score, and we went to sleep before long. He thought I was asleep first, but I wasn't, and lay there for hours trying to decide whether that front pattern and the back pattern really did move together or separately.

On a pattern like this, by daylight, there is a lack of sequence, a defiance of law, that is a constant irritant to a normal mind.

The color is hideous enough, and unreliable enough, and infuriating enough, but the pattern is torturing.

You think you have mastered it, but just as you get well underway in following, it turns a back somersault and there you are. It slaps you in the face, knocks you down, and tramples upon you. It is like a bad dream.

The outside pattern is a florid arabesque, reminding one of a fungus. If you can imagine a toadstool in joints, an interminable string of toadstools, budding and sprouting in endless convolutions—why, that is something like it.

That is, sometimes!

There is one marked peculiarity about this paper, a thing nobody seems to notice but myself, and that is that it changes as the light changes.

When the sun shoots in through the east window—I always watch for that first long, straight ray—it changes so quickly that I never can quite believe it.

That is why I watch it always.

By moonlight—the moon shines in all night when there is a moon—I wouldn't know it was the same paper.

At night in any kind of light, in twilight, candlelight, lamplight, and worst of all by moonlight, it becomes bars! The outside pattern I mean, and the woman behind it is as plain as can be.

I didn't realize for a long time what the thing was that showed behind, that dim subpattern, but now I am quite sure it is a woman.

By daylight she is subdued, quiet. I fancy it is the pattern that keeps her so still. It is so puzzling. It keeps me quiet by the hour.

I lie down ever so much now. John says it is good for me, and to sleep all I can.

Indeed he started the habit by making me lie down for an hour after each meal.

It is a very bad habit I am convinced, for you see I don't sleep.

And that cultivates deceit, for I don't tell them I'm awake—Oh no!

The fact is I am getting a little afraid of John.

He seems very queer sometimes, and even Jennie has an inexplicable look.

It strikes me occasionally, just as a scientific hypothesis,—that perhaps it is the paper!

I have watched John when he did not know I was looking, and come into the room suddenly on the most innocent excuses, and I've caught him several times *looking at the paper*! And Jennie, too. I caught Jennie with her hand on it once.

She didn't know I was in the room, and when I asked her in a quiet, a very quiet voice, with the most restrained manner possible, what she was doing with the paper—she turned around as if she had been caught stealing, and looked quite angry—asked me why I should frighten her so!

Then she said that the paper stained everything it touched, that she had found yellow smooches on all my clothes and John's, and she wished we would be more careful!

Did not that sound innocent? But I know she was studying that pattern, and I am determined that nobody shall find it out but myself!

Life is very much more exciting now than it used to be. You see I have something more to expect, to look forward to, to watch. I really do eat better, and am more quiet than I was.

John is so pleased to see me improve! He laughed a little the other day, and said I seemed to be flourishing in spite of my wallpaper.

I turned it off with a laugh. I had no intention of telling him it was *because* of the wallpaper—he would make fun of me. He might even want to take me away.

I don't want to leave now until I have found it out. There is a week more, and I think that will be enough.

I'm feeling ever so much better! I don't sleep much at night, for it is so interesting to watch developments; but I sleep a good deal in the daytime.

In the daytime it is tiresome and perplexing.

There are always new shoots on the fungus, and new shades of yellow all over it. I cannot keep count of them, though I have tried conscientiously.

It is the strangest yellow, that wallpaper! It makes me think of all the yellow things I ever saw—not beautiful ones like buttercups, but old foul, bad yellow things.

But there is something else about that paper—the smell! I noticed it the moment we came into the room, but with so much air and sun it was not bad. Now we have had a week of fog and rain, and whether the windows are open or not, the smell is here.

It creeps all over the house.

I find it hovering in the dining room, skulking in the parlor, hiding in the hall, lying in wait for me on the stairs.

It gets into my hair.

Even when I go to ride, if I turn my head suddenly and surprise it—there is that smell!

Such a peculiar odor, too! I have spent hours in trying to analyze it, to find what it smelled like.

It is not bad—at first, and very gentle, but quite the subtlest, most enduring odor I ever met.

In this damp weather it is awful, I wake up in the night and find it hanging over me.

It used to disturb me at first. I thought seriously of burning the house—to reach the smell.

But now I am used to it. The only thing I can think of that it is like is the *color* of the paper! A yellow smell.

There is a very funny mark on this wall, low down, near the mopboard. A streak that runs round the room. It goes behind every piece of furniture, except the bed, a long, straight, even *smooch*, as if it had been rubbed over and over.

I wonder how it was done and who did it, and what they did it for. Round and round and round—round and round and round—it makes me dizzy!

I really have discovered something at last.

Through watching so much at night, when it changes so, I have finally found out.

The front pattern *does* move—and no wonder! The woman behind shakes it!

Sometimes I think there are a great many women behind, and sometimes only one, and she crawls around fast, and her crawling shakes it all over.

Then in the very bright spots she keeps still, and in the very shady spots she just takes hold of the bars and shakes them hard.

And she is all the time trying to climb through. But nobody could climb through that pattern—it strangles so; I think that is why it has so many heads.

They get through, and then the pattern strangles them off and turns them upside down, and makes their eyes white!

If those heads were covered or taken off it would not be half so bad.

I think the woman gets out in the daytime!

And I'll tell you why—privately—I've seen her!

I can see her out of every one of my windows!

It is the same woman, I know, for she is always creeping, and most women do not creep by daylight.

I see her on that long road under the trees, creeping along, and when a carriage comes she hides under the blackberry vines.

I don't blame her a bit. It must be very humiliating to be caught creeping by daylight!

I always lock the door when I creep by daylight. I can't do it at night, for I know John would suspect something at once.

And John is so queer now, that I don't want to irritate him. I wish he would take another room! Besides, I don't want anybody to get that woman out at night but myself.

I often wonder if I could see her out of all the windows at once.

But, turn as fast as I can, I can only see out of one at one time.

And though I always see her, she *may* be able to creep faster than I can turn!

I have watched her sometimes away off in the open country, creeping as fast as a cloud shadow in a high wind.

If only that top pattern could be gotten off from the under one! I mean to try it, little by little.

I have found out another funny thing, but I shan't tell it this time! It does not do to trust people too much.

There are only two more days to get this paper off, and I believe John is beginning to notice. I don't like the look in his eyes.

And I heard him ask Jennie a lot of professional questions about me. She had a very good report to give.

She said I slept a good deal in the daytime.

260

John knows I don't sleep very well at night, for all I'm so quiet!

He asked me all sorts of questions, too, and pretended to be very loving and kind. As if I couldn't see through him!

Still, I don't wonder he acts so, sleeping under this paper for three months.

It only interests me, but I feel sure John and Jennie are secretly affected by it.

Hurrah! This is the last day, but it is enough. John to stay in town overnight, and won't be out until this evening.

Jennie wanted to sleep with me—the sly thing! but I told her I should undoubtedly rest better for a night all alone.

That was clever, for really I wasn't alone a bit! As soon as it was moonlight and that poor thing began to crawl and shake the pattern, I got up and ran to help her.

I pulled and she shook, I shook and she pulled, and before morning we had peeled off yards of that paper.

A strip about as high as my head and half around the room.

And then when the sun came and that awful pattern began to laugh at me, I declared I would finish it today!

We go away tomorrow, and they are moving all my furniture down again to leave things as they were before.

Jennie looked at the wall in amazement, but I told her merrily that I did it out of pure spite at the vicious thing.

She laughed and said she wouldn't mind doing it herself, but I must not get tired.

How she betrayed herself that time!

But I am here, and no person touches this paper but me,—not *alive*!

She tried to get me out of the room—it was too patent! But I said it was so quiet and empty and clean now that I believed I would lie down again and sleep all I could; and not to wake me even for dinner—I would call when I woke.

So now she is gone, and the servants are gone, and the things are gone, and there is nothing left but that great bedstead nailed down, with the canvas mattress we found on it.

We shall sleep downstairs tonight, and take the boat home tomorrow.

I quite enjoy the room, now it is bare again.

How those children did tear about here!

This bedstead is fairly gnawed!

But I must get to work.

I have locked the door and thrown the key down into the front path.

I don't want to go out, and I don't want to have anybody come in, 'til John comes.

I want to astonish him.

I've got a rope up here that even Jennie did not find. If that woman does get out, and tries to get away, I can tie her!

But I forgot I could not reach far without anything to stand on!

This bed will *not* move!

I tried to lift and push it until I was lame, and then I got so angry I bit off a little piece at one corner—but it hurt my teeth.

Then I peeled off all the paper I could reach standing on the floor. It sticks horribly and the pattern just enjoys it! All those strangled heads and bulbous eyes and waddling fungus growths just shriek with derision!

I am getting angry enough to do something desperate. To jump out of the window would be admirable exercise, but the bars are too strong even to try.

Besides I wouldn't do it. Of course not. I know well enough that a step like that is improper and might be misconstrued.

I don't like to look out of the windows even—there are so many of those creeping women, and they creep so fast.

I wonder if they all come out of that wallpaper as I did?

But I am securely fastened now by my well hidden rope—you don't get *me* out in the road there!

I suppose I shall have to get back behind the pattern when it comes at night, and that is hard!

It is so pleasant to be out in this great room and creep around as I please!

I don't want to go outside. I won't, even if Jennie asks me to.

For outside you have to creep on the ground, and everything is green instead of yellow.

But here I can creep smoothly on the floor, and my shoulder just fits in that long smooch around the wall, so I cannot lose my way.

Why there's John at the door!

It is no use, young man, you can't open it!

How he does call and pound!

Now he's crying for an axe.

It would be a shame to break down that beautiful door!

"John dear!" said I in the gentlest voice, "the key is down by the front steps, under a plantain leaf!"

That silenced him for a few moments.

Then he said—very quietly indeed, "Open the door, my darling!"

"I can't," said I. "The key is down by the front door under a plantain leaf!"

And then I said it again, several times, very gently and slowly, and said it so often that he had to go and see, and he got it of course, and came in. He stopped short by the door.

"What is the matter?" he cried. "For God's sake, what are you doing!"

I kept on creeping just the same, but I looked at him over my shoulder.

"I've got out at last," said I, "in spite of you and Jane. And I've pulled off most of the paper, so you can't put me back!"

Now why should that man have fainted? But he did, and right across my path by the wall, so that I had to creep over him every time!

—*Charlotte Perkins Gilman (1860-1935)*

Young Goodman Brown came forth at sunset into the street of Salem village; but put his head back, after crossing the threshold, to exchange a parting kiss with his young wife. And Faith, as the wife was aptly named, thrust her own pretty head into the street, letting the wind play with the pink ribbons of her cap while she called to Goodman Brown.

"Dearest heart," whispered she, softly and rather sadly, when her lips were close to his ear, "prithee put off your journey until sunrise and sleep in your own bed tonight. A lone woman is troubled with such dreams and such thoughts that she's afeared of herself sometimes. Pray tarry with me this night, dear husband, of all nights in the year."

"My love and my Faith," replied young Goodman Brown, "of all nights in the year, this one night must I tarry away from thee. My journey, as thou callest it, forth and back again, must needs be done 'twixt now and sunrise. What, my sweet, pretty wife, dost thou doubt me already, and we but three months married?"

"Then God bless you!" said Faith, with the pink ribbons; "and may you find all well when you come back."

"Amen!" cried Goodman Brown. "Say thy prayers, dear Faith, and go to bed at dusk, and no harm will come to thee."

So they parted; and the young man pursued his way until, being about to turn the corner by the meeting house, he looked back and saw the head of Faith still peeping after him with a melancholy air, in spite of her pink ribbons.

"Poor little Faith!" thought he, for his heart smote him. "What a wretch am I to leave her on such an errand! She talks of dreams, too. Methought as she spoke there was trouble in her face, as if a dream had warned her what work is to be done tonight. But no, no; 'twould kill her to think it. Well, she's a blessed angel on earth; and after this one night I'll cling to her skirts and follow her to heaven."

With this excellent resolve for the future, Goodman Brown felt himself justified in making more haste on his present evil purpose. He had taken a dreary road, darkened by all the gloomiest trees of the forest, which barely stood aside to let the narrow path creep through, and closed immediately behind. It was all as lonely as could be; and there is this peculiarity in such solitude, that the traveller knows not who may be concealed by the innumerable trunks and thick boughs overhead; so that with lonely footsteps he may yet be passing through an unseen multitude.

"There may be a devilish Indian behind every tree," said Goodman Brown to himself; and he glanced fearfully behind him as he added, "What if the devil himself should be at my very elbow!"

His head being turned back, he passed a crook of the road, and, looking forward again, beheld the figure of a man, in grave and decent attire, seated at the foot of an old tree. He arose at Goodman Brown's approach and walked onward side by side with him.

"You are late, Goodman Brown," said he. "The clock of the Old South was striking as I came through Boston; and that is full fifteen minutes agone."

"Faith kept me back a while," replied the young man, with a tremor in his voice, caused by the sudden appearance of his companion, though not wholly unexpected.

It was now deep dusk in the forest, and deepest in that part of it where these two were journeying. As nearly as could be discerned, the second traveller was about fifty years old, apparently in the same rank of life as Goodman Brown, and bearing a considerable resemblance to him, though perhaps more in expression than features. Still they might have been taken for father and son. And yet, though the elder person was as simply clad as the younger and as simple in manner too, he had an indescribable air of one who knew the world, and who would not have felt abashed at the governor's dinner table or in King William's court, were it possible that his affairs should call him thither. But the only thing about him that could be fixed upon as remarkable was his staff, which bore the likeness of a great black snake, so curiously wrought that it might almost be seen to twist and wriggle itself like a living serpent. This, of course, must have been an ocular deception, assisted by the uncertain light.

"Come, Goodman Brown," cried his fellow-traveller, "this is a dull pace for the beginning of a journey. Take my staff, if you are so soon weary."

"Friend," said the other, exchanging his slow pace for a full stop, "having kept covenant by meeting thee here, it is my purpose now to return whence I came. I have scruples touching the matter thou wot'st of."

"Sayest thou so?" replied he of the serpent, smiling apart. "Let us walk on, nevertheless, reasoning as we go; and if I convince thee not thou shalt turn back. We are but a little way in the forest yet."

"Too far! too far!" exclaimed the goodman, unconsciously resuming his walk. "My father never went into the woods on such an errand; nor his father before him. We have been a race of honest men and good Christians since the days of the martyrs; and shall I be the first of the name of Brown that ever took this path and kept—"

"Such company, thou wouldst say," observed the elder person, interpreting his pause. "Well said, Goodman Brown! I have been well acquainted with your family as with ever a one among the Puritans; and that's no trifle to say. I helped your grandfather, the constable, when he lashed the Quaker woman so smartly through the streets of Salem; and it was I that brought your father a pitch-pine knot, kindled at my own hearth, to set fire to an Indian village, in King Philip's war. They were my good friends, both; and many a pleasant walk have we had along this path, and returned merrily after midnight. I would fain be friends with you for their sake."

"If it be as thou sayest," replied Goodman Brown, "I marvel they never spoke of these matters; or, verily, I marvel not, seeing that the least rumor of the sort would have driven them from New England. We are a people of prayer, and good works to boot, and abide no such wickedness."

"Wickedness or not," said the traveller with the twisted staff, "I have a very general acquaintance here in New England. The deacons of many a church have drunk the communion wine with me; the selectmen of divers towns make me their chairman; and a majority of the Great and General Court are firm supporters of my interest. The governor and I, too—But these are state secrets."

"Can this be so?" cried Goodman Brown, with a stare of amazement at his undisturbed companion. "Howbeit, I have nothing to do with the governor and council; they have their own ways, and are no rule for a simple husbandman like me. But, were I to go on with thee, how should I meet the eye of that good old man, our minister, at Salem village: O, his voice would make me tremble both Sabbath day and lecture day."

Thus far the elder traveller had listened with due gravity; but now burst into a fit of irrepressible mirth, shaking himself so violently that his snakelike staff actually seemed to wriggle in sympathy.

"Ha! ha! ha!" shouted he again and again; then composing himself. "Well, go on, Goodman Brown, go on; but, prithee, don't kill me with laughing."

"Well, then, to end the matter at once," said Goodman Brown, considerably nettled, "there is my wife, Faith. It would break her dear little heart; and I'd rather break my own."

"Nay, if that be the case," answered the other, "e'en go thy ways, Goodman Brown. I would not for twenty old women like the one hobbling before us that Faith should come to any harm."

As he spoke, he pointed his staff at a female figure on the path, in whom Goodman Brown recognized a very pious and exemplary dame, who had taught him his catechism in youth, and was still his moral and spiritual adviser, jointly with the minister and Deacon Gookin.

"A marvel, truly, that Goody Cloyse should be so far in the wilderness at nightfall," said he. "But, with your leave, friend, I shall take a cut through the woods until we have left this Christian woman behind. Being a stranger to you, she might ask whom I was consorting with and whither I was going."

"Be it so," said his fellow-traveller. "Betake you to the woods, and let me keep the path."

Accordingly the young man turned aside, but took care to watch his companion, who advanced softly along the road until he had come within a staff's length of the old dame. She, meanwhile, was making the best of her way, with singular speed for so aged a woman, and mumbling some indistinct words—a prayer, doubtless—as she went. The traveller put forth his staff and touched her withered neck with what seemed the serpent's tail.

"The devil!" screamed the pious old lady.

"Then Goody Cloyse knows her old friend?" observed the traveller, confronting her and leaning on his writhing stick.

"Ah, forsooth, and is it your worship indeed?" cried the good dame. "Yea, truly is it, and in the very image of my old gossip, Goodman Brown, the grandfather of the silly fellow that now is. But—would your worship believe it?—my broomstick hath strangely disappeared, stolen, as I suspect, by that unhanged witch, Goody Cory, and that, too, when I was all anointed with the juice of smallage, and cinquefoil, and wolf's bane—"

"Mingled with fine wheat and the fat of a new-born babe," said the shape of old Goodman Brown.

"Ah, your worship knows the recipe," cried the old lady, cackling aloud. "So, as I was saying, being all ready for the meeting and no horse to ride on, I made up my mind to foot it; for they tell me there is a nice young man to be taken into communion tonight. But now your good worship will lend me your arm, and we shall be there in a twinkling."

"That can hardly be," answered her friend. "I may not spare you my arm, Goody Cloyse; but here is my staff, if you will."

So saying, he threw it down at her feet, where, perhaps, it assumed life, being one of the rods which its owner had formerly let to the Egyptian magi. Of this fact, however, Goodman Brown could not take cognizance. He had cast up his eyes in astonishment, and, looking down again, beheld neither Goody Cloyse nor the serpentine staff, but his fellow-traveller alone, who waited for him as calmly as if nothing had happened.

"That old woman taught me my catechism," said the young man; and there was a world of meaning in this simple comment.

They continued to walk onward, while the elder traveller exhorted his companion to make good speed and persevere in the path, discoursing so aptly that his arguments seemed rather to spring up in the bosom of his auditor than to be suggested by himself. As they went, he plucked a branch of maple to serve for a walking stick, and began to strip it of the twigs and little boughs, which were wet with evening dew. The moment his fingers touched them they became strangely withered and dried up as with a week's sunshine. Thus the pair proceeded, at a good free pace, until suddenly, in a gloomy hollow of the road, Goodman Brown sat himself down on the stump of a tree and refused to go any farther.

"Friend," said he, stubbornly, "my mind is made up. Not another step will I budge on this errand. What if a wretched old woman do choose to go to the devil when I thought she was going to heaven: is that any reason why I should quit my dear Faith and go after her?"

"You will think better of this by and by," said his acquaintance, composedly.

"Sit here and rest yourself a while; and when you feel like moving again, there is my staff to help you along."

Without more words, he threw his companion the maple stick, and was as speedily out of sight as if he had vanished into the deepening gloom. The young man sat a few moments by the roadside, applauding himself greatly, and thinking with how clear a conscience he should meet the minister in his morning walk, nor shrink from the eye of good old Deacon Gookin. And what calm sleep would be his that very night, which was to have been spent so wickedly, but so purely and sweetly now, in the arms of Faith! Amidst these pleasant and praiseworthy meditations, Goodman Brown heard the tramp of horses along the road, and deemed it advisable to conceal himself within the verge of the forest, conscious of the guilty purpose that had brought him thither, though now so happily turned from it.

On came the hoof tramps and the voices of the riders, two grave old voices, conversing soberly as they drew near. These mingled sounds appeared to pass along the road, within a few yards of the young man's hiding place; but, owing doubtless to the depth of the gloom at that particular spot, neither the travellers nor their steeds were visible. Though their figures brushed the small boughs by the wayside, it could not be seen that they intercepted, even for a moment, the faint gleam from the strip of bright sky athwart which they must have passed. Goodman Brown alternately crouched and stood on tiptoe, pulling aside the branches and thrusting forth his head as far as he durst without discerning so much as a shadow. It vexed him the more, because he could have sworn, were such a thing possible, that he recognized the voices of the minister and Deacon Gookin, jogging along quietly, as they were wont to do, when bound to some ordination or ecclesiastical council. While yet within hearing, one of the riders stopped to pluck a switch.

"Of the two, reverend sir," said the voice like the deacon's, "I had rather miss an ordination dinner than tonight's meeting. They tell me that some of our community are to be here from Falmouth and beyond, and others from Connecticut and Rhode Island, besides several of the Indian powwows, who, after their fashion, know almost as much deviltry as the best of us. Moreover, there is a goodly young woman to be taken into communion."

"Mighty well, Deacon Gookin!" replied the solemn old tones of the minister. "Spur up, or we shall be late. Nothing can be done, you know, until I get on the ground."

The hoofs clattered again; and the voices, talking so strangely in the empty air, passed on through the forest, where no church had ever been gathered or solitary Christian prayed. Whither, then, could these holy men be journeying so deep into the heathen wilderness? Young Goodman Brown caught hold of a tree for support, being ready to sink down on the ground, faint and overburdened with the heavy sickness of his heart. He looked up to the sky, doubting whether there really was a heaven above him. Yet there was the blue arch, and the stars brightening in it.

"With heaven above and Faith below, I will yet stand firm against the devil!" cried Goodman Brown.

While he still gazed upward into the deep arch of the firmament and had lifted his hands to pray, a cloud, though no wind was stirring, hurried across the zenith and hid the brightening stars. The blue sky was still visible except directly overhead, where this black mass of cloud was sweeping swiftly northward. Aloft in the air, as if from the depths of the cloud, came a confused and doubtful sound of voices. Once the listener fancied that he could distinguish the accents of townspeople of his own, men and women, both pious and ungodly, many of whom he had met at the communion table, and had seen others rioting at the tavern. The next moment, so indistinct were the sounds, he doubted whether he had heard aught but the murmur of the old forest, whispering without a wind. Then came a stronger swell of those familiar tones, heard daily in the sunshine at Salem village, but never until now from a cloud of night.

There was one voice, of a young woman, uttering lamentations, yet with an uncertain sorrow, and entreating for some favor, which, perhaps, it would grieve her to obtain; and all the unseen multitude, both saints and sinners, seemed to encourage her onward.

"Faith!" shouted Goodman Brown, in a voice of agony and desperation; and the echoes of the forest mocked him, crying, "Faith! Faith!" as if bewildered wretches were seeking her all through the wilderness.

The cry of grief, rage, and terror was yet piercing the night, when the unhappy husband held his breath for a response. There was a scream, drowned immediately in a louder murmur of voices, fading into far-off laughter, as the dark cloud swept away, leaving the clear and silent sky above Goodman Brown. But something fluttered lightly down through the air and caught on the branch of a tree. The young man seized it, and beheld a pink ribbon.

"My Faith is gone!" cried he, after one stupefied moment. "There is no good on earth; and sin is but a name. Come, devil; for to thee is this world given."

And, maddened with despair, so that he laughed loud and long, did Goodman Brown grasp his staff and set forth again, at such a rate that he seemed to fly along the forest path rather than to walk or run. The road grew wilder and drearier and more faintly traced, and vanished at length, leaving him in the heart of the dark wilderness, still rushing onward with the instinct that guides mortal man to evil. The whole forest was peopled with frightful sounds—the creaking of the trees, the howling of wild beasts, and the yell of Indians; while sometimes the wind tolled like a distant bell, and sometimes gave a broad roar around the traveller, as if all Nature were laughing him to scorn. But he was himself the chief horror of the scene, and shrank not from its other horrors.

"Ha! ha! ha!" roared Goodman Brown when the wind laughed at him. "Let us hear which will laugh loudest. Think not to frighten me with your deviltry. Come witch, come wizard, come Indian powwow, come devil himself, and here comes Goodman Brown. You may as well fear him as he fears you."

In truth, all through the haunted forest there could be nothing more frightful than the figure of Goodman Brown. On he flew among the black pines, brandishing his staff with frenzied gestures, now giving vent to an inspiration of horrid blasphemy, and now shouting forth such laughter as set all the echoes of the forest laughing like demons around him. The fiend in his own shape is less hideous than when he rages in the breast of man. Thus sped the demoniac on his course, until, quivering among the trees, he saw a red light before him, as when the felled trunks and branches of a clearing have been set on fire, and throw up their lurid blaze against the sky, at the hour of midnight. He paused, in a lull of the tempest that had driven him onward, and heard the swell of what seemed a hymn, rolling solemnly from a distance with the weight of many voices. He knew the tune; it was a familiar one in the choir of the village meeting house. The verse died heavily away, and was lengthened by a chorus, not of human voices, but of all the sounds of the benighted wilderness pealing in awful harmony together. Goodman Brown cried out; and his cry was lost to his own ear by its unison with the cry of the desert.

In the interval of silence he stole forward until the light glared full upon his eyes. At one extremity of an open space, hemmed in by the dark wall of the forest, arose a rock, bearing some rude, natural resemblance either to an altar or a pulpit, and surrounded by four blazing pines, their tops aflame, their stems untouched, like candles at an evening meeting. The mass of foliage that had overgrown the summit of the rock was all on fire, blazing high into the night and fitfully illuminating the whole field. Each pendent twig and leafy festoon was in a blaze. As the red light arose and fell, a numerous congregation alternately shone forth, then disappeared in shadow, and again grew, as it were, out of the darkness, peopling the heart of the solitary woods at once.

"A grave and dark-clad company," quoth Goodman Brown.

In truth they were such. Among them, quivering to and fro between gloom and splendor, appeared faces that would be seen next day at the council board of the province, and others which, Sabbath after Sabbath, looked devoutly heavenward, and benignantly over the crowded pews, from the holiest pulpits in the land. Some affirm that the lady of the governor was there. At least there were high dames well known to her, and wives of honored husbands, and widows, a great multitude, and ancient maidens, all of excellent repute, and fair young girls, who trembled lest their mothers should espy them. Either the sudden gleams of light flashing over the obscure field bedazzled Goodman Brown, or he recognized a score of the church members of Salem village famous for their especial sanctity. Good old Deacon Gookin had arrived, and waited at the skirts of that venerable saint, his reverend pastor. But, irreverently consorting with these grave, reputable, and pious people, these elders of the church, these chaste dames and dewy virgins, there were men of dissolute lives and women of spotted fame, wretches given over to all mean and filthy vice, and suspected even of horrid crimes. It was strange to see that the good shrank not from the wicked, nor were the sinners abashed by the saints. Scattered also among their palefaced enemies were the Indian priests, or powwows, who had often scared their native forest with more hideous incantations than any known to English witchcraft.

"But where is Faith?" thought Goodman Brown, and, as hope came into his heart, he trembled.

Another verse of the hymn arose, a slow and mournful strain, such as the pious love, but joined to words which expressed all that our nature can conceive of sin, and darkly hinted at far more. Unfathomable to mere mortals is the lore of fiends. Verse after verse was sung; and still the chorus of the desert swelled between like the deepest tone of a mighty organ; and with the final peal of that dreadful anthem there came a sound, as if the roaring wind, the rushing streams, the howling beasts, and every other voice of the unconverted wilderness were mingling and according with the voice of guilty man in homage to the prince of all. The four blazing pines threw up a loftier flame, and obscurely discovered shapes and visages of horror on the smoke wreaths above the impious assembly. At the same moment the fire on the rock shot redly forth and formed a glowing arch above its base, where now appeared a figure. With reverence be it spoken, the figure bore no slight similitude, both in garb and manner, to some grave divine of the New England churches.

"Bring forth the converts!" cried a voice that echoed through the field and rolled into the forest.

At the word, Goodman Brown stepped forth from the shadow of the trees and approached the congregation, with whom he felt a loathful brotherhood by the sympathy of all that was wicked in his heart. He could have well nigh sworn that the shape of his own dead father beckoned him to advance, looking downward from a smoke wreath, while a woman, with dim features of despair, threw her hand to warn him back. Was it his mother? But he had no power to retreat one step, nor to resist, even in thought, when the minister and good old Deacon Gookin seized his arms and led him to the blazing rock. Thither came also the slender form of a veiled female, led between Goody Cloyse, that pious teacher of the catechism, and Martha Carrier, who had received the devil's promise to be queen of hell. A rampant hag was she. And there stood the proselytes beneath the canopy of fire.

"Welcome, my children," said the dark figure, "to the communion of your race. Ye have found thus young your nature and your destiny. My children, look behind you!"

They turned; and flashing forth, as it were, in a sheet of flame, the fiend worshippers were seen; the smile of welcome gleamed darkly on every visage.

"There," resumed the sable form, "are all whom ye have reverenced from youth. Ye deemed them holier than yourselves, and shrank from your own sin, contrasting it with their lives of righteousness and prayerful aspirations heavenward. Yet here are they all my worshipping assembly. This night it shall be granted you to know their secret deeds; how hoarybearded elders of the church have whispered wanton words to the young maids of their households; how many a woman, eager for widows' weeds, has given her husband a drink at bedtime and let him sleep his last sleep in her bosom; how beardless youths have made haste to inherit their fathers' wealth; and how fair damsels—blush not, sweet ones—have dug little graves in the garden, and bidden me, the sole guest, to an infant's funeral. By the sympathy of your human hearts for sin ye shall scent out all the places—whether in church, bed chamber, street, field, or forest—where crime has been committed, and shall exult to behold the whole earth one stain of guilt, one mighty blood spot. Far more than this. It shall be yours to penetrate, in every bosom, the deep mystery of sin, the fountain of all wicked arts, and which inexhaustibly supplies more evil impulses than human power—than my power at its utmost—can make manifest in deeds. And now, my children, look upon each other.''

They did so; and, by the blaze of the hell-kindled torches, the wretched man beheld his Faith, and the wife her husband, trembling before that unhallowed altar.

''Lo, there ye stand, my children,'' said the figure, in a deep and solemn tone, almost sad with its despairing awfulness, as if his once angelic nature could yet mourn for our miserable race. ''Depending upon one another's hearts, yet had still hoped that virtue were not all a dream. Now are ye undeceived. Evil is the nature of mankind. Evil must be your only happiness. Welcome again, my children, to the communion of your race.''

''Welcome,'' repeated the fiend worshippers, in one cry of despair and triumph.

And there they stood, the only pair, as it seemed, who were yet hesitating on the verge of wickedness in this dark world. A basin was hollowed, naturally, in the rock. Did it contain water, reddened by the lurid light? or was it blood? or, perchance, a liquid flame? Herein did the shape of evil dip his hand and prepare to lay the mark of baptism upon their foreheads, that they might be partakers of the mystery of sin, more conscious of the secret guilt of others, both in deed and thought, than they could now be of their own. The husband cast one look at his pale wife, and Faith at him. What polluted wretches would the next glance show them to each other, shuddering alike at what they disclosed and what they saw!

''Faith! Faith!'' cried the husband, ''look up to heaven, and resist the wicked one.''

Whether Faith obeyed, he knew not. Hardly had he spoken when he found himself amid calm night and solitude, listening to a roar of the wind which died heavily away through the forest. He staggered against the rock, and felt it chill and damp; while a hanging twig, that had been all on fire, besprinkled his cheek with the coldest dew.

The next morning young Goodman Brown came slowly into the street of Salem village, staring around him like a bewildered man. The good old minister was taking a walk along the graveyard to get an appetite for breakfast and meditate his sermon, and bestowed a blessing, as he passed, on Goodman Brown. He shrank from the venerable saint as if to avoid an anathema. Old Deacon Gookin was at domestic worship, and the holy words of his prayer were heard through the open window. ''What God doth the wizard pray to?'' quoth Goodman Brown. Goody Cloyse, that excellent old Christian, stood in the early sunshine at her own lattice, catechizing a little girl who had brought her a pint of morning's milk. Goodman Brown snatched away the child as from the grasp of the fiend himself. Turning the corner by the meeting house, he spied the head of Faith, with the pink ribbons, gazing anxiously forth, and bursting into such joy at the sight of him that she skipped along the street and almost kissed her husband before the whole village. But Goodman Brown looked sternly and sadly into her face, and passed on without a greeting.

Had Goodman Brown fallen asleep in the forest and only dreamed a wild dream of a witch meeting?

Be it so, if you will; but, alas; it was a dream of evil omen for young Goodman Brown. A stern, a sad, a darkly meditative, a distrustful, if not a desperate, man did he become from the night of that fearful dream. On the Sabbath day, when the congregation were singing a holy psalm, he could not listen, because an anthem of sin rushed loudly upon his ear and drowned all the blessed strain. When the minister spoke from the pulpit, with power and fervid eloquence and with his hand on the open Bible, of the sacred truths of our religion, and of saintlike lives and triumphant deaths, and of future bliss or misery unutterable, then did Goodman Brown turn pale, dreading lest the roof should thunder down upon the gray blasphemer and his bearers. Often, awaking suddenly at midnight, he shrank from the bosom of Faith; and at morning or eventide, when the family knelt down at prayer, he scowled, and muttered to himself, and gazed sternly at his wife, and turned away. And when he had lived long, and was borne to his grave, a hoary corpse, followed by Faith, an aged woman, and children and grandchildren, a goodly procession, besides neighbors not a few, they carved no hopeful verse upon his tombstone; for his dying hour was gloom.

—*Nathaniel Hawthorne (1804-1864)*

A CLEAN, WELL-LIGHTED PLACE

It was late and every one had left the cafe except an old man who sat in the shadow the leaves of the tree made against the electric light. In the day time the street was dusty, but at night the dew settled the dust and the old man liked to sit late because he was deaf and now at night it was quiet and he felt the difference. The two waiters inside the cafe knew the old man was a little drunk, and while he was a good client they knew that if he became too drunk he would leave without paying, so they kept watch on him.

"Last week he tried to commit suicide," one waiter said.

"Why?"

"He was in despair."

"What about?"

"Nothing."

"How do you know it was nothing?"

"He has plenty of money."

They sat together at a table that was close against the wall near the door of the cafe and looked at the terrace where the tables were all empty except where the old man sat in the shadow of the leaves of the tree that moved slightly in the wind. A girl and a soldier went by in the street. The street light shone on the brass number on his collar. The girl wore no head covering and hurried beside him.

"The guard will pick him up," one waiter said.

"What does it matter if he gets what he's after?"

"He had better get off the street now. The guard will get him. They went by five minutes ago."

The old man sitting in the shadow rapped on his saucer with his glass. The younger waiter went over to him.

"What do you want?"

The old man looked at him. "Another brandy," he said.

"You'll be drunk," the waiter said. The old man looked at him. The waiter went away.

"He'll stay all night," he said to his colleague. "I'm sleepy now. I never get into bed before three o'clock. He should have killed himself last week."

The waiter took the brandy bottle and another saucer from the counter inside the cafe and marched out to the old man's table. He put down the saucer and poured a glass full of brandy.

"You should have killed yourself last week," he said to the deaf man. The old man motioned with his finger. "A little more," he said. The waiter poured on into the glass so that the brandy slopped over and ran down the stem into the top saucer of the pile. "Thank you," the old man said. The waiter took the bottle back inside the cafe. He sat down at the table with his colleague again.

"He's drunk now," he said.

"He's drunk every night."

"What did he want to kill himself for?"

"How should I know."

"How did he do it?"

"He hung himself with a rope."

"Who cut him down?"

"His niece."

"Why did they do it?"

"Fear for his soul."

"How much money has he got?"

"He's got plenty."

"He must be eighty years old."

"Anyway I should say he was eighty."

"I wish he would go home. I never get to bed before three o'clock. What kind of hour is that to go to bed?"

"He stays up because he likes it."

"He's lonely. I'm not lonely. I have a wife waiting in bed for me."

"He had a wife once too."

"A wife would be no good to him now."

"You can't tell. He might be better with a wife."

"His niece looks after him."

"I know. You said she cut him down."

"I wouldn't want to be that old. An old man is a nasty thing."

"Not always. This old man is clean. He drinks without spilling. Even now, drunk. Look at him."

"I don't want to look at him. I wish he would go home. He has no regard for those who must work."

The old man looked from his glass across the square, then over at the waiters.

"Another brandy," he said, pointing to his glass. The waiter who was in a hurry came over.

"Finished," he said, speaking with that omission of syntax stupid people employ when talking to drunken people or foreigners. "No more tonight. Close now."

"Another," said the old man.

"No. Finished." The waiter wiped the edge of the table with a towel and shook his head.

The old man stood up, slowly counted the saucers, took a leather coin purse from his pocket and paid for the drinks, leaving half a peseta tip.

The waiter watched him go down the street, a very old man walking unsteadily but with dignity.

"Why didn't you let him stay and drink?" the unhurried waiter asked. They were putting up the shutters. "It is not half-past two."

"I want to go home to bed."

"What is an hour?"

"More to me than to him."

"An hour is the same."

"You talk like an old man yourself. He can buy a bottle and drink at home."

"It's not the same."

"No, it is not," agreed the waiter with a wife. He did not wish to be unjust. He was only in a hurry."

"And you? You have no fear of going home before your usual hour?"

"Are you trying to insult me?"

"No, hombre, only to make a joke."

"No," the waiter who was in a hurry said, rising from pulling down the metal shutters. "I have confidence. I am all confidence."

"You have youth, confidence, and a job," the older waiter said. "You have everything."

"And what do you lack?"

"Everything but work."

"You have everything I have."

"No. I have never had confidence and I am not young."

"Come on. Stop talking nonsense and lock up."

"I am of those who like to stay late at the cafe," the older waiter said. "With all those who do not want to go to bed. With all those who need a light for the night."

"I want to go home and into bed."

"We are of two different kinds," the older waiter said. He was now dressed to go home. "It is only a question of youth and confidence although those things are very beautiful. Each night I am reluctant to close up because there may be some one who needs the cafe."

"Hombre, there are bodegas open all night long."

"You do not understand. This is a clean and pleasant cafe. It is well lighted. The light is very good and also, now, there are shadows of the leaves."

"Good night," said the younger waiter.

"Good night," the other said. Turning off the electric light he continued the conversation with himself. It is the light of course but it is necessary that the place be clean and pleasant. You do not want music. Certainly you do not want music. Nor can you stand before a bar with dignity although that is all that is provided for these hours. What did he fear? It was not fear or dread. It was nothing that he knew too well. It was all a nothing and a man was nothing too. It was only that and light was all it needed and a certain cleanness and order. Some lived in it and never felt it but he knew it all was nada y pues nada y nada y pues nada. Our nada who are in nada, nada be thy name thy kingdom nada thy will be nada in nada as it is in nada. Give us this nada our daily nada and nada us our nada as we nada our nada and nada us not into nada but deliver us from nada; pues nada. Hail nothing full of nothing, nothing is with thee. He smiled and stood before a bar with a shining stream pressure coffee machine.

"What's yours?" aksed the barman."

"Nada."

"Otro loco mas," said the barman and turned away.

"A little cup," said the waiter.

The barman poured it for him.

"The light is very bright and pleasant but the bar is unpolished," the waiter said.

The barman looked at him but did not answer. It was too late at night for conversation.

"You want another copita?" the barman asked.

"No, thank you," said the waiter and went out. He disliked bars and bodegas. A clean, well-lighted cafe was a very different thing. Now, without thinking further, he would go home to his room. He would lie in the bed and finally, with daylight, he would go to sleep. After all, he said to himself, it is probably only insomnia. Many must have it.

Ernest Hemingway (1899-1961)

TO BUILD A FIRE

Day had broken cold and gray, exceedingly cold and gray, when the man turned aside from the main Yukon trail and climbed the high earth-bank, where a dim and little-traveled trail led eastward through the fat spruce timberland. It was a steep bank, and he paused for breath at the top, excusing the act to himself by looking at his watch. It was nine o'clock. There was no sun nor hint of sun, though there was not a cloud in the sky. It was a clear day, and yet there seemed an intangible pall over the face of things, a subtle gloom that made the day dark, and that was due to the absence of sun. This fact did not worry the man. He was used to the lack of sun. It had been days since he had seen the sun, and he knew that a few more days must pass before that cheerful orb, due south, would just peep above the sky-line and dip immediately from view.

The man flung a look back along the way he had come. The Yukon lay a mile wide and hidden under three feet of ice. On top of this ice were as many feet of snow. It was all pure white, rolling in gentle undulations where the ice-jams of the freeze-up had formed. North and south, as far as his eye could see, it was unbroken white, save for a dark hairline that curved and twisted from around the spruce-covered island to the south, and that curved and twisted away into the north, where it disappeared behind another spruce-covered island. This dark hair-line was the trail—the main trail—that led south five hundred miles to the Chilcoot Pass, Dyea, and salt water; and that led north seventy miles to Dawson, and still on to the north a thousand miles to Nulato, and finally to St. Michael on Bering Sea, a thousand miles and half a thousand more.

But all this—the mysterious, far-reaching hair-line trail, the absence of sun from the sky, the tremendous cold, and the strangeness and weirdness of it all—made no impression on the man. It was not because he was long used to it. He was a newcomer in the land, a *chechaquo*, and this was his first winter. The trouble with him was that he was without imagination. He was quick and alert in the things of life, but only in the things, and not in the significances. Fifty degrees below zero meant eighty-odd degrees of frost. Such fact impressed him as being cold and uncomfortable, and that was all. It did not lead him to meditate upon his frailty as a creature of temperature, and upon man's frailty in general, able only to live within certain narrow limits of heat and cold; and from there on it did not lead him to the conjectural field of immortality and man's place in the universe. Fifty degrees below zero stood for a bite of frost that hurt and that must be guarded against by the use of mittens, ear-flaps, warm moccasins, and thick socks. Fifty degrees below zero was to him just precisely fifty degrees below zero. That there should be anything more to it than that was a thought that never entered his head.

As he turned to go on, he spat speculatively. There was a sharp, explosive crackle that startled him. He spat again. And again, in the air, before it could fall to the snow, the spittle crackled. He knew that at fifty below spittle crackled on the snow, but this spittle had crackled in the air. Undoubtedly it was colder than fifty below—how much colder he did not know. But the temperature did not matter. He was bound for the old claim on the left fork of Henderson Creek, where the boys were already. They had come over across the divide from the Indian Creek country, while he had come the roundabout way to take a look at the possibilities of getting out logs in the spring from the islands in the Yukon. He would be in to camp by six o'clock; a bit after dark, it was true, but the boys would be there, a fire would be going, and a hot supper would be ready. As for lunch, he pressed his hand against the protruding bundle under his jacket. It was also under his shirt, wrapped up in a handkerchief and lying against the naked skin. It was the only way to keep the biscuits from freezing. He smiled agreeably to himself as he thought of those biscuits, each cut open and sopped in bacon grease, and each enclosing a generous slice of fried bacon.

He plunged in among the big spruce trees. The trail was faint. A foot of snow had fallen since the last sled had passed over, and he was glad he was without a sled, traveling light. In fact, he carried nothing but the lunch wrapped in the handkerchief. He was surprised, however, at the cold. It certainly was cold, he concluded, as he rubbed his numb nose and cheek-bones with his mittened hand. He was a warm-whiskered man, but the hair on his face did not protect the high cheek-bones and the eager nose that thrust itself agressively into the frosty air.

At the man's heels trotted a dog, a big native husky, the proper wolfdog, gray-coated and without any visible or temperamental difference from its brother, the wild wolf. The animal was depressed by the tremendous cold. It knew that it was no time for traveling. Its instinct told it a truer tale than was told to the man by the man's judgment. In reality, it was not merely colder than fifty below zero; it was colder than sixty below, than seventy below. It was seventy-five below zero. Since the freezing point is thirty-two above zero, it meant that one hundred and seven degrees of frost obtained. The dog did not know anything about thermometers. Possibly in its brain there was no sharp consciousness of a condition of very cold such as was in the man's brain. But the brute had its instinct. It experienced a vague but menacing apprehension that subdued it and made it slink along at the man's heels, and that made it question eagerly every unwonted movement of the man as if expecting him to go into camp or to seek shelter somewhere and build a fire. The dog had learned fire, and it wanted fire, or else to burrow under the snow and cuddle its warmth away from the air.

The frozen moisture of its breathing had settled on its fur in a fine powder of frost, and especially were its jowls, muzzle, and eyelashes whitened by its crystalled breath. The man's red beard and mustache were likewise frosted, but more solidly, the deposit taking the form of ice and increasing with every warm, moist breath he exhaled. Also, the man was chewing tobacco, and the muzzle of ice held his lips so rigidly that he was unable to clear his chin when he expelled the juice. The result was that a crystal beard of the color and solidity of amber was increasing its length on his chin. If he fell down it would shatter itself, like glass, into brittle fragments. But he did not mind the appendage. It was the penalty all tobacco chewers paid in that country, and he had been out before in two cold snaps. They had not been so cold as this, he knew, but by the spirit thermometer at Sixty Mile he knew they had been registered at fifty below and at fifty-five.

He held on through the level stretch of woods for several miles, crossed a wide flat of nigger-heads, and dropped down a bank to the frozen bed of a small stream. This was Henderson Creek, and he knew he was ten miles from the forks. He looked at his watch. It was ten o'clock. He was making four miles an hour, and he calculated that he would arrive at the forks at half-past twelve. He decided to celebrate that event by eating his lunch there.

The dog dropped in again at his heels, with a tail drooping discouragement, as the man swung along the creek-bed. The furrow of the old sled-trail was plainly visible, but a dozen inches of snow covered the marks of the last runners. In a month no man had come up or down that silent creek. The man held steadily on. He was not much given to thinking, and just then particularly he had nothing to think about save that he would eat lunch at the forks and that at six o'clock he would be in camp with the boys. There was nobody to talk to; and, had there been, speech would have been impossible because of the ice-muzzle on his mouth. So he continued monotonously to chew tobacco and to increase the length of his amber beard.

Once in a while the thought reiterated itself that it was very cold and that he had never experienced such cold. As he walked along he rubbed his cheek-bones and nose with the back of his mittened hand. He did this automatically, now and again changing hands. But rub as he would, the instant he stopped his cheek-bones went numb, and the following instant the end of his nose went numb. He was sure to frost his cheeks; he knew that, and experienced a pang of regret that he had not devised a nose-strap of the sort Bud wore in cold snaps. Such a strap passed across the cheeks, as well, and saved them. But it didn't matter much, after all. What were frosted cheeks? A bit painful, that was all; they were never serious.

Empty as the man's mind was of thoughts, he was keenly observant and he noticed the changes in the creek, the curves and bends and timber-jams, and always he sharply noted where he placed his feet. Once, coming around a bend, he shied abruptly, like a startled horse, curved away from the place where he had been walking, and retreated several paces back along the trail. The creek he knew was frozen clear to the bottom,—no creek could contain water in that arctic winter,—but he knew also that there were springs that bubbled out from the hillsides and ran along under the snow and on top of the ice of the creek. He knew that the coldest snaps never froze these springs, and he knew likewise their danger. They were traps. They hid pools of water under the snow that might be three inches deep, or three feet. Sometimes a skin of ice half an inch thick covered them, and in turn was covered by the snow. Sometimes there were alternate layers of water and ice-skins, so that when one broke through he kept on breaking through for a while, sometimes wetting himself to the waist.

That was why he had shied in such panic. He had felt the give under his feet and heard the crackle of a snow-hidden ice-skin. And to get his feet wet in such a temperature meant trouble and danger. At the very least it meant delay, for he would be forced to stop and build a fire, and under its protection to bare his feet while he dried his socks and moccasins. He stood and studied the creek-bed and its banks, and decided that the flow of water came from the right. He reflected a while, rubbing his nose and cheeks, then skirted to the left, stepping gingerly and testing the footing for each step. Once clear of the danger, he took a fresh chew of tobacco and swung along at his four-mile gait.

In the course of the next two hours he came upon several similar traps. Usually the snow above the hidden pools had a sunken, candied appearance that advertised the danger. Once again, however, he had a close call; and once, suspecting danger, he compelled the dog to go on in front. The dog did not want to go. It hung back until the man shoved it forward, and then it went quickly across the white, unbroken surface. Suddenly it broke through, floundered to one side, and got away to firmer footing. It had wet its forefeet and legs, and almost immediately the water that clung to it turned to ice. It made quick efforts to lick the ice off its legs, then dropped down in the snow and began to bite out the ice that had formed between the toes. This was a matter of instinct. To permit the ice to remain would mean sore feet. It did not know this. It merely obeyed the mysterious prompting that arose from the deep crypts of its being. But the man knew, having achieved a judgment on the subject, and he removed the mitten from his right hand and helped tear out the ice-particles. He did not expose his fingers more than a minute, and was astonished at the swift numbness that smote them. It certainly was cold. He pulled on the mitten hastily, and beat the hand savagely across his chest.

At twelve o'clock the day was at its brightest. Yet the sun was too far south on its winter journey to clear the horizon. The bulge of the earth intervened between it and Henderson Creek, where the man walked under a clear sky at noon and cast no shadow. At half-past twelve, to the minute, he arrived at the forks of the creek. He was pleased at the speed he had made. If he kept it up, he would certainly be with the boys by six. He unbuttoned his jacket and shirt and drew forth his lunch. The action consumed no more than a quarter of a minute, yet in that brief moment the numbness laid hold of the exposed fingers. He did not put the mitten on, but, instead, struck the fingers a dozen sharp smashes against his leg. Then he sat down on a snow-covered log to eat. The sting that followed upon the striking of his fingers against his leg ceased so quickly that he was startled. He had had no chance to take a bite of biscuit.

He struck the fingers repeatedly and returned them to the mitten, baring the other hand for the purpose of eating. He tried to take a mouthful, but the ice-muzzle prevented. He had forgotten to build a fire and thaw out. He chuckled at his foolishness, and as he chuckled he noted the numbness creeping into the exposed fingers. Also, he noted that the stinging which had first come to his toes when he sat down was already passing away. He wondered whether the toes were warm or numb. He moved them inside the moccasins and decided that they were numb.

He pulled the mitten on hurriedly and stood up. He was a bit frightened. He stamped up and down until the stinging returned into the feet. It certainly was cold, was his thought. That man from Sulphur Creek had spoken the truth when telling how cold it sometimes got in the country. And he had laughed at him at the time! That showed one must not be too sure of things. There was no mistake about it, it *was* cold. He strode up and down, stamping his feet and threshing his arms, until reassured by the returning warmth. Then he got out matches and proceeded to make a fire. From the undergrowth, where high water of the previous spring had lodged a supply of seasoned twigs, he got his firewood. Working carefully from a small beginning, he soon had a roaring fire, over which he thawed the ice from his face and in the protection of which he ate his biscuits. For the moment the cold of space was outwitted. The dog took satisfaction in the fire, stretching out close enough for warmth and far enough away to escape being singed.

When the man had finished, he filled his pipe and took his comfortable time over a smoke. Then he pulled on his mittens, settled the ear-flaps of his cap firmly about his ears, and took the creek trail up the left fork. The dog was disappointed and yearned back toward the fire. The man did not know cold. Possibly all the generations of his ancestry had been ignorant of cold, of real cold, of cold one hundred and seven degrees below freezing point. But the dog knew; all its ancestry knew, and it had inherited the knowledge. And it knew that it was not good to walk abroad in such fearful cold. It was the time to lie snug in a hole in the snow and wait for a curtain of cloud to be drawn across the face of outer space whence this cold came. On the other hand, there was no keen intimacy between the dog and the man. The one was the toil-slave of the other and the only caresses it had ever received were the caresses of the whiplash and of harsh and menacing throat-sounds that threatened the whiplash. So the dog made no effort to communicate its apprehension to the man. It was not concerned in the welfare of the man; it was for its own sake that it yearned back toward the fire. But the man whistled, and spoke to it with the sound of whiplashes, and the dog swung in at the man's heel and followed after.

The man took a chew of tobacco and proceeded to start a new amber beard. Also, his moist breath quickly powdered with white his mustache, eyebrows, and lashes. There did not seem to be so many springs on the left fork of the Henderson, and for half an hour the man saw no signs of any. And then it happened. At a place where there were no signs, where the soft, unbroken snow seemed to advertise solidity beneath, the man broke through. It was not deep. He wet himself halfway to the knees before he floundered out to the first crust.

He was angry, and cursed his luck aloud. He had hoped to get into camp with the boys at six o'clock, and this would delay him an hour, for he would have to build a fire and dry out his foot-gear. This was imperative at that low temperature—he knew that much; and he turned aside to the bank, which he climbed. On top, tangled in the underbrush about the trunks of several small spruce trees, was a high-water deposit of dry firewood—sticks and twigs, principally, but also larger portions of seasoned branches and fine, dry, last-year's grasses. He threw down several large pieces on top of the snow. This served for a foundation and prevented the young flame from drowning itself in the snow it otherwise would melt. The flame he got by touching a match to a small shred of birch bark that he took from his pocket. This burned even more readily than paper. Placing it on the foundation, he fed the young flame with wisps of dry grass and with the tiniest dry twigs. He worked slowly and carefully, keenly aware of his danger. Gradually, as the flame grew stronger, he increased the size of the twigs with which he fed it. He squatted in the snow, pulling the twigs out from their entanglement in the brush and feeding directly to the flame. He knew there must be no failure. When it is seventy-five below zero, a man must not fail in his first attempt to build a fire—that is, if his feet are wet. If his feet are dry, and he fails, he can run along the trail for half a mile and restore his circulation. But the circulation of wet and freezing feet cannot be restored by running when it is seventy-five below. No matter how fast he runs, the wet feet will freeze the harder.

All this the man knew. The old-timer on Sulphur Creek had told him about it the previous fall, and now he was appreciating the advice. Already all sensation had gone out of his feet. To build the fire he had been forced to remove his mittens, and the fingers had quickly gone numb. His pace of four miles an hour had kept his heart pumping blood to the surface of his body and to all the extremities. But the instant he stopped, the action of the pump eased down. The cold of space smote the unprotected tip of the planet, and he, being on that unprotected tip, received the full force of the blow. The blood of his body recoiled before it. The blood was alive, like the dog, and like the dog it wanted to hide away and cover itself up from the fearful cold. So long as he walked four miles an hour, he pumped that blood, willy-nilly, to the surface; but now it ebbed away and sank down into the recesses of his body. The extremities were the first to feel its absence. His wet feet froze the faster, and his exposed fingers numbed the faster, though they had not yet begun to freeze. Nose and cheeks were already freezing, while the skin of all his body chilled as it lost its blood.

But he was safe. Toes and nose and cheeks would be only touched by the frost, for the fire was beginning to burn with strength. He was feeding it with twigs the size of his finger. In another minute he would be able to feed it with branches the size of his wrist, and then he could remove his wet foot-gear, and, while it dried, he could keep his naked feet warm by the fire, rubbing them at first, of course, with snow. The fire was a success. He was safe. He remembered the advice of the old-timer on Sulphur Creek, and smiled. The old-timer had been very serious in laying down the law that no man must travel alone in the Klondike after fifty below. Well, here he was; he had had the accident; he was alone; and he had saved himself. Those old-timers were rather womanish, some of them, he thought. All a man had to do was to keep his head, and he was all right. Any man who was a man could travel alone. But it was surprising, the rapidity with which his cheeks and nose were freezing. And he had not thought his fingers could go lifeless in so short a time. Lifeless they were, for he could scarcely make them move together to grip a twig, and they seemed remote from his body and from him. When he touched a twig, he had to look and see whether or not he had hold of it. The wires were pretty well down between him and his finger-ends.

All of which counted for little. There was the fire, snapping and crackling and promising life with every dancing flame. He started to untie his moccasins. They were coated with ice; the thick German socks were like sheaths of iron halfway to the knees; and the moccasin strings were like rods of steel all twisted and knotted as by some conflagration. For a moment he tugged with his numb fingers, then, realizing the folly of it, he drew his sheath-knife.

But before he could cut the strings, it happened. It was his own fault or, rather, his mistake. He should not have built the fire under the spruce tree. He should have built it in the open. But it had been easier to pull the twigs from the brush and drop them directly on the fire. Now the tree under which he had done this carried a weight of snow on its boughs. No wind had blown for weeks, and each bough was fully freighted. Each time he had pulled a twig he had communicated a slight agitation to the tree—an imperceptible agitation, so far as he was concerned, but an agitation sufficient to bring about the disaster. High up in the tree one bough capsized its load of snow. This fell on the boughs beneath, capsizing them. This process continued, spreading out and involving the whole tree. It grew like an avalanche, and it descended without warning upon the man and the fire, and the fire was blotted out! Where it had burned was a mantle of fresh and disordered snow.

The man was shocked. It was as though he had just heard his own sentence of death. For a moment he sat and stared at the spot where the fire had been. Then he grew very calm. Perhaps the old-timer on Sulphur Creek was right. If he had only had a trail-mate he would have been in no danger now. The trail-mate could have built the fire. Well, it was up to him to build the fire over again, and this second time there must be no failure. Even if he succeeded, he would most likely lose some toes. His feet must be badly frozen by now, and there would be some time before the second fire was ready.

Such were his thoughts, but he did not sit and think them. He was busy all the time they were passing through his mind. He made a new foundation for a fire, this time in the open, where no treacherous tree could blot it out. Next, he gathered dry grasses and tiny twigs from the high-water flotsam. He could not bring his fingers together to pull them out, but he was able to gather them by the handful. In this way he got many rotten twigs and bits of green moss that were undesirable, but it was the best he could do. He worked methodically, even collecting an armful of the larger branches to be used later when the fire gathered strength. And all the while the dog sat and watched him, a certain yearning wistfulness in its eyes, for it looked upon him as the fire-provider, and the fire was slow in coming.

When all was ready, the man reached in his pocket for a second piece of birch bark. He knew the bark was there, and, though he could not feel it with his fingers, he could hear its crisp rustling as he fumbled for it. Try as he would, he could not clutch hold of it. And all the time, in his consciousness, was the knowledge that each instant his feet were freezing. This thought tended to put him in a panic, but he fought against it and kept calm. He pulled on his mittens with his teeth, and threshed his arms back and forth, beating his hands with all his might against his sides. He did this sitting down, and he stood up to do it; and all the while the dog sat in the snow, its wolf-brush of a tail curled around warmly over its forefeet, its sharp wolf-ears pricked forward intently as it watched the man. And the man, as he beat and threshed with his arms and hands, felt a great surge of envy as he regarded the creature that was warm and secure in its natural covering.

After a time he was aware of the first far-away signals of sensation in his beaten fingers. The faint tingling grew stronger till it evolved into a stinging ache that was excruciating, but which the man hailed with satisfaction. He stripped the mitten from his right hand and fetched forth the birch bark. The exposed fingers were quickly going numb again. Next he brought out his bunch of sulphur matches. But the tremendous cold had already driven the life out of his fingers. In his efforts to separate one match from the others, the whole bunch fell in the snow. He tried to pick it out of the snow, but failed. The dead fingers could neither touch nor clutch. He was very careful. He drove the thought of his freezing feet, and nose, and cheeks, out of his mind, devoting his whole soul to the matches. He watched, using the sense of vision in place of that of touch, and then he saw his fingers on each side of the bunch, he closed them—that is, he willed to close them, for the wires were down, and the fingers did not obey. He pulled the mitten on the right hand, and beat it fiercely against his knee. Then, with both mittened hands, he scooped the bunch of matches, along with much snow, into his lap. Yet he was no better off.

After some manipulation he managed to get the bunch between the heels of his mittened hands. In this fashion he carried it to his mouth. The ice crackled and snapped when by a violent effort he opened his mouth. He drew the lower jaw in, curled the upper lip out of the way, and scraped the bunch with his upper teeth in order to separate a match. He succeeded in getting one, which he dropped on his lap. He was no better off. He could not pick it up. Then he devised a way. He picked it up in his teeth and scratched it on his leg. Twenty times he scratched before he succeeded in lighting it. As it flamed he held it with his teeth to the birch bark. But the burning brimstone went up his nostrils and into his lungs, causing him to cough spasmodically. The match fell into the snow and went out.

The old-timer on Sulphur Creek was right, he thought in the moment of controlled despair that ensued: after fifty below, a man should travel with a partner. He beat his hands, but failed in exciting any sensation. Sudden he bared both hands, removing the mittens with his teeth. He caught the whole bunch between the heels of his hands. His arm muscles not being frozen enabled him to press the hand-heels tightly against the matches. Then he scratched the bunch along his leg. It flared into flame, seventy sulphur matches at once! There was no wind to blow them out. He kept his head to one side to escape the strangling fumes, and held the blazing bunch to the birch bark. As he so held it, he became aware of sensation in his hand. His flesh was burning. He could smell it. Deep down below the surface he could feel it. The sensation developed into pain that grew acute. And still he endured it, holding the flame of the matches clumsily to the bark that would not light readily because his own burning hands were in the way, absorbing most of the flame.

At last, when he could endure no more, he jerked his hands apart. The blazing matches fell sizzling into the snow, but the birch bark was alight. He began laying dry grasses and the tiniest twigs on the flame. He could not pick and choose, for he had to lift the fuel between the heels of his hands. Small pieces of rotten wood and green moss clung to the twigs, and he bit them off as well as he could with his teeth. He cherished the flame carefully and awkwardly. It meant life, and it must not perish. The withdrawl of blood from the surface of his body now made him begin to shiver, and he grew more awkward. A large piece of green moss fell squarely on the little fire. He tried to poke it out with his fingers, but his shivering frame made him poke too far, and he disrupted the nucleus of the little fire, the burning grasses and tiny twigs separating and scattering. He tried to poke them together again, but in spite of the tenseness of the effort, his shivering got away with him, and the twigs were hopelessly scattered. Each twig gushed a puff of smoke and went out. The fire-provider had failed. As he looked apathetically about him, his eyes chanced on the dog, sitting across the ruins of the fire from him, in the snow, making restless, hunching movements, slightly lifting one forefoot and then the other, shifting its weight back and forth on them with wistful eagerness.

The sight of the dog put a wild idea into his head. He remembered the tale of the man, caught in a blizzard, who killed a steer and crawled inside the carcass, and so was saved. He would kill the dog and bury his hands in the warm body until the numbness went out of them. Then he could build another fire. He spoke to the dog, calling it to him; but in his voice was a strange note of fear that frightened the animal, who had never known the man to speak in such way before. Something was the matter, and its suspicious nature sensed danger—it knew not what danger, but somewhere, somehow, in its brain arose an apprehension of the man. It flattened its ears down at the sound of the man's voice, and its restless, hunching movements and the liftings and shiftings of its forefeet became more pronounced; but it would not come to the man. He got on his hands and knees and crawled toward the dog. This unusual posture again excited suspicion, and the animal sidled mincingly away.

The man sat up in the snow for a moment and struggled for calmness. Then he pulled on his mittens, by means of his teeth, and got upon his feet. He glanced down at first in order to assure himself that he was really standing up, for the absence of sensation in his feet left him unrelated to the earth. His erect position in itself started to drive the webs of suspicion from the dog's mind; and when he spoke peremptorily,

280

with the sound of whiplashes in his voice, the dog rendered its customary allegiance and came to him. As it came within reaching distance, the man lost his control. His arms flashed out to the dog, and he experienced genuine surprise when he discovered that his hands could not clutch, that there was neither bend nor feeling in the fingers. He had forgotten for the moment that they were frozen and that they were freezing more and more. All this happened quickly, and before the animal could get away, he encircled its body with his arms. He sat down in the snow, and in this fashion held the dog, while it snarled and whined and struggled.

But it was all he could do, hold its body encircled in his arms and sit there. He realized that he could not kill the dog. There was no way to do it. With his helpless hands he could neither draw nor hold his sheathknife nor throttle the animal. He released it, and it plunged wildly away, with tail between its legs, and still snarling. It halted forty feet away and surveyed him curiously, with ears sharply pricked forward. The man looked down at his hands in order to locate them, and found them hanging on the ends of his arms. It struck him as curious that one should have to use his eyes in order to find out where his hands were. He began threshing his arms back and forth, beating the mittened hands against his sides. He did this for five minutes, violently, and his heart pumped enough blood up to the surface to put a stop to his shivering. But no sensation was aroused in the hands. He had an impression that they hung like weights on the ends of his arms, but when he tried to run the impression down, he could not find it.

A certain fear of death, dull and oppressive, came to him. This fear quickly became poignant as he realized that it was no longer a mere matter of freezing his fingers and toes, or of losing his hands and feet, but that it was a matter of life and death with the chances against him. This threw him into a panic, and he turned and ran up the creek-bed along the old, dim trail. The dog joined in behind and kept up with him. He ran blindly, without intention, in fear such as he had never known in his life. Slowly, as he plowed and floundered through the snow, he began to see things again,—the banks of the creek, the old timber-jams, the leafless aspens, and the sky. The running made him feel better. He did not shiver. Maybe, if he ran on, his feet would thaw out; and, anyway, if he ran far enough, he would reach camp and the boys. Without doubt he would lose some fingers and toes and some of his face; but the boys would take care of him, and save the rest of him when he got there. And at the same time there was another thought in his mind that said he would never get to the camp and the boys; that it was too many miles away, that the freezing had too great a start on him, and that he would soon be stiff and dead. This thought he kept in the background and refused to consider. Sometimes it pushed itself forward and demanded to be heard, but he thrust it back and strove to think of other things.

It struck him as curious that he could run at all on feet so frozen that he could not feel them when they struck the earth and took the weight of his body. He seemed to himself to skim along above the surface, and to have no connection with the earth. Somewhere he had once seen a winged Mercury, and he wondered if Mercury felt as he felt when skimming over the earth.

His theory of running until he reached camp and the boys had one flaw in it: he lacked the endurance. Several times he stumbled, and finally he tottered, crumpled up, and fell. When he tried to rise, he failed. He must sit and rest, he decided, and next time he would merely walk and keep on going. As he sat and regained his breath, he noted that he was feeling quite warm and comfortable. He was not shivering, and it even seemed that a warm glow had come to his chest and trunk. And yet, when he touched his nose or cheeks, there was no sensation. Running would not thaw them out. Nor would it thaw out his hands and feet. Then the thought came to him that the frozen portions of his body must be extending. He tried to keep this thought down, to forget it, to think of something else; he was aware of the panicky feeling that it caused, and he was afraid of the panic. But the thought asserted itself, and persisted, until it produced a vision of his body totally frozen. This was too much, and he made another wild run along the trail. Once he slowed down to a walk, but the thought of the freezing extending itself made him run again. And all the time the dog ran with him, at his heels. When he fell down a second time, it curled its tail over its forefeet and sat in front of him, facing him, curiously eager and intent. The warmth and security of the animal angered him, and he cursed it till it flattened down its ears appeasingly. This time the shivering came more quickly upon the man. He was losing in his battle with the frost. It was creeping into his body from all sides. The thought of it drove him on, but he ran no more than a hundred feet, when he staggered and pitched headlong. It was his last panic. When he had recovered his breath and control, he sat up and entertained in his mind the conception of meeting death with dignity. However, the conception did not come to him in such terms. His idea of it was that he had been making a fool of himself, running around like a chicken with its head cut off—such was the simile that occurred to him. Well, he was bound to freeze anyway, and he might as well take it decently. With this new-found peace of mind came the first glimmerings of drowsiness. A good idea, he thought, to sleep off to death. It was like taking an anaesthetic. Freezing was not so bad as people thought. There were lots worse ways to die.

He pictured the boys finding his body next day. Suddenly he found himself with them, coming along the trail and looking for himself. And, still with them, he came around a turn in the trail and found himself lying in the snow. He did not belong with himself anymore, for even then he was out of himself, standing with the boys and looking at himself in the snow. It certainly was cold, was his thought. When he got back to the States he could tell the folks what real cold was. He drifted on from this to a vision of the old-timer on Sulphur Creek. He could see him quite clearly, warm and comfortable, and smoking a pipe.

"You were right, old hoss; you were right," the man mumbled to the old-timer of Sulphur Creek.

Then the man drowsed off into what seemed to him the most comfortable and satisfying sleep he had ever known. The dog sat facing him and waiting. The brief day drew to a close in a long, slow twilight. There were no signs of a fire to be made, and, besides, never in the dog's experience had it known a man to sit like that in the snow and make no fire. As the twilight drew on, its eager yearning for the fire mastered it, and with a great lifting and shifting of forefeet, it whined softly, then flattened its ears down in anticipation of being chidded by the man. But the man remained silent. Later, the dog whined loudly. And still later it crept close to the man and caught the scent of death. This made the animal bristle and back away. A little longer it delayed, howling under the stars that leaped and danced and shone brightly in the cold sky. Then it turned and trotted up the trail in the direction of the camp it knew, where were the other food-providers and fire-providers.

—*Jack London (1876-1916)*

282

THE MASQUE OF THE RED DEATH

The "Red Death" had long devastated the country. No pestilence had ever been so fatal or so hideous. Blood was its Avatar and its seal—the redness and the horror of blood. There were sharp pains, and sudden dizziness, and then profuse bleeding at the pores, with dissolution. The scarlet stains upon the body, and especially upon the face of the victim, were the pest ban which shut him out from the aid and from the sympathy of his fellow-men; and the whole seizure, progress, and termination of the disease, were the incidents of half-an-hour.

But the Prince Prospero was happy and dauntless and sagacious. When his dominions were half-depopulated, he summoned to his presence a thousand hale and light-hearted friends from among the knights and dames of his court, and with these retired to the deep seclusion of one of his castellated abbeys. This was an extensive and magnificent structure, the creation of the prince's own eccentric yet august taste. A strong and lofty wall girdled it in. This wall had gates of iron. The courtiers, having entered, brought furnaces and massy hammers and welded the bolts. They resolved to leave means neither of ingress or egress to the sudden impulses of despair from without or of frenzy from within. The abbey was amply provisioned. With such precautions the courtiers might bid defiance to contagion. The external world could take care of itself. In the meantime it was folly to grieve or to think. The prince had provided all the appliances of pleasure. There were buffoons, there were improvisatori, there were ballet dancers, there were musicians, there was beauty, there was wine. All these and security were within. Without was the "Red Death."

It was toward the close of the fifth or sixth month of his seclusion, and while the pestilence raged most furiously abroad, that the Prince Prospero entertained his thousand friends at a masked ball of the most unusual magnificence.

It was a voluptuous scene, that masquerade. But first let me tell of the rooms in which it was held. There were seven—an imperial suite. In many palaces, however, such suites form a long and straight vista, while the folding doors slide back nearly to the walls on either hand, so that the view of the whole extent is scarcely impeded. Here the case was very different, as might have been expected from the duke's love of the *bizarre*. The apartments were so irregularly disposed that the vision embraced but little more than one at a time. There was a sharp turn at every twenty or thirty yards, and at each turn a novel effect. To the right and left, in the middle of each wall, a tall and narrow Gothic window looked out upon a closed corridor which pursued the windings of the suite. These windows were of stained glass whose color varied in accordance with the prevailing hue of the decorations of the chamber into which it opened. That at the eastern extremity was hung, for example, in blue, and vividly blue were its windows. The second chamber was purple in its ornaments and tapestries, and here the panes were purple. The third was green throughout, and so were the casements. The fourth was furnished and lighted with orange, the fifth with white, the sixth with violet. The seventh apartment was closely shrouded in black velvet tapestries that hung all over the ceiling and down the walls, falling in heavy folds upon a carpet of the same material and hue. But in this chamber only the color of the windows failed to correspond with the decorations. The panes here were scarlet —a deep blood-color. Now in no one of the seven apartments was there any lamp or candelabrum amid the profusion of golden ornaments that lay scattered to and fro or depended from the roof. There was no light of any kind emanating from lamp or candle within the suite of chambers; but in the corridors that followed the suite there stood opposite to each window a heavy tripod bearing a brazier of fire that projected its rays through the tinted glass and so glaringly illumined the room. And thus were produced a multitude of gaudy and fantastic appearances. But in the western or black chamber the effect of the firelight that streamed upon the dark hangings, through the blood-tinted panes, was ghastly in the extreme, and produced so wild a look upon the countenances of those who entered that there were few of the company bold enough to set foot within its precincts at all.

It was in this apartment also that there stood against the western wall a gigantic clock of ebony. Its pendulum swung to and fro with a dull, heavy, monotonous clang; and when the minute-hand made the circuit of the face, and the hour was to be stricken, there came from the brazen lungs of the clock a sound which was clear and loud, and deep, and exceedingly musical, but of so peculiar a note and emphasis that, at each lapse of an hour, the musicians of the orchestra were constrained to pause momentarily in their performance to hearken to the sound; and thus the waltzers perforce ceased their evolutions, and there was a brief disconcert of the whole gay company, and while the chimes of the clock yet rang it was observed that the giddiest grew pale, and the more aged and sedate passed their hands over their brows as if in confused reverie or meditation; but when the echoes had fully ceased a light laughter at once pervaded the assembly; the musicians looked at each other and smiled as if at their own nervousness and folly, and made whispering vows each to the other that the next chiming of the clock should produce in them no similar emotion, and then, after the lapse of sixty minutes (which embrace three thousand and six hundred seconds of the time that flies), there came yet another chiming of the clock, and then were the same disconcert and tremulousness and meditation as before.

But in spite of these things it was a gay and magnificent revel. The tastes of the duke were peculiar. He had a fine eye for colors and effects. He disregarded the *decora* of mere fashion. His plans were bold and fiery, and his conceptions glowed with barbaric lustre. There are some who would have thought him mad. His followers felt that he was not. It was necessary to hear, and see, and touch him to be *sure* that he was not.

He had directed, in great part, the moveable embellishments of the seven chambers, upon occasion of this great *fête*; and it was his own guiding taste which had given character to the masqueraders. Be sure they were grotesque. There were much glare and glitter and piquancy and phantasm—much of what has been since seen in *Hernani*. There were arabesque figures with unsuited limbs and appointments. There were delirious fancies such as the madman fashions. There were much of the beautiful, much of the wanton, much of the *bizarre*, something of the terrible, and not a little of that which might have excited disgust. To and fro in the seven chambers there stalked, in fact, a multitude of dreams. And these—the dreams—writhed in and about, taking hue from the rooms, and causing the wild music of the orchestra to seem as the echo of their steps, and, anon, there strikes the ebony clock which stands in the hall of the velvet; and then, for a moment, all is still, and all is silent save the voice of the clock. The dreams are stiff-frozen as they stand. But the echoes of the chime die away—they have endured but an instant—and a light, half-subdued laughter floats after them as they depart. And now again the music swells, and the dreams live, and writhe to and fro more merrily than ever, taking hue from the many tinted windows through which stream the rays from the tripods. But to the chamber which lies most eastwardly of the seven, there are now none of the maskers who venture; for the night is waning away; and there flows a ruddier light through the blood-colored panes; and the blackness of the sable-drapery appalls; and to him whose foot falls upon the sable carpet, there comes from the near clock of ebony a muffled peal more solemnly emphatic than any which reaches *their* ears who indulge in the more remote gaieties of the other apartments.

But these other apartments were densely crowded, and in them beat feverishly the heart of life. And the revel went whirlingly on, until at length there commenced the sounding of midnight upon the clock. And then the music ceased, as I have told; and the evolutions of the waltzers were quieted; and there was an uneasy cessation of all things as before. But now there were twelve strokes to be sounded by the bell of the clock; and thus it happened, perhaps, that more of thought crept, with more of time, into the meditations of the thoughtful among those who revelled. And thus, too, it happened, perhaps, that before the last echoes of the last chime had utterly sunk into silence, there were many individuals in the crowd who had found leisure to become aware of the presence of a masked figure which had arrested the attention of no single individual before. And the rumor of this new presence having spread itself whisperingly around, there arose at length from the whole company a buzz, or murmur, expressive of disapprobation and surprise—then, finally, of terror, of horror, and of disgust.

In an assembly of phantasms such as I have painted, it may well be supposed that no ordinary appearance could have excited such sensation. In truth the masquerade license of the night was nearly unlimited; but the figure in question had out-Heroded Herod, and gone beyond the bounds of even the prince's indefinite decorum. There are chords in the hearts of the most reckless which cannot be touched without emotion. Even with the utterly lost, to whom life and death are equally jests, there are matters of which no jest can be made. The whole company indeed seemed now deeply to feel that in the costume and bearing of the stranger neither wit nor propriety existed. The figure was tall and gaunt, and shrouded from head to foot in the habiliments of the grave. The mask which concealed the visage was made so nearly to resemble the countenance of a stiffened corpse that the closest scrutiny must have had difficulty in detecting the cheat. And yet all this might have been endured, if not approved, by the mad revellers around. But the mummer had gone so far as to assume the type of the Red Death. His vesture was dabbled in *blood*—and his broad brow, with all the features of the face, was besprinkled with the scarlet horror.

When the eyes of Prince Prospero fell upon this spectral image (which with a slow and solemn movement, as if more fully to sustain its *rôle*, stalked to and fro among the waltzers) he was seen to be convulsed in the first moment with a strong shudder either of terror or distaste; but in the next his brow reddened with rage.

''Who dares?'' he demanded hoarsely of the courtiers who stood near him—''who dares insult us with this blasphemous mockery? Seize him and unmask him, that we may know whom we have to hang at sunrise from the battlements!''

It was in the eastern or blue chamber in which stood the Prince Prospero as he uttered these words. They rang throughout the seven rooms loudly and clearly—for the prince was a bold and robust man, and the music had become hushed at the waving of his hand.

It was in the blue room where stood the prince, with a group of pale courtiers by his side. At first, as he spoke, there was a slight rushing movement of this group in the direction of the intruder, who, at the moment was also near at hand, and now, with deliberate and stately step, made closer approach to the speaker. But, from a certain nameless awe with which the mad assumptions of the mummer had inspired the whole party, there were found none who put forth hand to seize him; so that unimpeded he passed within a yard of the prince's person; and while the vast assembly, as if with one impulse, shrank from the centers of the rooms to the walls, he made his way uninterruptedly, but with the same solemn and measured step which had distinguished him from the first, through the blue chamber to the purple—through the purple to the green—through the green to the orange—through this again to the white—and even thence to the violet, ere a decided movement had been made to arrest him. It was then, however, that the Prince Prospero, maddening with rage and the shame of his own momentary cowardice, rushed hurriedly through the six chambers, while none followed him on account of a deadly terror that had seized upon all. He bore aloft a drawn dagger, and had approached in rapid impetuosity, to within three or four feet of the retreating figure, when the latter, having attained the extremity of the velvet apartment, turned suddenly and confronted his pursuer. There was a sharp cry—and the dagger dropped gleaming upon the sable carpet, upon which, instantly afterwards, fell prostrate in death the Prince Prospero. Then, summoning the wild courage of despair, a throng of the revellers at once threw themselves into the black apartment, and, seizing the mummer, whose tall figure stood erect and motionless within the shadows of the ebony clock, gasped in unutterable horror at finding the grave cerements and corpse-like mask which they handled with so violent a rudeness, untenanted by any tangible form.

And now was acknowledged the presence of the Red Death. He had come like a thief in the night; and one by one dropped the revellers in the blood-bedewed halls of their revel, and died each in the despairing posture of his fall; and the life of the ebony clock went out with that of the last of the gay; and the flames of the tripods expired; and darkness and decay and the Red Death held illimitable dominion over all.

—*Edgar Allan Poe* (*1809-1849*)

THE SNAKE

It was almost dark when young Dr. Phillips swung his sack to his shoulder and left the tide pool. He climbed up over the rocks and squashed along the street in his rubber boots. The street lights were on by the time he arrived at his little commercial laboratory on the cannery street of Monterey. It was a tight little building, standing partly on piers over the bay water and partly on the land. On both sides the big corrugated-iron sardine canneries crowded in on it.

Dr. Phillips climbed the wooden steps and opened the door. The white rats in their cages scampered up and down the wire, and the captive cats in their pens mewed for milk. Dr. Phillips turned on the glaring light over the dissection table and dumped his clammy sack on the floor. He walked to the glass cages by the window where the rattlesnakes lived, leaned over and looked in.

The snakes were bunched and resting in the corners of the cage, but every head was clear; the dusty eyes seemed to look at nothing, but as the young man leaned over the cage the forked tongues, black on the ends and pink behind, twittered out and waved slowly up and down. Then the snakes recognized the man and pulled in their tongues.

Dr. Phillips threw off his leather coat and built a fire in the tin stove; he set a kettle of water on the stove and dropped a can of beans into the water. Then he stood staring down at the sack on the floor. He was a slight young man with the mild, pre-occupied eyes of one who looks through a microscope a great deal. He wore a short blond beard.

The draft ran breathily up the chimney and a glow of warmth came from the stove. The little waves washed quietly about the piles under the building. Arranged on shelves about the room were tier above tier of museum jars containing the mounted marine specimens the laboratory dealt in.

Dr. Phillips opened a side door and went into his bedroom, a book-lined cell containing an army cot, a reading light and an uncomfortable wooden chair. He pulled off his rubber boots and put on a pair of sheepskin slippers. When he went back to the other room the water in the kettle was already beginning to hum.

He lifted his sack to the table under the white light and emptied out two dozen common starfish. These he laid out side by side on the table. His preoccupied eyes turned to the busy rats in the wire cages. Taking grain from a paper sack, he poured it into the feeding troughs. Instantly the rats scrambled down from the wire and fell upon the food. A bottle of milk stood on a glass shelf between a small mounted octopus and a jellyfish. Dr. Phillips lifted down the milk and walked to the cat cage, but before he filled the containers he reached in the cage and gently picked out a big rangy alley tabby. He stroked her for a moment and then dropped her in a small black painted box, closed the lid and bolted it and then turned on a petcock which admitted gas into the killing chamber. While the short soft struggle went on in the black box he filled the saucers with milk. One of the cats arched against his hand and he smiled and petted her neck.

The box was quiet now. He turned off the petcock, for the airtight box would be full of gas.

On the stove the pan of water was bubbling furiously about the can of beans. Dr. Phillips lifted out the can with a big pair of forceps, opened it, and emptied the beans into a glass dish. While he ate he watched the starfish on the table. From between the rays little drops of milky fluid were exuding. He bolted his beans and when they were gone he put the dish in the sink and stepped to the equipment cupboard. From this he took a microscope and a pile of little glass dishes. He filled the dishes one by one with sea water from a tap and arranged them in a line beside the starfish. He took out his watch and laid it on the table under the pouring white light. The waves washed with little sighs against the piles under the floor. He took an eyedropper from a drawer and bent over the starfish.

At that moment there were quick soft steps on the wooden stairs and a strong knocking at the door. A slight grimace of annoyance crossed the young man's face as he went to open. A tall, lean woman stood in the doorway. She was dressed in a severe dark suit—her straight black hair, growing low on a flat forehead, was mussed as though the wind had been blowing it. Her black eyes glittered in the strong light.

She spoke in a soft throaty voice, "May I come in? I want to talk to you."

"I'm very busy just now," he said half-heartedly. "I have to do things at times." But he stood away from the door. The tall woman slipped in.

"I'll be quiet until you can talk to me."

He closed the door and brought the uncomfortable chair from the bedroom. "You see," he apologized, "the process is started and I must get to it." So many people wandered in and asked questions. He had little routines of explanations for the commoner processes. He could say them without thinking. "Sit here. In a few minutes I'll be able to listen to you."

The tall woman leaned over the table. With the eyedropper the young man gathered fluid from between the rays of the starfish and squirted it into a bowl of water, and then he drew some milky fluid and squirted it in the same bowl and stirred the water gently with the eyedropper. He began his little patter of explanation.

"When starfish are sexually mature they release sperm and ova when they are exposed at low tide. By choosing mature specimens and taking them out of the water, I give them a condition of low tide. Now I've mixed the sperm and eggs. Now I put some of the mixture in each one of these ten watch glasses. In ten minutes I will kill those in the first glass with menthol, twenty minutes later I will kill the second group and then a new group every twenty minutes. Then I will have arrested the process in stages, and I will mount the series on microscope slides for biologic study." He paused. "Would you like to look at this first group under the microscope?"

"No, thank you."

He turned quickly to her. People always wanted to look through the glass. She was not looking at the table at all, but at him. Her black eyes were on him, but they did not seem to see him. He realized why—the irises were as dark as the pupils, there was no color line between the two. Dr. Phillips was piqued at her answer. Although answering questions bored him, a lack of interest in what he was doing irritated him. A desire to arouse her grew in him.

"While I'm waiting the first ten minutes I have something to do. Some people don't like to see it. Maybe you'd better step into that room until I finish."

"No," she said in her soft flat tone. "Do what you wish. I will wait until you can talk to me." Her hands rested side by side on her lap. She was completely at rest. Her eyes were bright but the rest of her was almost in a state of suspended animation. He thought, "Low metabolic rate, almost as low as a frog's, from the looks." The desire to shock her out of her inanition possessed him again.

He brought a little wooden cradle to the table, laid out scalpels and scissors and rigged a big hollow needle to a pressure tube. Then from the killing chamber he brought the limp dead cat and laid it in the cradle and tied its legs to hooks in the sides. He glanced sidewise at the woman. She had not moved. She was still at rest.

The cat grinned up into the light, its pink tongue stuck out between its needle teeth. Dr. Phillips deftly snipped open the skin at the throat; with a scalpel he slit through and found an artery. With flawless technique he put the needle in the vessel and tied it in with gut. "Embalming fluid," he explained. "Later I'll inject yellow mass into the veinous system and red mass into the arterial system—for bloodstream dissection—biology classes."

He looked around at her again. Her dark eyes seemed veiled with dust. She looked without expression at the cat's open throat. Not a drop of blood had escaped.

The incision was clean. Dr. Phillips looked at his watch. "Time for the first group." He shook a few crystals of menthol into the first watch-glass.

The woman was making him nervous. The rats climbed about on the wire of their cage again and squeaked softly. The waves under the building beat with little shocks on the piles.

The young man shivered. He put a few lumps of coal in the stove and sat down. "Now," he said. "I haven't anything to do for twenty minutes." He noticed how short her chin was between lower lip and point. She seemed to awaken slowly, to come up out of some deep pool of consciousness. Her head raised and her dark dusty eyes moved about the room and then came back to him.

"I was waiting," she said. Her hands remained side by side on her lap. "You have snakes?"

"Why, yes," he said rather loudly. "I have about two dozen rattlesnakes. I milk out the venom and send it to the anti-venom laboratories."

She continued to look at him but her eyes did not center on him, rather they covered him and seemed to see in a big circle all around him. "Have you a male snake, a male rattlesnake?"

"Well, it just happens I know I have. I came in one morning and found a big snake in—in coition with a smaller one. That's very rare in captivity. You see, I do know I have a male snake."

"Where is he?"

"Why, right in the glass cage by the window there."

Her head swung slowly around but her two quiet hands did not move. She turned back toward him. "May I see?"

He got up and walked to the case by the window. On the sand bottom the knot of rattleshakes lay entwined, but their heads were clear. The tongues came out and flickered a moment and then waved up and down feeling the air for vibrations. Dr. Phillips nervously turned his head. The woman was standing beside him. He had not heard her get up from the chair. He had heard only the splash of water among the piles and the scampering of the rats on the wire screen.

She said softly, "Which is the male you spoke of?"

He pointed to a thick, dusty grey snake lying by itself in one corner of the cage. "That one. He's nearly five feet long. He comes from Texas. Our Pacific coast snakes are usually smaller. He's been taking all the rats, too. When I want the others to eat I have to take him out."

The woman stared down at the blunt dry head. The forked tongue slipped out and hung quivering for a long moment. "And you're sure he's a male."

"Rattlesnakes are funny," he said glibly. "Nearly every generalization proves wrong. I don't like to say anything definite about rattlesnakes, but—yes—I can assure you he's male."

Her eyes did not move from the flat head. "Will you sell him to me?"

"Sell him?" he cried. "Sell him to you?"

"You do sell specimens, don't you?"

"Oh—yes. Of course I do. Of course I do."

"How much? Five dollars? Ten?"

"Oh! Not more than five. But—do you know anything about rattlesnakes? You might be bitten."

She looked at him for a moment. "I don't intend to take him. I want to leave him here, but—I want him to be mine. I want to come here and look at him and feed him and to know he's mine." She opened a little purse and took out a five-dollar bill. "Here! Now he is mine."

Dr. Phillips began to be afraid. "You could come to look at him without owning him."

"I want him to be mine."

"Oh, Lord!" he cried. "I've forgotten the time. He ran to the table. "Three minutes over. It won't matter much." He shook menthol crystals into the second watch-glass. And then he was drawn back to the cage where the woman still stared at the snake.

She asked, "What does he eat?"

"I feed them white rats, rats from the cage over there."

"Will you put him in the other cage? I want to feed him."

"But he doesn't need food. He's had a rat already this week. Sometimes they don't eat for three or four months. I had one that didn't eat for over a year."

In her low monotone she asked, "Will you sell me a rat?"

He shrugged his shoulders. "I see. You want to watch how rattlesnakes eat. All right. I'll show you. The rat will cost twenty-five cents. It's better than a bullfight if you look at it one way, and it's simply a snake eating his dinner if you look at it another." His tone had become acid. He hated people who made sport of natural processes. He was not a sportsman but a biologist. He could kill a thousand animals for knowledge, but not an insect for pleasure. He'd been over this in his mind before.

She turned her head slowly toward him and the beginning of a smile formed on her thin lips. "I want to feed my snake," she said. "I'll put him in the other cage." She had opened the top of the cage and dipped her hand in before he knew what she was doing. He leaped forward and pulled her back. The lid banged shut.

"Haven't you any sense?" he asked fiercely. "Maybe he wouldn't kill you, but he'd make you damned sick in spite of what I could do for you."

"You put him in the other cage, then," she said quietly.

Dr. Phillips was shaken. He found that he was avoiding the dark eyes that didn't seem to look at anything. He felt that it was profoundly wrong to put a rat into the cage, deeply sinful; and he didn't know why. Often he had put rats in the cage when someone or other had wanted to see it, but this desire tonight sickened him. He tried to explain himself out of it.

"It's a good thing to see," he said. "It shows you how a snake can work. It makes you have respect for a rattlesnake. Then, too, lots of people have dreams about the terror of snakes making the kill. I think because it is a subjective rat. The person is the rat. Once you see it the whole matter is objective. The rat is only a rat and the terror is removed."

He took a long stick equipped with a leather noose from the wall. Opening the trap he dropped the noose over the big snake's head and tightened the thong. A piercing dry rattle filled the room. The thick body writhed and slashed about the handle of the stick as he lifted the snake out and dropped it in the feeding cage. It stood ready to strike for a time, but the buzzing gradually ceased. The snake crawled into a corner, made a big figure eight with its body and lay still.

"You see," the young man explained, "these snakes are quite tame. I've had them a long time. I suppose I could handle them if I wanted to, but everyone who does handle rattlesnakes gets bitten sooner or later. I just don't want to take the chance." He glanced at the woman. He hated to put in the rat. She had moved over in front of the new cage; her black eyes were on the stony head of the snake again.

She said, "Put in a rat."

Reluctantly he went to the rat cage. For some reason he was sorry for the rat, and such a feeling had never come to him before. His eyes went over the mass of swarming white bodies climbing up the screen toward him. "Which one?" he thought. "Which one shall it be?" Suddenly he turned angrily to the woman. "Wouldn't you rather I put in a cat? Then you'd see a real fight. The cat might even win, but if it did it might kill the snake. I'll sell you a cat if you like."

She didn't look at him. "Put in a rat," she said. "I want him to eat."

290

He opened the rat cage and thrust his hand in. His fingers found a tail and he lifted a plump, red-eyed rat out of the cage. It struggled up to try to bite his fingers and, failing, hung spread out and motionless from its tail. He walked quickly across the room, opened the feeding cage and dropped the rat in on the sand floor. "Now, watch it," he cried.

The woman did not answer him. Her eyes were on the snake where it lay still. Its tongue, flicking in and out rapidly, tasted the air of the cage.

The rat landed on its feet, turned around and sniffed at its pink naked tail and then unconcernedly trotted across the sand, smelling as it went. The room was silent. Dr. Phillips did not know whether the water sighed among the piles or whether the woman sighed. Out of the corner of his eye he saw her body crouch and stiffen.

The snake moved out smoothly, slowly. The tongue flicked in and out. The motion was so gradual, so smooth that it didn't seem to be motion at all. In the other end of the cage the rat perked up in a sitting position and began to lick down the fine white hair on its chest. The snake moved on, keeping always a deep S curve in its neck.

The silence beat on the young man. He felt the blood drifting up in his body. He said loudly, "See! He keeps the striking curve ready. Rattlesnakes are cautious, almost cowardly animals. The mechanism is so delicate. The snake's dinner is to be got by an operation as deft as a surgeon's job. He takes no chances with his instruments."

The snake had flowed to the middle of the cage by now. The rat looked up, saw the snake and then unconcernedly went back to licking its chest.

"It's the most beautiful thing in the world," the young man said. His veins were throbbing. "It's the most terrible thing in the world."

The snake was close now. Its head lifted a few inches from the sand. The head weaved slowly back and forth, aiming, getting distance, aiming. Dr. Phillips glanced again at the woman. He turned sick. She was weaving too, not much, just a suggestion.

The rat looked up and saw the snake. It dropped to four feet and back up, and then—the stroke. It was impossible to see, simply a flash. The rat jarred as though under an invisible blow. The snake backed hurriedly into the corner from which it had come, and settled down, its tongue working constantly.

"Perfect!" Dr. Phillips cried. "Right between the shoulder blades. The fangs must almost have reached the heart."

The rat stood still, breathing like a little white bellows. Suddenly it leaped in the air and landed on its side. Its legs kicked spasmodically for a second and it was dead.

The woman relaxed, relaxed sleepily.

"Well," the young man demanded, "it was an emotional bath, wasn't it?"

She turned her misty eyes to him. "Will he eat it now?" she asked.

"Of course he'll eat it. He didn't kill it for a thrill. He killed it because he was hungry."

The corners of the woman's mouth turned up a trifle again. She looked back at the snake. "I want to see him eat it."

Now the snake came out of its corner again. There was no striking curve in its neck, but it approached the rat gingerly, ready to jump back in case it attacked. It nudged the body gently with its blunt nose, and drew away. Satisfied that it was dead, the snake touched the body all over with its chin, from head to tail. It seemed to measure the body and to kiss it. Finally it opened its mouth and unhinged its jaws at the corners.

Dr. Phillips put his will against his head to keep it from turning toward the woman. He thought, "If she's opening her mouth, I'll be sick. I'll be afraid." He succeeded in keeping his eyes away.

The snake fitted its jaws over the rat's head and then with a slow peristaltic pulsing, began to engulf the rat. The jaws gripped and the whole throat crawled up, and the jaws gripped again.

Dr. Phillips turned away and went to his work table. "You've made me miss one of the series," he said bitterly. "The set won't be complete." He put one of the watch glasses under a low-power microscope and looked at it, and then angrily he poured the contents of all the dishes into the sink. The waves had fallen so that only a wet whisper came up through the floor. The young man lifted a trapdoor at his feet and dropped the starfish down into the black water. He paused at the cat, crucified in the cradle and grinning comically into the light. Its body was puffed with embalming fluid. He shut off the pressure, withdrew the needle and tied the vein.

"Would you like some coffee?" he asked.

"No, thank you. I shall be going pretty soon."

He walked to her where she stood in front of the snake cage. The rat was swallowed, all except an inch of pink tail that stuck out of the snake's mouth like a sardonic tongue. The throat heaved again and the tail disappeared. The jaws snapped back into their sockets, and the big snake crawled heavily to the corner, made a big eight and dropped its head on the sand.

"He's asleep now," the woman said. "I'm going now. But I'll come back and feed my snake every little while. I'll pay for the rats. I want him to have plenty. And sometime—I'll take him away with me." Her eyes came out of their dusty dream for a moment. "Remember, he's mine. Don't take his poison. I want him to have it. Goodnight." She walked swiftly to the door and went out. He heard her footsteps on the stairs, but he could not hear her walk away on the pavement.

Dr. Phillips turned a chair around and sat down in front of the snake cage. He tried to comb out his thought as he looked at the torpid snake. "I've read so much about psychological sex symbols," he thought. "It doesn't seem to explain. Maybe I'm too much alone. Maybe I should kill the snake. If I knew—no, I can't pray to anything."

For weeks he expected her to return. "I will go out and leave her alone here when she comes," he decided. "I won't see the damned thing again."

She never came again. For months he looked for her when he walked about in the town. Several times he ran after some tall woman thinking it might be she. But he never saw her again—ever.

—*John Steinbeck* (*1902-1969*)

CIRCE

Needle in air, I stopped what I was making. From the upper casement, my lookout on the sea, I saw them disembark and find the path; I heard that whole drove of mine break loose on the beautiful strangers. I slipped down the ladder. When I heard men breathing and sandals kicking the stones, I threw open the door. A shaft of light from the zenith struck my brow, and the wind let out my hair. Something else swayed my body outward.

"Welcome!" I said—the most dangerous word in the world.

Heads lifted to the smell of my bread, they trooped inside—and with such a grunting and frisking at their heels to the very threshold. Star-gazers! They stumbled on my polished floor, strewing sand, crowding on each other, sizing up the household for gifts (thinking already of sailing away), and sighted upwards where the ladder went, to the sighs of the island girls who peeped from the kitchen door. In the hope of a bath, they looked in awe at their hands.

I left them thus, and withdrew to make the broth.

With their tear-bright eyes they watched me come in with the great winking tray, and circle the room in a winding wreath of steam. Each in turn with a pair of black-nailed hands swept up his bowl. The first were trotting at my heels while the last still reached with their hands. Then the last drank too, and dredging their snouts from the bowls, let go and shuttled in to the company.

That moment of transformation—only the gods really like it! Men and beasts almost never take in enough of the wonder to justify the trouble. The floor was swaying like a bridge in battle. "Outside!" I commanded. "No dirt is allowed in this house!" In the end, it takes phenomenal neatness of housekeeping to put it through the heads of men that they are swine. With my wand seething in the air like a broom, I drove them all through the door—twice as many hooves as there had been feet before—to join their brothers, who rushed forward to meet them now, filthily rivaling, but welcoming. What tusks I had given them!

As I shut the door on the sight, and drew back into my privacy—deathless privacy that heals everything, even the effort of magic—I felt something from behind press like the air of heaven before a storm, and reach like another wand over my head.

I spun around, thinking, O gods, it has failed me, it's drying up. Before everything, I think of my power. One man was left.

"What makes you think you're different from anyone else?" I screamed; and he laughed.

Before I'd believe it, I ran back to my broth. I had thought it perfect—I'd allowed no other woman to come near it. I tasted, and it was perfect—swimming with oysters from my reef and flecks of golden pork, redolent with leaves of bay and basil and rosemary, with the glass of island wine tossed in at the last: it has been my infallible recipe. Circe's broth: all the gods have heard of it and envied it. No, the fault had to be in the drinker. If a man remained, unable to leave that magnificent body of his, then enchantment had met with a hero. Oh, I knew those prophecies as well as the back of my hand—only nothing is here to warn me when it is *now*.

The island girls, those servants I support, stood there in the kitchen and smiled at me. I threw kettle and all at their withering heels. Let them learn that unmagical people are put into the world to jusify and serve the magical—not to smile at them!

I whirled back again. The hero stood as before. But his laugh had gone too, after his friends. His gaze was empty, as though I were not in it—I was invisible. His hand groped across the rushes of a chair. I moved beyond him and bolted the door against the murmurous outside. Still invisibly, I took away his sword. I sent his tunic away to the spring for washing, and I, with my own hands, gave him his bath. Then he sat and dried himself before the fire— carefully, the only mortal man on an island in the sea. I rubbed oil on his shadowy shoulders, and on the rope of curls in which his jaw was set. His rapt ears still listened to the human silence there.

"I know your name," I said in the voice of a woman, "and you know mine by now."

I took the chain from my waist, it slipped shining to the floor between us, where it lay as if it slept, as I came forth. Under my palms he stood warm and dense as a myrtle grove at noon. His limbs were heavy, braced like a sleep-walker's who has wandered, alas, to cliffs above the sea. When I passed before him, his arm lifted and barred my way. When I held up the glass he opened his mouth. He fell among the pillows, his still-open eyes two clouds stopped over the sun, and I lifted and kissed his hand.

It was he who in a burst of speech announced the end of day. As though the hour brought a signal to the wanderer, he told me a story, while the owl made comment outside. He told me of the monster with one eye—he had put out the eye, he said. Yes, said the owl, the monster is growing another, and a new man will sail along to blind it again. I had heard it all before, from man and owl. I didn't want his story, I wanted his secret.

When Venus leaned at the window, I called him by name, but he had talked himself into a dream, and his dream had him fast. I now saw through the cautious herb that had protected him from my broth. From the first, he had found some way to resist my power. He must laugh, sleep, ravish, he must talk and sleep. Next it would be he must die. I looked an age into that face above the beard's black crescent, the eyes turned loose from mine like the statues' that sleep on the hill. I took him by the locks of his beard and hair, but he rolled away with his snore to the very floor of sleep—as far beneath my reach as the drowned sailor dropped out of his, in the tale he told of the sea.

I thought of my father the Sun, who went on his divine way untroubled, ambitionless—unconsumed; suffering no loss, no heroic fear of corruption through his constant shedding of light, needing no story, no retinue to vouch for where he had been—even heroes could learn of the gods!

Yet I knew they keep something from me, asleep and awake. There exists a mortal mystery, that, if I knew where it was, I could crush like an island grape. Only frailty, it seems, can divine it—and I was not endowed with that property. They live by frailty! By the moment! I tell myself that it is only a mystery, and mystery is only uncertainty. (There is no mystery in magic! Men are swine: let it be said, and no sooner said than done.) Yet mortals alone can divine where it lies in each other, can find it and prick it in all its peril, with an instrument made of air. I swear that only to possess that one, trifling secret, I would willingly turn myself into a harmless dove for the rest of eternity!

When presently he leapt up, I had nearly forgotten he would move again—as a golden hibiscus startles you, all flowers, when you are walking in some weedy place apart.

Yes, but he would not dine. Dinner was carried in, but he would not dine with me until I would undo that day's havoc in the pigsty. I pointed out that his portion was served in a golden bowl—the very copy of that bowl my own father the Sun crosses back in each night after his journey of the day. But he cared nothing for beauty that was not of the world, he did not want the first taste of anything new. He wanted his men back. In the end, it was necessary for me to cloak myself and go down in the dark, under the willows where the bones are hung to the wind, into the sty; and to sort out and bring up his friends again from their muddy labyrinth. I had to pass them back through the doorway as themselves. I could not skip or brush lightly over one—he named and counted. Then he could look at them all he liked, staggering up on their hind legs before him. Their jaws sank asthmatically, and he cried, "Do you know me?"

"It's Odysseus!" I called, to spoil the moment. But with a shout he had already sprung to their damp embrace.

Reunions, it seems, are to be celebrated. (I have never had such a thing.) All of us feasted together on meat and bread, honey and wine, and the fire roared. We heard out the flute player, we heard out the story, and the fair-haired sailor, whose name is now forgotten, danced on the table and pleased them. When the fire was black, my servants came languishing from the kitchen, and all the way up the ladder to the beds above they had to pull the drowsy-kneed star-gazers, spilling laughter and songs all the way. I could hear them calling away to the girls as they would call them home. But the pigsty was where they belonged.

Hand in hand, we climbed to my tower room. His cheeks were grave and his eyes black, put out with puzzles and solutions. We conversed of signs, omens, premonitions, riddles and dreams, and ended in fierce, cold sleep. Strange man, as unflinching and as wound up as I am. His short life and my long one have their ground in common. Passion is our ground, our island—do others exist?

His sailors came jumping down in the morning, full of themselves and stories. Preparing the breakfast, I watched them tag one another, run rough-and-tumble around the table, regaling the house. "What did *I* do? How far did *I* go with it?" and in a reckless reassurance imitating the sounds of pigs at each other's backs. They were certainly more winsome now than they could ever have been before; I'd made them younger, too, while I was about it. But tell me of one that appreciated it! Tell me one now who looked my way until I had brought him his milk and figs.

When he made his appearance, we devoured a god's breakfast—all, the very sausages, taken for granted. The kitchen girls simpered and cried that if this went on, we'd be eaten out of house and home. But I didn't care if I put the house under greater stress for this one mortal than I ever dreamed of for myself—even on those lonely dull mornings when mist wraps the island and hides every path of the sea, and when my heart is black.

But a stir was upon them all from the moment they rose from the table. Treading on their napkins, tracking the clean floor with honey, they deserted me in the house and collected, arms wound on each other's shoulders, to talk beneath the sky. There they were in a knot, with him in the center of it. He folded his arms and sank his golden weight on one leg, while every ear on the island listened. I stood in the door and waited.

He walked up and said, "Thank you, Circe, for the hospitality we have enjoyed beneath your roof."

"What is the occasion for a speech?" I asked.

"We are setting sail," he said. "A year's visit is visit enough. It's time we were on our way."

Ever since the morning Time came and sat on the world, men have been on the run as fast as they can go, with beauty flung over their shoulders. I ground my teeth. I raised my wand in his face.

"You've put yourself to great trouble for us. You may have done too much," he said.

"I undid as much as I did!" I cried. "That was hard."

He gave me a pecking, recapitulating kiss, his black beard thrust at me like a shoe. I kissed it, his mouth, his wrist, his shoulder, I put my eyes to his eyes, through which I saw seas toss, and to the cabinet of his chest.

He turned and raised an arm to the others. "Tomorrow."

The knot broke and they wandered apart to the shore. They were not so forlorn when they could eat acorns and trot quickly where they would go.

It was as though I had no memory, to discover how early and late the cicadas drew long sighs like the playing out of all my silver shuttles. Wasn't it always the time of greatest heat the Dog Star running with the Sun? The sea the color of honey looked sweet even to the tongue, the salt and vengeful sea. My grapes had ripened all over again while we stretched and drank our wine, and I ordered the harvest gathered and pressed—but this wine, I made clear to the servants, was to store. Hospitality is one thing, but I must consdier how my time is endless, how I shall need wine endlessly. They smiled; but magic is the tree, and intoxication is just the little bird that flies in it to sing and flies out again. But the wanderers were watching the sun and waiting for the stars.

Now the night wind was rising. I went my way over the house as I do by night to see if all is well and holding together. From the rooftop I looked out. I saw the vineyards spread out like wings on the hill, the servants' huts and the swarthy groves, the sea awake, and the eye of the black ship. I saw in the moonlight the dance of the bones in the willows. "Old, displeasing ones!" I sang to them on the wind. "There's another now more displeasing than you! Your bite would be sweeter to my mouth than the soft kiss of a wanderer." I looked up at Cassiopeia, who sits there and needs nothing, pale in her chair in the stream of heaven. The old Moon was still at work. "Why keep it up, old woman?" I whispered to her, while the lions roared among the rocks; but I could hear plainly the crying of birds nearby and along the mournful shore.

I swayed, and was flung backward by my torment. I believed that I lay in disgrace and my blood ran green, like the wand that breaks in two. My sight returned to me when I awoke in the pigsty, in the red and black aurora of flesh, and it was day.

They sailed from me, all but one.

The youngest—Elpenor was his name—fell from my roof. He had forgotten where he had gone to sleep. Drunk on the last night, the drunkest of them all—so as not to be known any longer as only the youngest—he'd gone to sleep on the rooftop, and when they called him, his step went off into air. I saw him beating down through the light with rosy fists, as though he'd never left his mother's side till then.

They all ran from the table as though a star had fallen. They stood or they crouched above Elpenor fallen in my yard, low-voiced now like conspirators—as indeed they were. They wept for Elpenor lying on his face, and for themselves, as *he* wept for them the day they came, when I had made them swine.

He knelt and touched Elpenor, and like a lover lifted him; then each in turn held the transformed boy in his arms. They brushed the leaves from his face, and smoothed his red locks, which were still in their tangle from his brief attempts at love-making and from his too-sound sleep.

I spoke from the door. "When you dig the grave for that one, and bury him in the lonely sand by the shadow of your fleeing ship, write on the stone: 'I died for love.' "

I thought I spoke in epitaph—in the idiom of man. But when they heard me, they left Elpenor where he lay, and ran. Red-limbed, with linens sparkling, they sped over the windy path from house to ship like a rainbow in the sun, like new butterflies turned erratically to sea. While he stood in the prow and shouted to them, they loaded the greedy ship. They carried off their gifts from me—all unappreciated, unappraised.

I slid out of their path. I had no need to see them set sail, knowing as well as if I'd been ahead of them all the way, the far and wide, misty and islanded, bright and indelible and menacing world under which they all must go. But foreknowledge is not the same as the last word.

My cheek against the stony ground, I could hear the swine like summer thunder. These were with me still, pets now, once again—grumbling without meaning. I rose to my feet. I was sickened, with child. The ground fell away before me, blotted with sweet myrtle, with high oak that would have given me a ship too, if I were not tied to my island, as Cassiopeia must be to the sticks and stars of her chair. We were a rim of fire, a ring on the sea. His ship was a moment's gleam on a wave. The little son, I knew, was to follow—follow and slay him. That was the story. For whom is a story enough? For the wanderers who will tell it—it's where they must find their strange felicity.

I stood on my rock and wished for grief. It would not come. Though I could shriek at the rising moon, and she, so near, would wax or wane, there was still grief, that couldn't hear me—grief that cannot be round or plain or solid-bright or running on its track, where a curse could get at it. It has no heavenly course; it is like mystery, and knows where to hide itself. At last it does not even breathe. I cannot find the dusty mouth of grief. I am sure now grief is a ghost—only a ghost in Hades, where ungrateful Odysseus is going—waiting on him.

—Eudora Welty (1909-   )

THE DOOR

Everything (he kept saying) is something it isn't. And everybody is always somewhere else. Maybe it was the city, being in the city, that made him feel how queer everything was and that it was something else. Maybe (he kept thinking) it was the names of the things. The names were tex and frequently koid. Or they were flex and oid or they were duroid (sani) or flexsan (duro), but everything was glass (but not quite glass) and the thing that you touched (the surface, washable, crease-resistant) was rubber, only it wasn't quite rubber and you didn't quite touch it but almost. The wall, which was glass but thrutex, turned out on being approached not to be a wall, it was something else, it was an opening or doorway—and the doorway (through which he saw himself approaching) turned out to be something else, it was a wall. And what he had eaten not having agreed with him.

He was in a washable house, but he wasn't sure. Now about those rats, he kept saying to himself. He meant the rats that the Professor had driven crazy by forcing them to deal with problems which were beyond the scope of rats, the insoluble problems. He meant the rats that had been trained to jump at the square card with the circle in the middle, and the card (because it was something it wasn't) would give way and let the rat into a place where the food was, but then one day it would be a trick played on the rat, and the card would be changed, and the rat would jump but the card wouldn't give way, and it was an impossible situation (for a rat) and the rat would go insane and into its eyes would come the unspeakably bright imploring look of the frustrated, and after the convulsions were over and the frantic racing around, then the passive stage would set in and willingness to let anything be done to it, even if it was something else.

He didn't know which door (or wall) or opening in the house to jump at, to get through, because one was an opening that wasn't a door (it was a void, or koid) and the other was a wall that wasn't an opening, it was a sanitary cupboard of the same color. He caught a glimpse of his eyes staring into his eyes, in the thrutex, and in them was the expression he had seen in the picture of the rats—weary after convulsions and the frantic racing around, when they were willing and did not mind having anything done to them. More and more (he kept saying) I am confronted by a problem which is incapable of solution (for this time even if he chose the right door, there would be no food behind it) and that is what madness is, and things seeming different from what they are. He heard, in the house where he was, in the city to which he had gone (as toward a door which might, or might not, give way), a noise—not a loud noise but more of a low prefabricated humming. I came from a place in the base of the wall (or state) where the flue carrying the filterable air was, and not far from the Minipiano, which was made of the same material nailbrushes are made of, and which was under the stairs. "This, too, has been tested," she said, pointing, but not at it, "and found viable." I wasn't a loud noise, he kept thinking, sorry that he had seen his eyes, even though it was through his own eyes that he had seen them.

First will come the convulsions (he said), then the exhaustion, then the willingness to let anything be done. "And you better believe it *will* be."

All his life he had been confronted by situations which were incapable of being solved, and there was a deliberateness behind all this, behind this changing of the card (or door), because they would always wait till you had learned to jump at the certain card (or door)— the one with the circle—and then they would change it on you. There have been so many doors changed on me, he said, in the last twenty years, but it is now becoming clear that it is an impossible situation, and the question is whether to jump again, even though they ruffle you in the rump with a blast of air—to make you jump. He wished he wasn't standing by the Minipiano. First they would teach you the prayers and the Psalms, and that would be the right door (the one with the circle), and the long sweet words with the holy sound, and that would be the one to jump at to get where the food was. Then one day you jumped and it didn't give way, so that all you got was a bump on the nose, and the first bewilderment, the first young bewilderment.

I don't know whether to tell her about the door they substituted or not, he said, the one with the equation on it and the picture of the omoeba reproducing itself by division. Or the one with the photostatic copy of the check for thirty-two dollars and fifty cents. But the jumping was so long ago, although the bump is . . . how those old wounds hurt! Being crazy this way wouldn't be so bad if only, if only. If only when you put your foot forward to take a step, the ground wouldn't come up to meet your foot the way it does. And the same way in the street (only I may never get back to the street unless I jump at the right door), the curb coming up to meet your foot, anticipating ever so delicately the weight of the body, which is somewhere else. "We could take your name," she said, "and send it to you." And it wouldn't be so bad if only you could read a sentence all the way through without jumping (your eye) to something else on the same page; and then (he kept thinking) there was that man out in Jersey, the one who started to chop his trees down, one by one, the man who began talking about how he would take his house to pieces, brick by brick, because he faced a problem incapable of solution, probably, so he began to hack at the trees in the yard, began to pluck with trembling fingers at the bricks in the house. Even if a house is not washable, it is worth taking down. It is not till later that the exhaustion sets in.

But it is inevitable that they will keep changing the doors on you, he said, becuase that is what they are for; and the thing is to get used to it and not let it unsettle the mind. But that would mean not jumping, and you can't. Nobody can not jump. There will be no not-jumping. Among rats, perhaps, but among people never. Everybody has to keep jumping at a door (the one with the circle on it) because that is the way everybody is, specially some people. You wouldn't want me, standing here, to tell you, would you, about my friend the poet (deceased) who said, "My heart has followed all my days something I cannot name"? (It had the circle on it.) And like many poets, although few so beloved, he is gone. It killed him, the jumping. First, of course, there were the preliminary bouts, the convulsions, and the calm and the willingness.

I remember the door with the picture of the girl on it (only it was spring), her arms outstretched in loveliness, her dress (it was the one with the circle on it) uncaught, beginning the slow, clear, blinding cascade—and I guess we would all like to try that door again, for it seemed like the way and for a while it was the way, the door would open and you would go through winged and exalted (like any rat) and the food would be there, the way the Professor had it arranged, everything O.K., and you had chosen the right door for the world was young. The time they changed that door on me, my nose bled for a hundred hours—how do you like that, Madam? Or would you prefer to show me further through this so strange house, or you could take my name and send it to me, for although my heart has followed all my days something I cannot name, I am tired of the jumping and I do not know which way to go, Madam, and I am not even sure that I am not tried beyond the endurance of man (rat, if you will) and have taken leave of sanity. What are you following these days, old friend, after your recovery from the last bump? What is the name, or is it something you cannot name? The rats have a name for it by this time, perhaps, but I don't know what they call it. I call it plexikoid and it comes in sheets, something like insulating board, unattainable and ugli-proof.

And there was the man out in Jersey, because I keep thinking about his terrible necessity and the passion and trouble he had gone to all those years in the indescribable abundance of a house-holder's detail, building the estate and planting of the trees and in spring the lawn-dressing and in fall the bulbs for the spring burgeoning, and the watering of the grass on the long light evenings in summer and the gravel for the driveway (all had to be thought out, planned) and the decorative borders, probably, the perennials and the bug spray, and the building of the house from plans of the architect, first the sills, then the studs, then the full corn in the ear, the floors laid on the floor timbers, smoothed, and then the carpets upon the smooth floors and the curtains and the rods therefore. And then, almost without warning, he would be jumping at the same old door and it wouldn't give: they had changed it on him, making life no longer supportable under the elms in the elm shade, under the maples in the maple shade.

"Here you have the maximum of openness in a small room."

It was impossible to say (maybe it was the city) what made him feel the way he did, and I am not the only one either, he kept thinking—ask any doctor if I am. The doctors, they know how many there are, they even know where the trouble is only they don't like to tell you about the prefrontal lobe because that means making a hole in your skull and removing the work of centuries. It took so long coming, this lobe, so many, many years. (Is it something you read in the paper, perhaps?) And now, the strain being so great, the door having been changed by the Professor once too often . . . but it only means a whiff of ether, a few deft strokes, and the higher animal becomes a little easier in his mind and more like the lower one. From now on, you see, that's the way it will be, the ones with the small prefrontal lobes will win because the other ones are hurt too much by this incessant bumping. They can stand just so much, eh, Doctor? (And what is that, pray, that you have in your hand?) Still, you never can tell, eh, Madam?

He crossed (carefully) the room, the thick carpet under him softly, and went toward the door carefully, which was glass and he could see himself in it, and which, at his approach, opened to allow him to pass through; and beyond he half expected to find one of the old doors that he had known, perhaps the one with the circle, the one with the girl her arms outstretched in loveliness and beauty before him. But he saw instead a moving stairway, and descended in light (he kept thinking) to the street below and to the other people. As he stepped off, the ground came up slightly, to meet his foot.

—E.B. White (1899-1985)

Index